Contemporary Issues in Social Accounting

Audrey Paterson, Akira Yonekura, William Jackson and Darren Jubb

(G) Goodfellow Publishers Ltd

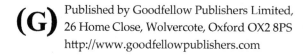

Published by Goodfellow Publishers Limited,
26 Home Close, Wolvercote, Oxford OX2 8PS
http://www.goodfellowpublishers.com

British Library Cataloguing in Publication Data: a catalogue record for this title is available from the British Library.

Library of Congress Catalog Card Number: on file.

ISBN: 978-1-911396-55-0

Copyright © Audrey Paterson, Akira Yonekura, William Jackson and Darren Jubb, 2018

 Design and typesetting by P.K. McBride, www.macbride.org.uk

Cover design by Cylinder

Printed by Baker and Taylor, www.baker-taylor.com

Contents

Case Studies

Foreword

The role of the management accountant is one of enabling, shaping and telling the organisation's value story. It is the story of how organisations create and preserve value. However, in the storytelling the questions of whose story and whose value are becoming increasingly important. There is an increasing demand for a diversity of narratives, depending on the stakeholder, societal impact, time orientation and governing principles. This book is timely as trust in global business and its leadership has been in decline, and organisations are struggling to report on new business models that have shifted value from tangible to intangible assets.

Through CIMA's sponsorship of the annual Accounting for Society and the Environment (ASE) research network workshop at Heriot-Watt University in Edinburgh, I have had the privilege to witness its great work. The interdisciplinary aspects of the network leads to a cross-fertilization of ideas and innovative thinking. Through consistent engagement and alignment of shared interests and language, the network brings credibility to issues in social accounting. The raised profile of these issues can then foster organisational debate and contribute to better business practices. From a personal standpoint, I particularly appreciated the friendly and almost family feel to the workshops, making it a safe space in which to foster thinking and debate. Given the diverse nature of the topics and issues covered, I have learned much from the different sessions, and have applied that knowledge to my own areas of management accounting research.

In 2019, CIMA and its professional community of Management Accountants will reach its centenary year. For almost 100 years, we have been promoting and developing the science of management accountancy. This has included the development of CIMA's code of ethics and the Global Management Accounting Principles; the purpose of which is to support CEOs, CFOs and boards of directors in benchmarking and improving their management accounting systems. It helps them to meet the needs of their organisations, effectively and efficiently, to achieve long-term economic performance, while generating positive value for society and minimising environmental impact.

At the heart of every Chartered Global Management Accountant (CGMA) designation holder is the code of ethics. These ethical obligations are built on: integrity and objectivity; professional competence and due care; confidentiality; and professional behaviour and conduct. They are a commitment to act in the public interest and maintain public confidence in management accounting through the highest professional standards. From 1919 to the present, through examples such as the Global Management Accounting Principles and the code of ethics, CIMA has continually sought to foster and maintain investigation and research into the best means and methods of developing and applying the science of management accountancy. I believe this book continues in this tradition.

We are in a period of change that the World Economic Forum has termed, 'the Fourth Industrial Revolution'. Technology and its possibilities are impacting on the evolution of organisations and finance. This is changing the way organisations construct and tell their value stories. It is also allowing organisations to engage with an ever-greater diversity of stakeholders, and explore the broader narrative that links business into the rest of society. Finance is struggling to respond to the emergent new conditions. However, social and environmental accounting can make a crucial new contribution to the wider understanding of business and society and the future role of finance in this new epoch. The issues in this book can help us reconsider, how, as finance professionals, we enable, shape and tell the value stories of our organisations and societies.

Dr Martin Farrar
Associate Technical Director, Research and Development – Management Accounting
CIMA
E: Martin.Farrar@aicpa-cima.com
November 2017.

Acknowledgements

Acknowledgements are always a tricky business. They can be sparing or effusive, but if they try to mention individuals then invariably they miss someone important. To avoid that we will just say that many people have been involved in the design, authoring, review and editing of this text and we would like to thank them all. They have done stalwart work in the face of our decision to adopt extremely tight deadlines and everyone came through when they really needed to. We are sure there must have been some personal cost at times. Certainly, there have been stresses and strains, but no one complained, and everyone delivered. We would also like to thank our colleagues Tim and Sally at Goodfellow Publishing who have always been supportive of our ideas and have been understanding when deadlines were pressing. Of course, everyone involved has family and friends who have shared the sacrifice and we would like to thank them for their forbearance.

Finally, we would like to acknowledge the importance of the Accounting for Society and the Environment (ASE) network. Through its regular workshops, which for the last few years have been  most valuably supported by CIMA, we have been able to develop the community of interested individuals that have allowed us to create this text. It is ultimately a community effort and without the ongoing research we would not be here today and the outlook for the future would be much less promising.

Audrey, Akira, William and Darren

Biographies

Zayyad Abdul-Baki is a PhD candidate at Heriot-Watt University. Prior to this, he worked as a lecturer at the University of Ilorin, Nigeria. Zayyad is an associate member of the Institute of Chartered Accountants of Nigeria (ICAN) and Chartered Institute of Public Finance and Accountancy, UK. Zayyad currently tutors on financial reporting and auditing at Heriot-Watt University and his research interests are financial reporting, accounting regulation and accountability.

Gbenga Adamolekun is a doctoral candidate at Heriot-Watt University. He is a member of the Chartered Institute of Security and Investment (CISI) as well as the Centre for Finance and Investment (CFI). He holds an MSc in Investment and Finance with distinction from Bournemouth University. Prior to research, Gbenga had an extensive experience working in the Finance industry in Nigeria. His research interest includes corporate finance, market microstructure, asset pricing, behavioural finance and development finance.

Alexander Anggono is a Senior Lecturer at Trunojoyo University, Indonesia. Prior to this, Alex had worked for 10 years in a public accounting firm. Alex currently lectures on both management accounting and public sector accounting courses. His primary research area is on behavioural accounting, with a specific emphasis on the public sector.

Yasser Barghathi is an Assistant Professor in Accounting at the Dubai Campus of Heriot-Watt University. During the previous academic year, he has taught auditing and assurance, international accounting and research methods. His research interest revolves around financial reporting quality and audit quality. He is also a professional accountant with over 15 years of experience in the areas of corporate accounting, financial reporting, and auditing. He is also a member of the Libyan Accountants and Auditors Association and CPA Australia.

Eleni Chatzivgeri is a Senior Lecturer in Accounting at Westminster Business School, London. She holds a BSc in Economics, an MSc in International Accounting and Finance and a PhD in Accounting and Finance. Prior to this she worked as a teaching assistant at Heriot-Watt University. Eleni's research interests include: issues arising from the adoption and application of International Financial Reporting Standards (IFRS), corporate finance, developing theories of compliance, exploring the success of NGOs lobbying for accounting change.

Kate Clements is Assistant Professor of Accountancy at Heriot Watt University. She qualified as a Chartered Accountant (ICAEW) with KPMG and has wide experience working in industry and in public practice. Kate specialises in teaching audit, financial accounting and tax.

Mercy Denedo is a PhD student in the School of Social Sciences at Heriot-Watt University where she is a teaching assistant on a number of accounting courses. Prior to this, she was a lecturer at Delta State University, Nigeria. Her research interest focuses on interdisciplinary studies on accountability and governance in the context of human rights, corporate social responsibility, counter accountability, stakeholders' engagement and sustainable development.

Yasser Eliwa is Lecturer of Accounting at Loughborough University. Prior to this, he worked as Senior Lecturer of Accounting at Brighton University for two years. Yasser currently lectures on financial accounting and reporting, and his primary area of research is financial reporting and analysis.

Mohamed (Mo) Elshinawy is a doctoral candidate at Heriot-Watt University. Mo holds a BSc in Business Administration and an MSc in Finance. Prior to this, he worked as an assistant lecturer at Cairo University, Egypt. He currently tutors on Governance and Accounting Ethics at Strathclyde University and Introduction to Accounting at Heriot-Watt University. His research interests include Behavioural Finance, Corporate Governance, and the governance of financial institutions.

Anees Farrukh is a PhD student in the School of Social Sciences at the Heriot-Watt University. The focus of his research is the educational crisis in Pakistan, with aims to shed light on the accountability and governance of educational NGOs in addressing this crisis. His future research plans fare to develop further into the field of accounting and education by conducting research on accountability, sustainability, educational policy and practice, social and environmental accounting and public-sector accounting.

William (Bill) Jackson is Head of Accounting at Heriot-Watt University and holds a PhD from the University of Edinburgh. Bill's research interests are primarily in the history of accounting, particularly where accounting interfaces with medical practice. Other interests are in the more contemporary interface between accounting and medical practice, the history of accounting and popular culture, management accounting practices in non-Anglo-Saxon contexts and the gendering of the accountancy profession.

Amber Jasmine Jackson is a freelance proof-reader and copy-editor. Amber holds a BA (Hons) in Classics from the University of Cambridge and a MSc in Late Antique, Islamic and Byzantine Studies from the University of Edinburgh. She is employed by EY as a Tax Advisor in the People Advisory Services practice, and specialises in Global Mobility consulting. She works with a variety of middle-market private sector clients, providing tax compliance and advisory services in conjunction with overseas EY teams. She is based in Edinburgh.

Darren Jubb is an Assistant Professor of Accountancy at Heriot-Watt University. Prior to this, Darren worked in professional accountancy practice for several years during which time he qualified as a Chartered Accountant with the

Institute of Chartered Accountants Scotland (ICAS). Darren currently lectures on financial accounting and audit courses, and his primary area of research is investigating the links between accounting, management and popular culture.

Stylianos Kotsias joined The American College of Greece in 2009, and since then he has been teaching accounting and finance courses. Since 2014, Stylianos is a visiting lecturer at ALBA Graduate Business School, teaching financial and management accounting courses. Stylianos holds a PhD Degree in Accounting from Heriot-Watt University in Edinburgh. His research interests lay upon the areas of accounting and financial accountability reforms in the Greek public sector.

Sunita Mathur is Assistant Professor in Accounting and Finance at the Dubai Campus of Heriot-Watt University. She has more than 15 years of international teaching experience in Higher Education and currently teaches Financial Reporting, Managing Corporate Value and Contemporary issues in Financial Accounting. Her research interest principally lies in Accounting Regulatory Frameworks, Corporate Social Responsibility and SMEs. She also supervises MSc dissertations on various subjects.

Vasileios Milios is a PhD candidate at Heriot-Watt University. He has completed his studies in Accounting (BSc, ATEI of Larisa) and in International Accounting and Finance (MSc, Heriot-Watt University). Vasileios' research interest mainly focuses on public sector accounting and accounting history and, more specifically, on the interplay between accounting and the political environment.

Bridget Efeoghene Ogharanduku is a PhD candidate in Accountancy at the Heriot-Watt University. Her main research interests focus on gender in the accounting profession and accounting history. She has taught on the social and environmental accounting course at the undergraduate level at Heriot-Watt University. Prior to this, Bridget has also held academic roles as a Graduate Assistant, Teaching Assistant and Assistant Lecturer at Delta State University, Nigeria. Her main teaching areas are in both financial and management accounting.

Audrey S Paterson is an Associate Professor in Accounting at Heriot-Watt University and holds a Bcom (Hons), MSc in Social Science Research and a PhD from the University of Edinburgh. Audrey is currently involved in several research networks including the Institute of Public Sector Accounting Research (IPSAR) and is the founder of the Accounting for Society and the Environment (ASE) research network which meets annually. Audrey is also responsible for the management of the PhD programme within the Department of Accounting, Economics & Finance.

Sebastian F Paterson is the Chief Executive Officer of Seallaidh na Beinne Moire, a community owned estate company formed in 2006 under the Scottish Land Reform Act 2003. In his present role, Sebastian manages South Uist

Estate's crofting, shooting and fishing assets, the South Uist Renewable Energy Windfarm and the recently constructed Lochboisdale Harbour; additionally, he is developing economic and social projects aimed at enhancing employment and retaining population on the estate. Sebastian received a Master's Degree with Distinction from Heriot-Watt University in 2015.

Stephen Rae is a postdoctoral researcher, and was awarded a PhD from Heriot-Watt University in 2016. His primary research interests lie in how and why companies release information. He received an MA in Accounting and Finance in 2010 and an MRes in the same in 2011, both also from Heriot Watt. He has a further research interest in quantitative methodologies and their uses following an earlier degree in Statistics, awarded in 2007.

Konstantinos Ritos is part of the Accounting Postgraduate Research team at Heriot-Watt University and parallel to researching, acts as a Student Representative for Accounting Postgraduate Researchers there. His previous studies include an MSc in International Accounting and Finance at Heriot-Watt University in 2016, where he graduated with a distinction, and a degree in Accounting and Finance from A.T.E.I. of Thessaloniki. Konstantinos has also previously worked in the accounting office of the Water and Sewer Supply of Thessaloniki public company for six months.

Chris Ryan is currently a Consultant with Deloitte in Finance Transformation, Chartered Accountant with ICAS and received a First-Class Honours degree from Heriot-Watt. Chris has worked with a wide variety of clients in both public and private sectors. His role primarily focuses on solving the key issues facing Finance Functions in organisations. The range of issues is broad and includes the social and ethical implications of the actions of the Finance Function and the resulting impact on the organisation's reputation, CSR and bottom line.

Mo Sherif is Associate Professor of Finance. He received his PhD from the University of Manchester, UK. He is an interdisciplinary Finance researcher whose initial contributions to the Finance literature are in Entrepreneurial and Behavioural Finance, Stock Trading Strategies and Asset Pricing fields. He is a fellow of the Higher Education Academy in the UK and a member of the American Finance Association in the USA. He is currently the Director of Postgraduate Taught Programmes in Finance (AEF) at SoSS and Senator at Heriot-Watt University.

Melanie Wilson is a Chartered Accountant, Chartered Tax Adviser and ethical entrepreneur with experience across the private, public and third sectors. Melanie is currently the MD of businesses with local to global client bases operating within professional practice and training. Melanie also currently lectures in tax and accounting subjects at Heriot Watt University. Melanie is currently engaged with both ICAEW and CIOT committees representing members and society regarding tax and education issues. Melanie's research interests are based in tax, including avoidance, contemporary and society issues.

Akira Yonekura is currently an Assistant Professor at Heriot-Watt University, Director of Undergraduate Teaching Programmes for Accounting, Economics & Finance and a member of the Accounting for Society and the Environment (ASE) research network. Akira's research and teaching interests involve a critical analysis of current and historical accounting and corporate governance practices in their socio-economic, political and cultural contexts.

Abdelrhman Yusuf is currently a doctoral researcher at Heriot-Watt University. He received his second MSc award from the University of Dundee. Yusuf has ten years of teaching experience with undergraduate and post-graduate students during which time he become an Associate Fellow of the Higher Education Academy (HEA). His research interests are corporate governance, social responsibility, strategic management, and shareholders' activism.

1 Contemporary Issues in Social Accounting

Audrey Paterson, Akira Yonekura, William Jackson and Darren Jubb

Introduction

The discipline of accounting has ancient roots. Indeed, there is evidence in historical artefacts indicating that records of account, in the form of clay tablets, regarding business, finance and taxation, date back to around 2500-3300 BC in Egypt and Mesopotamia. These early records were lists of expenditures, goods received and traded, and were kept by rulers for the purposes of gathering taxation and tracking expenditures on public works. They were further used to validate the use of taxes raised for the common good and to demonstrate the social responsibility of the rulers. Such records therefore suggest that for as long as societies have engaged in trade, records have been kept and used as a form of social accountability.

From these early roots, accounting as both a function and a profession has gone through a long evolutionary process. One of the first professional accounting organisations, the Edinburgh Society of Accountants, was founded in Scotland in 1854, with the Glasgow Institute of Accountants and Actuaries appearing soon after in the same year. These organisations established a distinct profession with a high level of reliability, responsibility and honesty. On these grounds, they sought out, and were granted, a royal charter. Following this, the Edinburgh institute adopted the title 'Chartered Accountant'. As economies grew and businesses expanded, the demand for accounting services increased, resulting in accounting and accountants becoming an integral part of business entities. This also led to the geographical expansion of professional accounting bodies, for example, the Institute of Chartered Accountants for England and Wales, which was formed in 1880. The establishment of professional accounting institutes however, was not isolated to the UK. In 1887, the American Institute of

Certified Public Accountants was created, along with several others appearing in Europe. More recently, in 1949, the Chartered Institute of Accountants of India was formed and more recently still, the Institute of Chartered Accountants of Nigeria was established in 1965. Indeed, there are now professional accounting organisations all over the world.

Accounting as we know it today can be described as concerning the book-keeping methods that are used to create financial records of business transactions which, in turn, lead to the preparation of statements concerning the assets, liabilities, and operating results of an entity. The accounting system is an arrangement consisting of a group of interacting, interrelated, or interdependent elements forming a complex whole which involves people, procedures, and resources used to gather, record, classify, summarise and report the financial (and increasingly non-financial) information of a business, government or other financial entity. While accounting can still, in some sense, be categorised as a technical topic, it has retained a social accountability orientation that contains similarities to its earliest origins, thus rendering it not only an institutional, but also a social, practice (Hopwood and Miller, 1994). Indeed, several strands of research demonstrate the role of accounting in management motivations for: social reporting/disclosure; as a tool for securing and maintaining legitimacy and societal expectations; demonstrating ethical and social accountability to stakeholders and the wider community and as a social accountability tool. Thus, social accounting can be defined as:

> *"the preparation and publication of an account about an organisation's social, environmental, employee community, customer and other stakeholder interactions and activities, and where possible, the consequence of those interactions and activities"* (Gray, 2000: 250).

For a considerable period, much of the academic writing and teaching on accounting has tended to ignore or pay scant attention to the concept of social accounting, despite it having wide ranging implications for both the profession and society. Over the last few decades we have seen an increasing amount of attention being given to the activities of business and the role that accounting plays in organisational decision-making. Much of this attention has been driven by the economic and financial crisis which have occurred in recent years and a succession of financial scandals, reports of unethical or questionable business and accounting practices, and by calls from the media and society to address these issues. In response to these calls there has been a strengthening of financial and business ethics, corporate responsibility and social accounting courses within the accounting teaching curriculum.

Accounting, as a profession, has maintained its prestigious status and attracts large numbers of students on undergraduate accounting programmes every year. Indeed, most universities offer accounting degrees as part of their portfolio of programmes. However, most of these degree programmes focus much of their teaching on private sector organisations, neglecting other key areas of the economy such as the public and third sectors, cooperatives and family businesses. The aim of this book is to fill this gap by introducing you to the applicability of social accounting and social responsibility to each of these sectors. The importance of social accounting with respect to sustainability, socially responsible investments, the role of social audits and taxation issues relating to these sectors is also generally neglected in the curriculum, thus a further aim of this book is to introduce you to these concepts and some general debates in these areas. To achieve these aims, we begin our discussion by considering both a historical and contemporary viewpoint of the relevance of accountability, ethics and corporate social responsibility to these sectors, highlighting along the way some serious issues and considerations that need to be accounted for within these sectors.

Accountability, ethics and the business world

The concepts of accountability, ethics and their relevance within the business world have grown considerably in recent years, within both the educational and professional context. This can be attributed to the work of philosophers and scholars within accounting and finance who have successfully connected ethical theory to real world problems (Paterson *et al.*, 2016). One of the main driving forces behind business is the desire to generate profit. Indeed, in Western capitalist societies the activities of business and the financial services industry, and their decision-making processes, are predominantly motivated by profit maximisation goals which can often lead to highly questionable decisions being made (Paterson *et al.*, 2016). We do not need to look too far into the business world to find examples that raise questions over the moral and ethical behaviour of organisations, regardless of the sector in which they are placed. Such scandals have resulted in growing demand for accountability across all sectors. Indeed, calls for these organisations to be held accountable for their actions, and for policies to be adopted to help prevent unethical expressions, which affect a wide range of stakeholders, feature highly in the media.

In Chapter 2, we introduce you to two interrelated concepts: social accountability and ethics, and discuss their importance to everyday life. We begin by first considering what accountability and business ethics are and why they are important. Following this we introduce a discussion on the codes of conduct that facilitate social ethics and accountability. To illustrate these concepts, the chapter includes examples of issues that require careful reflection and consideration when determining approaches to business activity and ensuring professional integrity. This is followed by a discussion on the limitations of ethics and codes of conduct.

■ History and dynamics of corporate social responsibility

Following our discussion of accountability, ethics and the business world we move on to considering the dynamics of social responsibility practices and concepts, to demonstrate how they have grown and shaped business practices, corporate regulations and reporting. We begin this discussion with a historical overview of the development of corporate social responsibility (CSR) from the mid-19th century industrial revolution, when commercial activities began to expand considerably, and the forms of business ownership began to evolve. This is an important starting point as it facilitates understanding of how organisations have responded and adapted to meet changing societal expectations; comply with regulatory bodies and institutionalise CSR within contemporary business environments and reporting frameworks.

Chapter 3 therefore considers CSR from a historical perspective and the driving forces which initiated changes to CSR practices within organisations. While CSR appears in many countries of the world, in terms of scholarly debates, it is more evident in Western economies. Early writings originated from the United States, however, over the last three decades increased attention has been given to this topic in Europe. In developing economies, there has been an ongoing debate about CSR over the last decade, especially in the context of globalisation, corruption and transnational business and reporting. The discussion and debate in this chapter provides the foundations needed to understand CSR from a contemporary perspective which will be presented in Chapter 4.

■ Corporate social responsibility

Whilst CSR has attracted attention from practitioners and academics from different disciplines over the years, the notion of CSR has yet to be constructed into a cohesive whole. Indeed, when investigating this concept, it is clear that there is no universal agreement on what CSR is, the rationale behind it, or the strategies for achieving it. However, the extant literature does provide a solid foundation in which to explore and integrate these widely divergent viewpoints on CSR. As previously mentioned, a prevalent objective of organisations is the desire to maximise the wealth of capital providers (shareholders). Opponents of this notion have, however, argued that organisational activities impact on other parties that are directly or indirectly related to the organisation. It is also the case that organisations can be affected by their stakeholder/shareholder behaviour through their buying power or voting rights. Thus, it can be argued that all of these parties should be considered in the decision making of an organisation for it to be financially viable in the long-run.

To expand on these ideas, Chapter 4 unveils and integrates insights into CSR issues by considering environmental, social, economic, stakeholder and voluntary dimensions of CSR activities carried out by organisations from the most basic level (economic responsibility) to the most developed level (philanthropic responsibility). The divergent theoretical arguments regarding the ethics and morality of corporate behaviour are also threaded throughout the discussion. Following this, the strategic approach to CSR implementation which assumes that corporations should absorb CSR as a key business issue rather than an *ad hoc* response to corporate social and economic failures is considered. Stakeholder engagement, CSR reporting and the frameworks often employed by organisations in communicating their CSR activities are also included.

Social accounting and sustainability

The concept of sustainability assumes that resources are finite, and should be used and managed conservatively while also considering the long-term priorities of society, the environment and the consequences of how and to what extent these resources are used. In simple terms, sustainability is about avoiding harm to the environment and the depletion of natural resources, thereby supporting a long-term ecological balance to ensure we leave the planet for future generations no worse than when we entered it. The concept of sustainability is currently the subject of much debate, indicating that it is of major importance. Providing the next generation of accounting students with greater knowledge of sustainability will have positive effects on the future of both professional practice and the movement towards a more sustainable world. As de Aguiar and Paterson (2017) show, it is an area that is positively received by both students and academics in higher education. Additionally, the subject creates valuable knowledge and skills for both groups.

To address this, Chapter 5 takes a closer look at sustainability developments. It begins with a discussion of the *triple bottom line* (TBL), a key concept influencing the development and practice of social and sustainability reporting. The emphasis is on both the positive aspects of the TBL as well as its limitations. This is followed by a discussion of major initiatives within the context of CSR and sustainability, including attempts by not-for-profit organisations as well as local governments and the EU. The chapter then takes a closer look at some of the key organisations involved in initiatives on CSR and sustainability reporting, before briefly discussing key reporting guidelines. Having outlined key initiatives and the organisations behind them, the chapter then moves on to a discussion of two key concepts in social and sustainability accounting: sustainability and accountability. We do this by first defining sustainability and providing examples of sustainability reports, including public sector accounting reports. The concept of accountability and socially and environmentally responsible actions, as well as the need for transparency and disclosure are then discussed.

Socially responsible investment

Having considered various issues and aspects of social accounting and their application including corporate social responsibility (CSR), we now turn our attention to another important aspect of business: how to attract and maintain financial investment to support and grow the organisation. Businesses require investment; without it, there is no financing for operations that foster growth. Many investors have their own set of priorities when committing cash to an organisation and this can encompass their social responsibility concerns. Such concerns have led to a practice known as *socially responsible investment* (SRI). This can loosely be defined as shareholders making investments with a desire for socially beneficial results, in addition to the more traditional desire for financial returns.

The concept of SRI has grown considerably in recent years, particularly in response to the media raising awareness of the ruthlessness of corporate activity and social inequality across the globe. Chapter 6, therefore, introduces the SRI concept. It begins with a brief outline of its evolution and continuing importance to the present day. The legitimacy of SRI in the 21st century and the influence of the United Nations Sustainable Development goals and principles on SRI are then discussed. This then leads into a discussion on SRI decision-making in the form of *environmental social governance* (ESG) a vital tool available to investors in selecting investments based on a combination of financial returns, social responsibility, and personal ethics. The importance of non-financial outcomes to investors is also discussed. This is followed by a discussion of some investment options that are available to investors before moving on to consider the performance of SRI investments.

■ Auditing for social aspects

As an early advocate of social responsibility, Goyder (1961), believed that stakeholders in local communities and wider society should demand greater accountability from organisations regarding their social, environmental and ethical impact. Social audit was put forward as a means of delivering such accountability to stakeholders. According to Goyder, if organisations are not willing to take control over their own social and environmental accountability, then society at large must take matters into its own hands. Social audit, therefore, began as an exercise at the level of civil society, carried out by parties external to the organisation being 'audited'. Since then, auditing for social aspects has developed to become a core element of the practice of accounting.

Chapter 7 provides an overview of the main developments within the social audit movement. The chapter discusses three types of social audit: external social audits, supply chain audits and the self-generated social audit. More specifically, it highlights the nature and scope of social audit, how the data used in social audits are collected and reported, and who is responsible for providing assurance in relation to social audits.

Having considered the foundations of social accounting and the concepts of CSR, sustainability, SRI and social audits, the book from here turns its attention to the applicability of these concepts to organisations in the public and third sectors as well as to cooperatives and family businesses.

■ Social accounting and the public sector

In modern societies, the public sector is the heart of democracy as it illustrates the sovereignty of citizens who transfer their power to sovereign governments (Jones and Pendlebury, 2010). The social nature of the public sector is undeniable as it is fundamentally different from the private sector. The main aim of the public sector is not profit maximisation but the creation of social value. The means that the definition of assets differs in public sector accounting as they are not expected to bring economic benefits, but are used instead to provide services and goods to citizens. However, social value cannot be clearly defined as, within public sector organisations, there is a complex framework of interests which derive from different perspectives. In this context, the role of accounting is very important as it must ensure democratic control over the use of funds (Pallot, 1992).

The global financial crisis of 2008 brought to the surface new and strident calls for the restructuring of the public sector. The call of Hopwood and Tompkins (1984) for researchers to explore the organisational, institutional and social nature of accounting practice thus became more relevant than ever. Chapter 8 presents the fundamental characteristics of public sector accounting and an examination of the environment in which public sector accounting operates. Our discussion focuses on who is responsible for the public sector crisis, the initiatives that have been undertaken, the heterogeneous challenges that the public sector faces, and how these issues could be addressed.

■ Social accounting and the third sector

In recent years, much attention has been paid to the roles and the responsibilities of not-for-profit or charitable organisations. These mission-based entities seek social impact rather than profitability for shareholders and comprise what is known as the *third sector* of economic activity (Lindsay *et al.*, 2014). Focus on these socially-driven entities and their performance has increased over recent years, primarily due to the alleged failure of third sector organisations (TSOs) to efficiently deploy financially sustainable services and achieve associated programmatic goals. Like public sector entities, TSOs are under pressure to be accountable for delivering value-added services to their constituents. However, the way TSOs are held accountable is different; they are expected to manage a 'double bottom line', in that they must deliver a measurable and meaningful social impact for their beneficiaries, while also responsibly and transparently accounting for the financial resources entrusted to them by their donors (The Scottish Government, 2011).

Chapter 9 discusses the nature and purpose of third sector organisations and the role that they play within society. This is followed by a discussion of what accountability means in the third sector and why it is important. The concept of third sector accountability is considered through three key lenses; an examination of the reporting framework applied by TSOs, scrutiny of 'The Non-for-Profit

Starvation Cycle' and investigation into TSO governance. The chapter then discusses the three forms of accountability typically found in TSOs, upward, downward and holistic.

Cooperatives and family businesses

Having considered social accounting within the private, public and third sectors and explored related concepts we move on to consider two further important economic sectors, namely cooperatives and family businesses. In contrast to public and private companies, the main purpose of a cooperative is the advancement of its members and not the pursuit of public interest. Cooperatives hold a profit motive for their members. While cooperatives provide a significant contribution to the economy, a large proportion of the UK's economy is also supported by family businesses. Family businesses, in contrast to cooperatives, public and third sector organisations, are driven by profit maximisation in the same way as large multi-national organisations. Indeed, it is estimated that family businesses account for almost 25% of the UK's gross domestic product (GDP). As such, these two areas are of increasing importance when considering accountability and the governance responsibilities of organisations. Likewise, given the importance of the role boards play in the success or failure of cooperative organisations and family businesses, and the importance of these organisations in the wider economy, it is prudent to develop some knowledge and understanding of the complex ways that these boards can be structured and the role that they play in achieving accountability and governance within the organisation and to the wider community.

Within Chapter 10 we begin with a short overview of the evolution of cooperatives and what constitutes a family business, followed by a discussion of the organisational model and governance structures and their effectiveness. To achieve this, we consider the following: who governs; board roles and board relationships with management; board size and director selection processes; and the importance of board member participation and the input of managers in relation to accountability and governance in these two sectors.

Taxation and social accounting

Taxation relates to transactions between taxpayers and the state, and, like all transactions, needs to be accounted for and reported in the interests of accountability and transparency to society. Taxes are essential for the functioning of a modern state, as they are typically the primary source of revenue for funding public services. Governments are charged with making choices about how to raise finance through the system of taxation and when and to what extent to offer incentives and waivers of taxation, which can result in foregoing revenues in some areas. Governments, therefore, also need to be held to account for the tax systems they create. Over the past 25 years, the minimal taxation paid by some large organisations has increasingly been a social and ethical issue and has become a high-profile concern for society and for governments. Thus, it is very timely to set tax within the context of Social Accounting in this text book.

Chapter 11 begins by presenting a broad overview of the objectives and scope of taxation before discussing issues surrounding the calculation of tax. The chapter then discusses taxation within the context of social responsibility, with an emphasis placed on entities other than private organisations, including NGOs, cooperatives and family businesses. Following this, the chapter considers the future direction of taxation within the context of social accountability and transparency.

Tomorrow's accounting and society's future

The purpose of this book is to introduce you to the notion of accounting for society, the historical development of corporate social responsibility, accountability and ethics and their importance to everyday life. We note that the practices we consider central to accounting are as old as human history and are essential to the functioning of complex societies. However, these foundations have come under critical scrutiny in recent years, particularly following the recent spate of global financial crises. Indeed, the reliance, accuracy and compliance of accounting information and the profession that generates it were heavily criticised alongside those other organisations that had also not foreseen or reacted to the global financial crisis adequately. In the book we show that such issues are not restricted to the private sector. Indeed, these issues are equally applicable to the public and third sectors as well as cooperatives and family businesses.

In the concluding chapter, we draw together the disparate strands of social accounting covered in this book. We acknowledge that, despite the growing trend of corporate accountability and the increasing revival of social accounting, there remains a significant gap between what organisations do, what they are willing to report, and the rights of society. We further note that globalisation and political uncertainty pose challenges to organisations in implementing social accounting practices. The chapter then moves on to consider how public sector, third sector, cooperatives and family businesses need to adapt and respond to demands for increased social responsibility, and to demonstrate this through a social accounting and accountability system. This is followed by a discussion of the future directions and potential developments within the social accounting arena.

While this book is targeted at undergraduate accounting students, the material is of interest and relevance to a wider audience. We hope that it will stimulate interest and thought in anyone wishing to develop knowledge and understanding of why social accounting, corporate social responsibility and the need to consider sustainability are important concepts and issues, not only for society of today, but for future generations.

To facilitate knowledge and understanding of the key concepts and issues covered in this book, each chapter is supported with end of chapter discussion questions. Mini case studies are also provided, at the end of the book, to stimulate discussion and reflection. Additionally, we have provided on the publisher's website, instructor's resources in the form of PowerPoint presentations and a set of multiple choice questions for each chapter. Solutions to the end of chapter discussion questions and the mini case studies are also available. Find these all at:

http://www.goodfellowpublishers.com/socialaccounting

References and further reading

de Aguiar, T. and Paterson, A. (2017). Sustainability on campus: knowledge creation through social and environmental reporting. *Studies in Higher Education*, pp.1-13.

Gauthier, Y., Leblanc, M., Farley, L. and Martel, L. (1997) *Introductory Guide to Environmental Accounting*. KPMG, Montreal.

Goyder, G. (1961). *The Responsible Company*. London: Blackwell.

Gray R.H. (2000). Current developments and trends in social and environmental auditing, reporting and attestation: A review and comment. *International Journal of Auditing*, **4**(3), 247-268.

Hopwood, A. G. and Miller, P., (eds.) (1994). *Accounting as a Social and Institutional Practice*. CUP, Cambridge.

Hopwood, A. and Tompkins, C. (1984) *Issues in Public Sector Accounting*. Oxford: Philip Allan Publishers Limited.

Jones, R. and Pendlebury, M. (2010) *Public Sector Accounting*. Harlow: Pearson Education Limited.

Lindsay, C., Osborne, S.P. and Bond, S. (2014). New public governance and employability services in an era of crisis: challenges for Third Sector Organizations in Scotland. *Public Administration*, **92**(1), 192-207.

Mathews M.R. and Perera M.H.B. (1995). *Accounting Theory and Development* (3rd Ed). Melbourne, Thomas Nelson Australia.

Pallot, J. (1992). Elements of a theoretical framework for public sector accounting, *Accounting, Auditing and Accountability Journal*, **5**(1), 38-59.

Paterson, A.S., Leung, D., Jackson, W., Macintosh, R. and O'Gorman, K. (eds.) (2016). *Research Methods for Accounting and Finance*. Goodfellow, Oxford.

Ramanathan, K. V. (1976). Toward a Theory of Social Accounting, *The Accounting Review*, 516–28.

The Scottish Government (2011). Renewing Scotland's Public Services. Priorities for reform in response to the Christie Commission. Available at: http://www.gov.scot

2 Accountability, Ethics, and the Business World

Audrey Paterson, Yasser Barghathi, Sunita Mathur and William Jackson

Introduction

The activities of business and the financial services industry, and their decision-making processes are predominantly motivated by profit maximisation criteria, which can often lead to highly questionable decisions being made (Paterson *et al.*, 2016). Indeed, we do not need to dig too far into the financial services world and the activities of business to find examples that demonstrate a distinct lack of consideration for society, the environment or human life, as well as activities that demonstrate questionable moral or ethical behaviour. The collapse of Enron, for example, was an outcome of unethical behaviour by the management and the accounting firm (Arthur Andersen), which resulted in great losses suffered by all of its stakeholders. Questionable business and accounting decisions are not restricted to the private sector but are also found within the public and third sectors. Cooperatives and family businesses are also not exempt from questionable business behaviour.

Within the public sector, the MHB Bank of Vietnam, which is part of the fully state-run Bank for Investment and Development of Vietnam, was exposed to fraudulent activities amounting to millions of dollars by three senior bankers and six securities officials (Channel News Asia, 2016). Petrobras, one of the largest state-owned oil organisations of Latin America also suffered from fraudulent activity of around $400m involving 35 members of which several were chief executives (Leahy, 2016; Guardian, 2014). The CEO within Age UK, a charity providing services and support for older people in the South Tyneside community, was charged with defrauding more than £700,000 from the organisation

(Cooney, 2015). The Co-operative Bank in the UK has been involved in a series of scandals including alleged drug-taking by former chairman Paul Flowers (Goodway, 2013). Family businesses, despite being run with a more hands-on and inclusive management style are also vulnerable to fraud. For example, Parmalat suffered four decades of fraudulent activity by Calisto Tanzi which ultimately led to its collapse (Guardian, 2004). Such scandals have led to growing demand for accountability across all sectors. Indeed, calls for these organisations to be held accountable for their actions, and for policies to be adopted to help prevent unethical actions that affect a wide range of stakeholders, feature highly in the media.

The concepts of ethics and social accountability have grown considerably in recent years in both the educational and professional contexts. This can be attributed to philosophers and scholars within accounting and finance successfully connecting ethical theory to real world problems (Paterson *et al.*, 2016). Within this chapter, we introduce you to two interrelated concepts: social accountability and ethics and their importance to everyday life. We begin by first considering what accountability and business ethics are and why they is important. Following this we introduce a discussion on the codes of conduct that facilitate social ethics and accountability. The chapter includes examples of important issues that require careful reflection and consideration when determining approaches to business activity and ensuring professional integrity. This is followed with a discussion on the limitations of ethics and codes of conduct.

Accountability concepts and relationships

Accountability, according to Bovens (2010), is a term that could embrace more than one meaning depending on the context in which it is used. A simple definition of accountability is taking, or being assigned, responsibility for something that you have done, or something you are supposed to do. From an ethics perspective, accountability is answerability, blameworthiness, liability, and the expectation of account-giving for one's actions. According to Day and Klein (1987), accountability is expected to be perceived differently in different contexts since it is a social and political process; they believe that accountability is mainly concerned about the definition of a certain type of conduct and how it is assessed. Sinclair (1995) stressed the importance of language in shaping accountability understanding. For example, an auditor views accountability as a financial matter, whereas a politician sees accountability as a political issue.

Accountability is arguably something that everyone should respect. It is a 'gold' concept that everyone agrees with and it is widely used in political discourse since it implies transparency and trustworthiness. However, it is also an 'elusive concept' that can mean different things to different people (Bovens, 2007). Laughlin (1990) justifies the linkage between finance and accountability based on the importance of finance for an organisation and a particular domain and, further, on the notion that the way finance is accounted for will influence how resources and responsibilities are accounted for.

A notable issue related to the term 'accountability' was indicated by Bovens (2007); that is the translation of the term into other languages. He indicates that accountability as a term does not exist in French, Portuguese, Spanish, German, Dutch or Japanese languages and, moreover, they do not distinguish between accountability and responsibility. The Arabic language appears not to have an equivalent word to accountability. The translation of 'responsibility' is commonly used to refer to this term.

Bovens (2010) describes accountability as a synonym to good governance. He points out that it has become a general term that refers to any mechanism by which powerful institutions can be made responsive to their stakeholders. In an extended discussion, accountability has been succinctly defined by Gray *et al.* (1996:38) as 'the duty to provide an account (by no means necessarily a financial account) or reckoning of those actions for which one is held responsible'. Accountability thus implies two 'responsibilities or duties'. First the accountor is responsible for performing a duty and then is responsible to account for that duty to whom he or she is responsible, the accountee (Gray *et al.*, 1996). However, Cooper and Owen (2007: 653) noted a shortfall in the accountability definition given by Gray *et al.* (1996). The issues of "effective utilization of information" and "associated power differentials" have not been addressed. They suggest for accountability to be achieved the accountees (stakeholders) should be given the power to hold the accountor to account. They argue that stakeholder accountability can be enhanced by empowerment.

An accountability framework is seen to imply justification and explanation of what an accountor has done. It also implies that accountability should be discharged. Jackson (1982) views accountability as follows:

> Basically, accountability involves explaining or justifying what has been done, what is currently being done and what has been planned. Accountability arises from a set of established procedures and relationships of varying formality. Thus, one party is accountable to another in the sense that one of the parties has the right to call upon the other to give an account of his activities. Accountability involves, therefore, the giving of information. (Jackson, 1982: 220)

In Stewart's (1984:16) words, an accountability relationship ends by providing an account (i.e. information). He describes the accountability relationship, as 'involving both the account and the holding to account'. Fitting the notion of providing an account in the accounting context, one could infer that providing accounting information represents a way for accountors to discharge their accountability to accountees.

Within an accountability framework there is a need to distinguish between: 'legal and non-legal; or moral or natural, rights and responsibilities' (Gray *et al.*

1996: 39). The most obvious rights and responsibilities are determined by law and are considered the lowest level of rights and responsibilities that, according to the accountability framework, the accountor must fulfil.

Having discussed the concept of accountability, we now move to what is referred to as accountability relationship which will be discussed based on two notions of accountability, namely narrow and wide notions of accountability.

■ The notion of narrow accountability (shareholders)

A narrow definition of accountability implies the existence of an explicit contract between two parties (accountor and accountee). Swift (2001) suggested a contract is essential in the (narrow) accountability relationship and that without it there will be no accountability. She states that:

> *"Narrow definitions conceive of accountability as being pertinent to contractual arrangements only, asserting that where accountability is not contractually bound there can be no act of accountability"* (Swift, 2001: 17).

The simple example to illustrate the narrow notion of the accountability relationship is that of a company's directors and shareholders (Gray *et al.* 1996). Directors (accountors) have the duty to look after shareholder's (accountees) resources, either financial or non-financial, (managing the company). They are also responsible for providing an account for their mission (i.e. to prepare and provide financial statements). Here the accountor takes on the responsibility to undertake the management and is responsible for delivering or discharging accountability by preparing and submitting the financial statements. The responsibility to discharge accountability is of great importance and represents the essence of accountability overall. Perks (1993) for example, states that: 'accountability means the obligation to give an account' (p. 23).

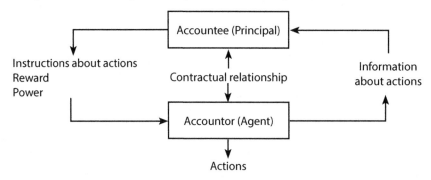

Figure 2.1: The accountability relationship. Source: Gray *et al.* (1996: 39).

Regardless of which sector the organisation is placed in (private, public, third sector etc.) it is argued that to understand accountability in a specific situation four questions must be answered; '(1) who is accountable (2) to whom, (3) how (by what means) and (4) for what?' (Perks, 1993:24). In the narrow notion of accountability managers are accountable for the funds they are entrusted with by shareholders or in the case of public sector organisations, government officials. They discharge their accountability by providing accounting information, although Gray *et al.* (1996) suggest that the discharge of accountability may not, and arguably should not, be only through financial information as managers could and should use narrative accounting to discharge such information. The accountability relationship can be illustrated simply as shown in Figure (2.1).

According to Swift (2001) the accountability relationship between two parties is usually represented in the form of a principal-agent relationship and a lot of accountability definitions support the notion that the accountability relationship is derived from agency theory. She stated:

> *These definitions underpinning the accountability framework are rooted in economic agency theory which asserts that agents are prey to opportunism if they remain unchecked by regulation or other social controls imposed by society.* (Swift, 2001:17).

However, Gray *et al.* (1996) emphasise the importance of distinguishing between an accountability relationship between a principal and an agent, and agency theory, which makes explicit assumptions about the purely self-interested motivations of the parties to the relationship that Gray *et al.* regard as inadequate to fully explain the parties' motivations.

■ The notion of wider accountability (stakeholders)

Accountability has been extended to include stakeholders other than only financial investors. Connolly and Dhanani (2013) indicated that the notion of wide accountability has recently come to the fore. Organisations have started to report on their social, political, and wider economic interests, not only to their financial investors but also to all of their stakeholders. This extension may be due to the influence that organisations have on the other stakeholders: 'If institutions [i.e. organisations] affect the lives of others, so the argument goes, they should be accountable to them [others]' (Steets, 2010: 41). However, Gallhofer and Haslam (1993) argue that an accountability relationship has an even wider scope than is portrayed by the discussion above. They claim:

> *Accountability is not so much about holding responsible and judging behavior; nor does it assume a simple agency-principal relation… accountability appears equivalent to the ability to render accounts conducive to well-being.* (Gallhofer and Haslam, 1993:326).

An accountability relationship, despite its simplest model representing only a two-way relationship between an accountee and an accountor, according to Gray *et al.* (1996) is also more flexible. An accountability relationship exists between employees and management, which, according to Stewart (1984), can be referred to as managerial accountability by which employees are accountor to the management in respect of performing their duties, meanwhile management are accountor to employees in respect of offering them a healthy and safe workplace (Gray *et al.* 1996).

The wider view of accountability is where an organisation's managers are held accountable to various groups in society, rather than only to shareholders (or perhaps also the creditors) as depicted by the narrow notion. The wider view also holds that they are accountable in respect of different issues besides the financial position and performance; e.g. reporting about social and economic issues of the company's performance known as corporate social reporting (CSR)[1].

■ Public accountability

Having discussed the accountability concept and the difference between the two views of accountability (*narrow* and *wide*) we now move on to discuss what is called 'public accountability'. The accountability concept and relationship should remain the same regardless of whether it is within private sector, public or third sector. However, there is a fundamental difference between the two in terms of the source of funds entrusted to the agent. In the private sector, the agent is entrusted with private finance while in the public sector the fund is public. According to Bovens (2007), public accountability can be defined as the:

> *Relationship between an actor and a forum, in which the actor has an obliga-tion to explain and to justify his or her conduct, the forum can pose questions and pass judgment, and the actor may face consequences.* (Bovens, 2007:450)

Boven's statement suggests that public accountability can still be seen as an agent entrusted with (public) funds being held accountable to a principal, but the nature and location of the principal is much less clearly defined. Public accountability can be found in public sector and not-for-profit sector (NPOs). The importance of public accountability to secure the use of public funds has increased in the recent past, mainly due to the financial crisis of 2008, and the increasing reliance on voluntary contributions from different stakeholders including individuals, national governments, and funding agencies (Crawford *et al.*, 2017). Reporting non-financial information will help NPOs in several ways. It will, for example, assist NPOs when improving operational progress. It will also be helpful in identifying the areas where good practice has taken place through which it would be easy to identify other areas that need to be improved (McConville, 2017).

Accountability in the private sector can arguably be discharged by provid-ing financial statements based on which the performance of the entity can be assessed. The public sector, on the other hand, will need more than financial accountability to measure the performance of the not-for-profit organization. Financial accountability on its own will not be sufficient and they (public sector organisations) will have to 'tell their stories' so that their performance is better

---

1 CSR has been used in the literature to refer to corporate social reporting but in recent years the abbreviation CSR is more commonly used to refer to corporate social responsibility.

measured, and accordingly public accountability will also require reporting on non-financial performance information (McConville, 2017). This is discussed more fully in later chapters.

It should be noted that although accountability is generally seen as beneficial (whether public or private) not all actors will view it in the same way. It rather depends on the viewpoint of the individual and whether they are the principal or the agent. It is much more likely to be favoured by the principal as their knowledge is improved and their assets more secure as a result. By contrast, it is less likely to be favoured by the agent who comes under scrutiny and is required to do extra work to justify their actions (Perks, 1993). Considering the relative restrictions that agents might suffer to their freedom in this accountability relationship, Coy *et al.* (2001) suggest that they (as accountors) might well seek ways to avoid such constraints.

As discussed above, public accountability refers to the agent being accountable for his/her actions to the principal by being obliged to report not only on the prudent use of funds, but also on the way that they deliver the necessary services to their stakeholders and conduct their operations in an ethical manner. Public accountability, therefore, is sometimes referred to as social accounting in which the reported information must consider the implications of the business on the social context. This leads to a discussion of what is commonly referred to as 'business ethics' or how business (and other operations) can be ethically conducted.

Business ethics

Business ethics is increasingly becoming a prominent issue in the business world, attracting a great deal of attention from the business community and researchers (Rashid and Ibrahim, 2008). Indeed, as the examples referred to above demonstrate, greater emphasis on ethics as well as organisational social responsibility is a vital issue in all sectors of business and society (Valentine and Fleischman, 2008).

According to Lopez-Gamero *et al.* (2008), ethics can be defined as the application of moral principles and values when making choices between right and wrong actions. Ethics in simple terms are rules and regulations or standards (explicit or implicit) that govern our actions in everyday activities. They help us to differentiate between 'right' and 'wrong'. Many believe that ethics are governed by or originate from several factors, such as an individual's society, culture, traditions, religion, faith, and family values. Similarly, business ethics reflect the philosophy of Business. It cannot be compared to subjects like Accounting, Engineering, Company Law or Finance, where there is a logical sequence of processes and procedures, following which help you to make decisions that are objectively correct. Business ethics can simply be defined as:

> *...the study of a business situation, activities and decisions where issues of right and wrong are addressed. By right and wrong we mean morally right and wrong as opposed to, for example, commercially, strategically or financially right or wrong* (Crane and Matten, 2010: 5)

Researchers have confirmed that recent private and public sector scandals involving unethical and immoral practices impose substantial consequences for their stakeholders (Cacioppe *et al.* 2008). For instance, Enron and Arthur Andersen created chaos in the business and accounting world when their unethical practices were reported in the media, quite aside from the costs of the company's collapse to their stakeholders (Rashid and Ibrahim, 2008). The collapse in 1987 of the National Bank of Fiji, where thousands of small depositors had deposited their hard-earned savings is another example (Valemei, 2014).

Any organisation that is operating within a society is a social organisation if it serves the society and is rewarded for its services. Yong (2008) believes a business has an obligation to recognise the whole society as part of its social responsibility, because it emerges from, operates in and benefits from that society. De George (1990) considers business as a social enterprise and that its mandate and limits have been set by society; although business's limits are based in morality, they are generally expressed in the form of written laws and regulations. The accounting profession for example, must maintain a high perception of ethical standards for it to provide users of accounting information with information that is both reliable and trusted. This is important, because it is generally held that the efficiency of capital markets is contingent on users' confidence in the information that they have received. Thus, agency theory emphasizes that the auditor's ethical behaviour is crucial in the process of financial reporting (Felton *et al.*, 2008). This then leads us to consider how individuals and organisations learn and develop ethical and moral standards.

■ A (very brief) history of ethics

Early philosophers such as Socrates, Plato and Aristotle examined and discussed various topics like virtue, wisdom, and human good, and how one must behave within the norms of society. Western moral philosophy took from the Greeks, who spent a lot of time contemplating what makes a 'good person'. According to the Greeks a 'good citizen' who 'contributed to the state' was a 'good person' (Gaffikin, 2007). In the modern period, 1600 AD to the present times, Hobbes (1588-1679), who is held to be the founder of modern ethics, indicated that ethics is influenced by the political order as well as the security of public authority. Of course, even without the conventions and laws of a civil society we might still have the inclination to be peaceful as well as to be kind and generous, but just leaving it at this would perhaps be contrary to self-preservation. Hobbes developed the notion of the social contract. This way people in a society enter into an agreement in their own best interests to avoid social conflict. Everyone agrees not to steal from, or kill, others in such an agreement. Such a contract in

2

written form would be imposed by a government, being a (relatively) neutral third party, which is why Hobbes believed that governments should be strong (Gaffikin, 2007).

The German philosopher Immanuel Kant (1724-1804) is generally considered the most important name in modern ethics. Kant believed that irrespective of whether actions like murder, theft and lying result in more happiness for the majority they should be absolutely prohibited. He proposed asking the following two questions before a person decides to act: (i) Can the person rationally will that everyone acts as he proposes? Unless the answer is yes, then the person should not perform the action. (ii) Is the action to merely use humans for the person's own purpose or does it respect the goals of all humans? Again, unless the answer is yes then the person should not perform the action. Kant believed that these questions were equivalent (Anscombe, n.d.).

The early 2000s saw some high-profile cases of diversion from the ethical standards, as mentioned earlier in the chapter, both in private as well as public sectors. To address the resultant lack of confidence in organisational ethics and financial reporting, in 2001 the US Congress passed the Sarbanes-Oxley Act which made securities fraud a criminal offence and greatly strengthened the penalties for organisational fraud. Likewise, following a series of public and third sector fraud cases other world governments have increased their accountability and transparency requirements through the implementation of acts and policies.

Pause for thought

"Donald Trump's regular jaunts to his Mar-a-Lago club in Florida appear to be costing taxpayers a small fortune. The president's three trips have probably cost the federal Treasury about $10 million, the Washington Post estimates, based on an October 2016 Government Accountability Office analysis of White House travel. By comparison, Barack Obama's travel expenses averaged just $12.1 million during each year of his presidency. In total, Obama's eight-year travel bill came to $97 million and unbelievably, Donald Trump is on pace to outspend him in less than one year." (McCarthy, 2017:58). Critics are concerned that the billionaire first family hasn't acknowledged that these trips are being paid for by America's people.

Q: Reflecting on the chapter discussion so far, should President Trump give back any of the $10 million of public (tax payers) money that he has spent on his three trips to Mar-a-Lago as President?

Having outlined the concept of accountability and introduced the importance of ethical considerations we now turn our attention to social accounting and its importance to organisational performance.

Social accounting

Social accounting assesses the impact of an organisation's action on the internal and external environment within which it operates. It is not just the systematic and regulated activities of the organisation; it is a combination of myriad subjects. Gray *et al.* (2014:3), defines social accounting as 'the process of communicating the social and environmental effects of organisations' economic actions to particular interest groups within society and to society at large.' He adds that reporting about such activities may require both financial and non-financial information. Therefore, here it becomes necessary to bring out the differences between traditional accounting and social accounting.

Traditional accounting quantifies the performance of the company mainly in terms of monetary, or material values, but in social accounting the performance of the company is measured in terms of its effect on society, the environment, and the effect of these on the sustainability of its activities. The differences between the two types of accounting can be summarized as follows:

> *a) Social accounting is not for financial or economic events, but for a lot of other activities like sustainability of socio economic activities, NGOs etc. b) Social accounting is not only providing information to the finance providers of the company but to an array of individuals and groups e.g. trade unions, local community members, employees etc. and c) Social accounting not only facilitates the financial judgment of the company but for a range of other activities e.g. behaviour of the organisation in terms of labour law, the effect on the environment etc.* (Gray *et al.*, 2014).

Figure 2.2: The pyramid of organisational social responsibility. Adapted from Gray (2014:40).

So, it can be said that traditional accounting is just a minor part of the entire universe of accounting and only a part of the broader aspect of social accounting. Gray *et al.* (2014) put forth the basic elements of the conventional accounting model, which would include a formal account that has been prepared by the organisation about social and environmental activities and communicated to all stakeholders (internal and external).

■ Social accounting relationships and systems

The period of 1995-2005 witnessed a steep increase in financial scandals and significant and repetitive losses suffered by investors and employees across all business sectors. Scientific claims of global warming too became more accepted and its effects began to be felt around the world. These crises emphasized the need for greater social accountability which was increasingly the focus of lobbying by human rights activists and environmentalists. This led to major changes in the activities of many organisations which, in response to the demands of public opinion and looming legislative changes, started to promote activities leading to environmental protection, consumer protection and employees' welfare. Indeed, organisations are increasingly under pressure to demonstrate social accountability to society to prove that they have more to offer than just increasing profit margins and/or continued existence.

Understanding the organisation-society relationship is a key perspective in comprehending the social responsibility of an organisation. The way each organisation takes on the responsibility varies. In small organisations, for example, the personal values of the owner tend to be closely aligned with those of the organisation and, if the organisation is to survive, they need to engage with current social trends. Greater problems arise when big organisations seek profit and growth as their sole objective. It is argued that organisations can benefit from adopting more rigorous accountability and ethical practice on several fronts. For example, an organisation can enrich its governance structures and accountability to all stakeholders through establishing clearer lines of communication that can facilitate discussion of the objectives and results of organisational activity. A robust system of accountability and strong ethical code can also help to solve the problem of incomplete information, which can affect relations between the organisation and its stakeholders. Organisation strategy and policy development can further be advanced through improved dialogue with all stakeholders, which can empower organisational decision-makers and management to anticipate, appreciate and balance stakeholders' interests, expectations and reactions to their activities.

From the above discussion, an accountability and ethical accounting system embodies both a strategic management tool and a communication tool that extends beyond traditional accounting systems. It is a systematic approach to the collection of information on the organisation's social and ethical performance. This information is useful for the management's strategic decision-making and enables organisational decision-makers to engage in effective dialogue with stakeholders and facilitates trust with the organisation's stakeholders.

It should be noted that Gray *et al.* (2014), offer two main reasons for organisations to be socially responsible: accountability and sustainability. Accountability, as discussed above is the responsibility of a manager to be accountable for his/her actions. Thus, the greater the power of managers the greater their responsibility to provide full and complete social and environmental information to the various stakeholders. Sustainability, on the other hand, is the careful use of the current resources for the benefit of the current stakeholders to ensure that the next generation is not affected. Managers, therefore, will need to develop and focus on balancing that fine line between competing needs – the need to move forward technologically and economically, and the need to protect the environment (natural and social) in which we and others live. The importance of sustainability will be discussed further throughout the text, but especially in Chapter 5.

A healthy social accountability initiative such as that discussed above, if effectively implemented by organisations in the private, public and other sectors, can have a deep positive impact on the morale of employees, leading to higher job satisfaction, greater productivity and a better employee–employer relationship. It will also help customers or consumers of products and services to make ethical choices if they are aware of the organisation's strength of social responsibility.

Having discussed the importance of social accountability and the potential benefits to organisations we now move on to consider ways in which organisations can enact a sense of ethical behaviour, through providing training to organisational actors and adoption of ethical codes of conduct.

Accountability and ethical training

Most managers at all levels of an organisation, irrespective of the size of the organisational unit they are handling, will face ethical dilemmas in their decision making processes constantly throughout their careers. Such ethical dilemmas come in various forms and give rise to complex situations. They could be extreme examples such as overstating profits, irregularly valuing assets, taking part in fraudulent activities such as bribery or corruption, withholding valuable information from shareholders, but, they can equally encompass mundane resource allocation decisions in which one group is prioritised over another, or simply making decisions with limited/inadequate information.

Knowing how to respond to ethical dilemmas can increase decision making effectiveness and keep the organisation on the right side of stakeholder sentiment. An effective response to ethical dilemmas can be achieved through the implementation of ethically based policies, practices, and programmes put in place by management. This is known as *'business ethics management'*, but the essence of it is equally applicable to other sectors. These workplace policies, or codes of ethics, are based on the company's mission, vision and philosophy, and are typically assembled into a handbook, made readily available to employees, to assist them in their ethical decision-making processes.

Training in ethical and social accountability can aid organisational actors in their understanding of the moral and ethical aspects of their business and financial decisions; empowering them to apply moral principles and values to their daily activities. It can further raise employees' understanding and compliance with the organisation's vision/mission and thus facilitate an acceptable balance between the organisation and its stakeholders. Such training is not only a process to educate individual employees on the organisation's activities, but is also a means to encourage individual reflection on their own position, which helps them to internalise good practice and thereby contribute to the organisation's vision/mission through a conscious alignment of their own actions and ethical behaviour.

Ethical and social accountability training, therefore, is not only a means to inform employees of the organisation's ethical management stance, but also allows each individual organisational member to be able to understand the purpose, need and vision of the organisation's ethical and social accountability code of conduct. The purpose of ethics training, according to Sacconi *et al.* (2002), is to develop employees' moral awareness so they are more able to identify and deal with ethical problems. Ethics training would also facilitate sharing and applying ethical values in the organisation (de Colle and Gonella, 2002). Thus, ethics training can provide organisational actors with a set of ethical capabilities that can enhance their ability to recognise ethical dilemmas and analyse and respond to these in an appropriate way (Awareness Raising Training). It can further augment decision making skills to interpret and apply organisational values in their everyday tasks and decision making as well as their interactions with organisational stakeholders (Function-specific Ethical Training). At an organisational level, ethics training such as awareness raising workshops, role play, crisis simulations etc, can strengthen the dissemination of organisational values and reinforce a shared ethics culture.

Designing and maintaining an effective organisational ethics and social accountability policy and code of conduct are the core responsibilities of the organisation's ethics and compliance officers. In the US an Ethics and Compliance Officer Association was set up in 1992 and more than 50% of Fortune 100 organisations have become members of it, which shows the importance that even the largest of businesses now place on these issues. Having a committee of this nature can help to support employees when they encounter workplace dilemmas that place them in a threatening position, e.g. whistle blowing. The aim of ethical codes and supporting organisational structures is, therefore, to provide a guidance mechanism that 'reasonably' helps to reduce the occurrence of unethical or illegal behaviour Kaptein and Schwarts (2008).

The key elements of such a programme could include:

■ Oversight by high-level personnel;

■ Due care in delegating substantial discretionary authority;

- Effective communication with all levels of employees;

- Reasonable steps to achieve compliance, which include systems for monitoring, auditing, and reporting suspected wrongdoing without fear of reprisal;

- Consistent enforcement of compliance standards including disciplinary mechanisms;

- Reasonable steps to respond to and prevent further similar offences upon detection of a violation.

■ Codes of conduct and ethics

Codes of conduct and ethics have recently attracted much attention in the academic literature following the many scandals that rocked the financial market in early 2000s, as well as the scandals that took place within the public and third sectors. Indeed, reports of unethical behaviour by some organisations have gripped the attention of the public who have called for action to be taken (Canary and Jennings, 2008). Such issues have affected public perceptions of the ethical behaviour, not only of these organizations, but the entire business world. As a result, it has become very critical for all organisations to have a code of conduct in place to govern the ethical standards of the organisation.

As our previous sections demonstrate, there are good and valid reasons for the implementation and adherence to both accountability and ethical codes of conduct, but such codes do not appear from nowhere and organisations that do not already have one, or have one that is out of date need to find ways of developing and implementing them. Fortunately, there are many useful organisations which provide sound principles and guidelines as exemplars. For instance, the accounting profession lays down a specific ethical code of conduct for all its members regardless of their status (student or professional) to which they are required to conform (Hellier and Bebbington, 2004) and many other organisations are open about the content of their own codes. But it is important that organisations seeking to enact their own code of conduct do not simply copy that of another and attempt to implement it without reference to their own context. They can use others' codes for inspiration and guidance but need to build a set of principles that are primarily relevant to their own organisation and its stakeholders, therefore a certain element of originality is necessary. Building a code where none exists is therefore a non-trivial task for the organisation, but typically they will have some common features.

A code of conduct can be defined as a document of formal written statements of organisational principles and values and the expected behaviour of employees. Kaptein and Schwarts (2008:113) have developed the following definition:

> *A business code is a distinct and formal document containing a set of prescriptions developed by and for a company to guide present and future behaviour on multiple issues of its managers and employees towards one another, the company, external stakeholders and/or society in general.*

An organisational code of ethics provides the main apparatus to institutional-ise the organisation's own specific set of moral values and practices. Typically, a code of ethics will outline the rights, duties and responsibilities of the organisa-tion towards its employees, stakeholders and the wider society. It is a statement of behaviour principles and rules of conduct which are designed to enrich the decision-making processes and orientation of organisational activity.

Such a construction provides external stakeholders with reference parameters on which they can develop their opinions of the ethical and moral reliability of the organisation and its reputation within the industry (Sacconi et al., 2002). On the other hand, a code of ethics can also be an indication for ethical behaviour commitment by the organization which can be seen as an attempt to regain the public confidence and trust (Hyatt, 2012). In the words of Stohl et al. (2009: 608), "codes of ethics are increasingly spreading around to become 'more common-place' because of the held perception that they are marketing instruments of legitimation". They added that such codes are also perceived as an evidence that organisation is committed to ethical behaviours.

A code of ethics also embodies the organisation's constitutional charter of moral rights and duties that expresses the responsibilities of the organisation (including all its members), states the ethical ideology and rules of conduct through which the organisation values are put into practice, and is used to provide a guide for individual behaviour. A well designed code, therefore, pro-vides a tool for the organisation through the provision of guiding principles for organisational activity and its reporting. As such, it can build trust, encourage stakeholder co-operation and help preserve the organisation's reputation and moral legitimisation.

An effective code of ethics is characterised by the implementation mechanisms associated with it. These include actions that the organisation needs to engage, establish or amend, to support and facilitate the dissemination and promotion of the code. It should also facilitate the dissemination of the shared values and rules of behaviour and provide monitoring of individual and organisational behaviour when necessary. It should further permit periodic review and updates to the code in line with organisational developments. A well-constructed code ideally focuses on what is right or wrong from an ethical viewpoint, and addresses potential conflicts of interest (Luckerath-Rovers and Bos, 2011; Hyatt, 2012). As such, it could govern the future behaviour of both organisation and employees more specifically. Furthermore, a code of ethics can address the responsibilities of the employees and the organisation to the wider community, i.e. stakeholders (Stohl et al., 2009).

While there can be significant benefits to organisations from the implemen-tation of an ethics and social accountability programme which is informed by regulations and standards put forward by government and institutes such as the Institute of Business Ethics (IBE), there are also potential limitations. For example, initiating a strong focus on compliance can lead to a 'follow-the-law' mindset in organisational members that can lead to decision making that lacks 'moral imagination' (Izraeli and Schwartz, 1998). Genuine reflection on complex decisions, of the sort that moral imagination implies, is an essential component in making good ethical and moral judgments, therefore decision makers should not unthinkingly adhere to codes without proper reflection on the resultant outcomes. A 'follow-the-law' mentality which adheres to actions being determined by a set of rules or rule-governed concerns also restricts the ability and effectiveness of organisational actors in responding to and dealing with potential ethical issues (de Colle and Werhane, 2008). Thus, a code of ethics may not be as effective as one might think. Indeed, Kaptein and Schwarts (2008) noted some limitations of code of ethics which include:

- Implementation of the code may cost the organisation more that it benefits.
- In some cases, a code of ethics is not able to influence behaviour, the sector code or law may work more efficiently.
- Some stakeholders view code of ethics as window dressing to provide an image that the organisation is ethically committed.

An additional constraint on the effectiveness of codes of ethics and conduct stems from differences in the cultures, attitudes and belief systems of individuals. Markus and Kitayama (2003) note differences in personalities and behaviour of people of the Western cultures (e.g. United States, Britain, etc.) and those belonging to the non-Western cultures (e.g. China, Japan, etc.). For example, people of Western cultures see themselves as more independent, self-reliant, more detached and not much concerned about the impact of their thoughts, actions and behaviour on others. Whereas people of the non-Western cultures are relatively more interdependent. These differences across cultures affect the way people see and feel the realities and their perception of what they consider to be ethical or unethical behaviour. For example, in the Asian-Pacific countries like India, China, Japan, employees hesitate to question their superiors, even if they feel that they are being asked to do something unethical. This is less likely be the case in North America and Europe.

Summary

This chapter has attempted to provide a background to the general debate on the need for organisations across all sectors to demonstrate accountability and ethical behaviour in their business activity. We have demonstrated that the concept of accountability is rather chameleon as it holds different meaning depending on the context and is, therefore, not simple to pin down. Likewise, we note that the question of ethical business behaviour is a subject that has troubled thinkers and policy makers for many decades. Indeed, the subject of business and accounting ethics has become substantially more complicated as organisations conduct business across multiple national boundaries and cultural settings. The activities of organisations have the potential to impact on all aspects of society and this drives the need for organisations to demonstrate good ethical and moral behaviour and accountability. A robust code of conduct/ethics is generally regarded as the hallmark of a profession. This has been recognised by the accounting profession and their implementation of a code by which it expects its members to behave. Members are expected to comply not only with the 'letter of the code' but also the 'spirit'. Other organisations demonstrate varying degrees of responsibility and compliance towards social accountability and ethical behaviour. Those with robust systems can potentially achieve a reduction of unethical or illegal behaviour and can use this to create strategic advantage.

■ Discussion questions

1 What is meant by 'Business Ethics Management' and how ethical decision-making can be made effective?

2 Define the term 'accountability' and distinguish between the wider and the narrower notions of accountability.

3 How can ethical issues be addressed?

4 Despite the potential benefits that can be achieved from implementation of code of ethics, there are also potential limitations. Discuss

References and further reading

Adams, J. S., Tashchian, A. and Shore, T. H. (2001). Codes of ethics as signals for ethical behavior, *Journal of Business Ethics*, **29**, 199-211.

Anscombe, E. (n.d.) Kantian ethics, Available at: http://www.citethisforme.com/guides/harvard/how-to-cite-a-website

Atakan, M. S., Burnaz, S. and Topcu, Y. I. (2008). An empirical investigation of the ethical perceptions of future managers with a special emphasis on gender - Turkish case. *Journal of Business Ethics*, **82**, 573-586.

Bovens, M. (2007). Analysing and assessing accountability: A conceptual framework. *European Law Journal*, **13**, 447-468.

Bovens, M. a. P. (2010). Two concepts of accountability: Accountability as a virtue and as a mechanism. *West European Politics*, **33**, 946-967.

Cacioppe, R., Forster, N. and Fox, M. (2008). A survey of managers' perceptions of organisation ethics and social responsibility and actions that may affect organisation' success. *Journal of Business Ethics*, **82**, 681-700.

Canary, H. E. and Jennings, M. (2008). Principles and influences in codes of ethics: A centering resonance analysis comparing pre-and post-Sarbanes-Oxley codes of ethics, *Journal of Business Ethics*, **80**, 263-278.

Channel News Asia (2016), Vietnam seeks death penalty for embezzlement by ex-chairman of state energy firm, Available at: http://www.channelnewsasia.com/news/asiapacific/vietnam-seeks-death-penalty-for-embezzlement-by-ex-chairman-of-state-energy-firm-9216538

Connolly, C. and Dhanani, A. (2013). Exploring the discharging of e-ccountability by charities. *Journal of Applied Accounting Research*, 14, n/a.

Cooney, R. (2015), Police look into allegations of fraud at Age UK South Tyneside, Available at://www.thirdsector.co.uk/police-look-allegations-fraud-age-uk-south-tyneside/finance/article/1371350

Cooper, S. M. and Owen, D. L. (2007). Organisation social reporting and stakeholder accountability: The missing link. *Accounting, Organizations and Society*, **32**, 649-667.

Coy, D., Fischer, M. and Gordon, T. (2001). Public accountability: A new paradigm for college and university annual reports. *Critical Perspectives on Accounting*, **12**, 1-31.

Crane, A. and Matten, D. (2010). *Business ethics*. 3th Ed, Oxford University.

Crawford, L., Morgan, G., Cordery, C., and Breen, O. (2017). For the love of humanity: Mobilising profession accounting knowledge into not-for-profit financial reporting practice. Paper presented to BAFA 2017 annual conference, Edinburgh, 10-12 April.

Day, P. and Klein, R. (1987). *Accountabilities: Five public services*, London: Tavistock.

de Colle, S. and Gonella, C (2002) The social and ethical alchemy: an integrative approach to social and ethical accountability, *Business Ethics: A European Review,* **11** (1):86-96.

de Colle, S., and Werhane, P. H. (2008). Moral motivation across ethical theories: What can we learn for designing corporate ethics programs? *Journal of Business Ethics*, **81**, 751–764.

De George, R. T. (1990). *Business Ethics*, New York, Macmillan.

Doran, C. (2014). Ethical Codes of Conduct: Theory and Application in Small and Medium Businesses. PhD Thesis, University of Salford.

Elias, R. Z. (2004). The impact of organisation ethical values on perceptions of earnings management. *Managerial Auditing Journal*, **19**, 84-98.

Felton, S., Dimnik, T. and Bay, D. (2008). Perceptions of accountants' ethics: evidence from their portrayal in cinema. *Journal of Business Ethics*, **83**, 217-232.

Ferrell, Fraedich, and Ferrel. (2005). *Business Ethics*. Boston, Houghton Mifflin Company.

Fiji Times, (2014), Fiji's biggest scandal, Available at: http://www.fijitimes.com/story.aspx?id=260705

Forde, S. (1998). Hugo Grotius on Ethics and War. *The American Political Science Review,* **92**(3), 639-648. doi:10.2307/2585486.

Gaffikin, M. (2007). Accounting research and theory: The age of neo-empiricism, *Australasian Accounting, Business and Finance Journal*, **1**, 1-19.

2

Gallhofer, S. and Haslam, J. (1993). Approaching organisation accountability: Fragments from the past. *Accounting and Business Research*, **23**, 320-330.

Goodway, N., (2013), Co-op drafts in 'bad bank' boss to tackle its £1bn black hole, Available at: http://www.independent.co.uk/news/business/news/co-op-drafts in bad-bank-boss-to-tackle-its-1bn-black-hole-8645089.html

Gray, R. (1983). Accounting, financial reporting and not-for-profit organizations. *British Accounting Review*, **15**, 3-23.

Gray, R. (1992). Accounting and environmentalism: An exploration of the challenge of gently accounting for accountability, transparency and sustainability. *Accounting, Organizations and Society*, **17**, 399-425.

Gray, R. H., Owen, D. and Adams, C. A. (1996). *Accounting and Accountability: Changes and challenges in organisation social and environmental reporting*, Harlow, Financial Times/Prentice Hall.

Gray, R. H., Owen, D. L. and Maunders, K. (1987). *Organisation Social Reporting: Accounting and accountability*, London, Prentice/Hall international.

Gray, R. H., Owen, D. L. and Maunders, K. T. (1991). Accountability, organisation social reporting and the external social audits. *Advances in Public Interest Accounting*, **4**, 1-21.

Gray, R., Adams, C, and Owen, D. (2014). *Accountability, Social Responsibility and Sustainability: Accounting for society and the environment.* Edinburgh, Pearson Education Ltd.

Gray, R., Adams, C. and Owen, D., 2014. Accountability, social responsibility and sustainability: Accounting for society and the environment. Pearson Higher Ed.

Gray, R., Dey, C., Owen, D., Evans, R. and Zadek, S. (1997). Struggling with the praxis of social accounting. *Accounting, Auditing and Accountability Journal*, **10**, 325-364.

Guardian, (2004) Parmalat dream goes sour, Available at: https://www.theguardian. com/business/2004/jan/04/corporatefraud.parmalat2

Guardian, (2013), The Co-op scandal: drugs, sex, religion … and the humiliation of a movement, Available at: https://www.theguardian.com/business/2013/nov/23/ coop-scandal-paul-flowers-mutual-societies

Guardian, (2014), Petrobras scandal: Brazilian oil executives among 35 charged, Available at: https://www.theguardian.com/world/2014/dec/12/ petrobras-scandal-brazilian-oil-executives-among-35-charged

Hartman, L. (2011). *Business Ethics*. New York, McGraw-Hill.

Helliar, C., and Bebbington, J., (2004), *Taking Ethics to Heart*, Institute of Chartered Accountants of Scotland Monograph, Edinburgh.

Hopwood, A. (1990). Accounting and organisation change. *Accounting, Auditing and Accountability Journal*, **3**, 7-17.

Hughes, C.L. (1998), The primacy of ethics: Hobbes and Levinas, *Continental Philosophy Review*, **31**(1), 79-94.

Hyatt, K. (2012), Research on organisation codes of ethics and its application to university honor codes, in *Handbook of Research on Teaching Ethics in Business and Management Education*, Wankel, C. and Stachowics-Stanusch, A. (Eds.), IGI Global, pp 310-326.

Ijiri, Y. (1983). On the accountability-based conceptual framework of accounting. *Journal of Accounting and Public Policy*, **2**, 75-81.

Izraeli, D. and Schwartz, M. (1998), What can we learn from the U.S. Federal Sentencing Guidelines for organizational ethics?', *Journal of Business Ethics*, **17**, 1045-1055.

Jackson, P. M. (1982). *The Political Economy of Bureaucracy*, Deddington Philip Allan.

Kaptein, M., and Schwarts, M. S. (2008). The Effectiveness of business codes: A critical examination of existing studies and the development of an integrated research model. *Journal of Business Ethics*, **77**, 111-127.

Laffan, B. (2003). Auditing and accountability in the European Union. *Journal of European Public Policy*, **10**, 762-777.

Laughlin, R. C. (1990). A model of financial accountability and the Church of England *Financial Accountability and Management*, **6**, 93-114.

Leahy, (2016). What is the Petrobras scandal that is engulfing Brazil?,Financial Times.

López-Gamero, M.D., Claver-Cortés, E. and Molina-Azorín, J.F. (2008), Complementary resources and capabilities for an ethical and environmental management: A qualitative/quantitative study, *Journal of Business Ethics*, **82**, 701-732.

Lovell, A. and Fisher, C. (2003). *Business Ethics and Values*, Harlow, FT Prentice Hall.

Luckerath-Rovers, M. and Bos, A. (2011). Code of conduct for non-executive and supervisory directors, *Journal of Business Ethics*, **100**, 465-481.

McCarthy, N. (2017). Trump's family trips cost taxpayers nearly as much in a month as Obama's cist in a whole year, Forbes.

Markus, H.R. and Kitayama, S. (2003). Culture, self, and the reality of the social. *Psychological Inquiry*, **14**(3-4), 277-283.

McConville, D. (2017). 'Telling your story' publicly: Voluntary and mandatory approaches to performance reporting. Paper presented to BAFA 2017 annual conference, Edinburgh, 10-12 April 2017. Viewed at 15/07/2017.

Normanton, E. L. (1966). *The Accountability and Audit of Governments*, Manchester, University of Manchester.

Paterson AS, Leung D, Jackson W, Macintosh R and O'Gorman K, Eds. (2016) *Research Methods for Accounting and Finance*, Goodfellow, Oxford.

Perks, R. W. (1993). *Accounting and Society*, London, Chapman and Hall.

Rashid, M. Z. and Ibrahim, S. (2008). The effect of culture and religiosity on business ethics: A cross-cultural comparison. *Journal of Business Ethics*, **82**, 907-917.

Sacconi, L., de Colle, S. and Baldin, E. (2002) *The Q-RES Project: The Quality of the Social and Ethical Responsibility of Corporations, Guidelines for Management,* EconomEtica - Inter-university center of research, University Milano Bicocca, Milan

Sinclair, A. (1995). The chameleon of accountability: Forms and discourses. *Accounting, Organizations and Society,* **20**, 219-237.

Solomon, J. (2013). *Organisation Governance and Accountability.* West Sussex, John Wiley and Sons Ltd.

Stewart, J. D. (1984). The role of information in public accountability. In: Hopwood, T. and Tomkins, C. (eds.) *Issues in Public Sector Accounting.* Deddington: Philip Allan.

Steets, J. (2010). *Accountability in Public Policy Partnerships,* Basingstoke, UK and New York, USA, Palgrave Macmillan.

Stohl, C., Stohl, M., and Popvva, L. (2009). A new generation of organisation codes of ethics. *Journal of Business Ethics,* **90**, 607-622.

Swift, T. (2001). Trust, reputation and organisation accountability to stakeholders. Business Ethics, *A European Review,* **10**, 16-16.

The Local. (2014). "Sweden's dirty secret: It arms dictators" by Tom Sullivan.

Tower, G. 1993. A public accountability model of accounting regulation. The British Accounting Review, 25, 61-85.

Tseng, H.-C., Duan, C.-H., Tung, H.-L. and Kung, H.-J. 2010. Modern business ethics research: Concepts, theories, and relationships. Journal of Business Ethics, 91, 587-597.

Valemei, R. (2014). Fiji's biggest scandal, The Fiji Times.

Valentine, S. and Fleischman, G. (2008). Professional ethical standards, organisation social responsibility, and the perceived role of ethics and social responsibility. *Journal of Business Ethics,* **82**, 657-666.

Yong, A. (2008). Cross-cultural comparisons of managerial perceptions on profit. *Journal of Business Ethics,* **82**, 775-791.

■   Some useful weblinks

http://www.channelnewsasia.com/news/asiapacific/vietnamese-bankers-arrested-over-fraud-worth-millions-8179806

https://fambiz.com/2015/05/05/fraud-in-the-family-business-it-can-easily-happen/

https://www.theguardian.com/world/2014/dec/12/petrobras-scandal-brazilian-oil-executives-among-35-charged

https://www.theguardian.com/business/2003/dec/31/italy.parmalat1

http://content.time.com/time/specials/packages/article/0,28804,2021097_2023262_2023247,00.html

3 | History and Dynamics of Corporate Social Responsibility

Bridget Ogharanduku, Zayyad Abdul-Baki,
Abdelrhman Yusuf and Sunita Mathur

Introduction

Although corporate social responsibility (CSR) is currently the subject of much debate in the contemporary global business environment it is not a new phenomenon; rather, it has a historical dimension. Despite its current growth and popularity, there is plenty of historical evidence of the concerns of businesses and businessmen for their employees and the communities in which they operated (Carroll, 2008). Indeed, as Chapter 2 illustrates, social accountability and CSR practices and reporting have evolved considerably over several decades. In order to appreciate the current debate on CSR and the context in which it has developed and flourished, in both developed and developing countries, it is necessary to have some understanding of the historical underpinnings of the concept. This chapter therefore, provides a historical perspective on CSR, beginning from the mid-19th century industrial revolution when commercial activities began to expand considerably, and the forms of business ownership started changing. It was during this period, that social inequality, employee welfare, working conditions, education, environmental concerns and the responsibilities of business gradually became important issues that required attention. A primary focus of this chapter is a discussion of the dynamics of social responsibility practices and concepts, in order to demonstrate how they have grown and shaped business practices and corporate regulations and reporting. Within this discussion we trace the evolution of CSR from the 1850s to present day. A range of issues from employee welfare, corporate philanthropy, social activism through to environmental and social impacts of business and the response of the state to these wider social issues are identified.

Following this, the chapter considers changes, practices and developments within organisations, society and regulatory bodies that have led to the institutionalisation of CSR in contemporary business environments and reporting frameworks. CSR practices and reporting abound in many countries of the world, but in terms of scholarly debates, are more evident in Western economies. Early writings in this area originated from the United States, however, over the last three decades, increased attention has been given to this topic in Europe. In developing economies, there has been an ongoing debate about CSR, particularly over the last decade and in the context of globalisation, corruption and transnational business and reporting. It is, therefore, also important to understand the social impact of negligent or deliberate actions of organisations, and steps that can be (or have been) taken to increase the social responsibility and CSR of organisations. The chapter considers the key players in CSR's growth and development and their roles in shaping CSR globally. We begin our investigation into the history and dynamics of CSR by looking at the origins, changes in meaning, practice and reporting of CSR practices.

The development of CSR – a brief description

Scholarly debates on the historical development of CSR have revolved around theory and practice. CSR as a business or management concept and practice is viewed from various perspectives and has been quite amorphous. Thus, it is difficult to arrive at a generalised definition of what CSR is, and the definitions keep evolving as the debate continues. In the last seventy years, several authors and businessmen defined CSR in diverse ways. Likewise, the practice of CSR has been described using different concepts. In the early years of the conceptual debate on CSR it was often referred to as social responsibility rather than as CSR (Carroll, 1979), because of the forms of business ownership during that period. Other concepts include the social responsiveness of businesses, corporate social performance, and so on. Possible definitions of CSR which may capture the social sensitivity of businesses are Davis and Carroll's definitions. Davis defines CSR as "businessmen's decisions and actions taken for reasons at least partially beyond the firm's direct economic or technical interest" (Davis, 1960:70). He argues that in the long run, the social contributions businesses make to society would bring economic gains, thereby paying it back for its socially responsible outlook. Apparently, this is a major argument in contemporary debates on the usefulness of CSR to businesses themselves (Carroll and Shabana, 2010). Carroll defines CSR as "encompassing the economic, legal, ethical and discretionary expectations that society has of organizations at a given point in time" (Carroll, 1979:500). CSR therefore, challenges businesses to look beyond the interests of shareholders and incorporate the changing needs and opinions of the wider society in which they operate.

CSR activities commenced long before the 19th century as business motivations during that period was mixed with public interest objectives and private economic objectives. Moreover, charters of corporation in developed societies were mainly given to businesses that were socially useful. That is, the law encouraged and permitted businesses primarily because they were of service to the community, rather than because they were a source of profit to their owners (Avi-Yonah, 2005). Therefore, businesses have historically made both economic and social contributions to the communities they operate in, but CSR in contemporary times focuses more on the social and environmental impacts of businesses. However, it is important to note that the economic impacts of businesses, when viewed in a wider context, are equally social contributions to society (Carroll, 2008), especially in developing economies. For example, economic impacts in terms of employment, provision of goods and services, tax revenue, research and development for improving the quality of products and services are social contributions to society in their own way. Therefore, when analysing CSR from a historical perspective, it is important not to lose sight of these dynamics.

Several factors have contributed to shaping CSR practices and reporting across the world at various times in history. The changing nature of business ownership and practices, as well as the political environment in which businesses operate, have shaped the development of CSR globally. Thus, the development of CSR practices and reporting originates from the interaction of various stakeholder groups and actions. This is depicted in Figure 3.1

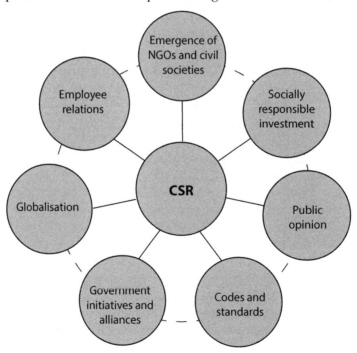

Figure 3.1: The development of CSR in a wider context

It is clear from Figure 3.1 that CSR did not develop in a vacuum. Rather, several changes and activities in the economic, corporate, professional and political environment have influenced the development of CSR practices and reporting globally. These factors are the main lenses through which this chapter analyses CSR from a historical perspective. CSR can be viewed as both a managerial concept in corporate debates as well as in business practices, but this chapter focuses more on CSR as a business practice. Chapter 4 elaborates on CSR as a managerial concept in corporate debates.

Early evidence of CSR practices in developed economies (1850s –1950s)

Carroll (1999) notes that the conceptualisation of CSR in contemporary business and management literature emerged in the 1950s, but there is evidence of practices that could be interpreted as CSR in developed countries before this period (Carroll, 2008). During the mid-19th century, businesses in Britain and America were concerned about employees, particularly in terms of improving their productivity and managing labour issues in factories, as these were common social challenges during the 1800s. This period was characterised by various criticisms against the emerging factory system, which was implicated as the source of various social ills, including labour unrest, poverty, slums, and child and female labour. In response to these social issues, an industrial welfare movement emerged which produced several schemes to prevent labour problems and improve employee performance. These welfare schemes included the provision of hospital clinics, bath houses, lunch rooms, profit sharing, recreational facilities, and so on (Wren, 2005: 268-70). These schemes could be interpreted as having both social and business impacts, but it is difficult to decisively ascertain whether businesses were doing these things for social or business reasons. In other words, were businesses improving their workers' welfare for purposes that extended beyond the economic interests of the business (Carroll, 2008)?

Employee welfare and philanthropy

There is evidence that many businesses made contributions to charitable organisations in the late 1800s and early 1900s, particularly in relation to World War I (Muirhead, 1999). However, it is difficult to ascribe much of this philanthropic activity to the business entity as opposed to its owners, because some early business leaders displayed extraordinary generosity (Carroll, 2008). For example, early capitalists like Andrew Carnegie and John D Rockefeller were renowned philanthropists whose charitable deeds were pursued individually and not on behalf of any company (Cochran, 2007). Moreover, several legal cases regarding corporate philanthropy during the late 19th century questioned its existence, which makes it difficult to explicitly ascribe philanthropic activities to the business (Carroll, 2008; Lee, 2008). For example, Wren (2005) refers to two cases in his book. The first case relates to the efforts made by the West Cork Railroad Company in Great Britain to compensate its employees for job losses due to the company's dissolution. The court ruled that the responsibilities of the board of directors excluded charity and their duty was to use the company's money exclusively for carrying out the business. On the other hand, in the second case which involved Steinway, the court permitted the piano company to purchase land to be used for a church, library and school for its employees, as the court saw the improvement of 'employee relations' as an important benefit to the company (Wren, 2005). It is obvious that the employees in the first case were of no economic benefit to the corporation as it had already ceased to exist, but in the second case the employees were still of economic importance to the business. Apparently, therefore, corporate philanthropy was legally restricted to causes that benefited the companies concerned.

Despite these legal challenges, there is evidence of many socially responsible actions undertaken by company management that impacted on the wider community, although they were never referred to as corporate social responsibility. Heald (1970), notes that in the years preceding the First World War, there was a significant growth in the contributions made by companies towards community related welfare programmes. For example, in 1875, a company in New York (R.H Macy) made contributions to an orphan asylum, and in the 1887 accounts of the company, gifts to charities were listed among miscellaneous expenses (Heald, 1970:7). Other examples include companies giving to the Young Men's Christian Association (YMCA) movement during the mid-1800s, and in 1893, community development, to improve the welfare of employees and their families, by George M. Pullman of the Pullman Palace Car Company, (Heald, 1970). Thus, early CSR practices were focused on employee welfare and philanthropy. On the other hand, many viewed corporate philanthropy from a negative perspective; as management practices that were inconsistent with the interests of shareholders. Moreover, it was argued that social workers and the government were more qualified with appropriate skills and expertise to handle social issues than were corporate managers. Such attitudes still existed late into the 20th century as economists like Milton Friedman argued that businesses were meant to enhance shareholders' wealth rather than cater to society, because they were not social enterprises (Lee, 2008).

New wave of corporate philanthropy

By the 1900s, businesses began to engage with social workers, leading to the emergence of a new perspective on philanthropy. Business leaders began to view social issues from the perspective of other stakeholders, and became more conscious of the objectives of social agencies (Carroll, 2008). Corporate philanthropy became more distinctly evident in society and was increasingly acceptable even within legal circles. For example, in 1953, The New Jersey Supreme Court gave approval for the A.P. Smith Manufacturing company to donate $1500 to Princeton University without violating shareholders' interests (Cochran, 2007). Cochran (2007) argues that an important feature of corporate philanthropy during the 1950s was that it was expected to be 'from the heart' and not overly focused on any gains for the business. Corporate philanthropic practices that also enhanced the firm's profit were viewed strictly as business decisions rather than philanthropic activities. However, it is difficult to explicitly delineate these activities into business and social decisions, as many social decisions had the potential to create goodwill for the businesses which contributed to its economic gains in the long run.

Although during this early part of the 20th century many businesses were socially sensitive to society and exhibited socially responsible business behaviours, many did not. Eberstadt (1973 cited in Carroll, 2008) claims that after the First World War many charters of incorporation were issued to business whether they were socially useful or not. This created large corporations that dominated the economy and possessed significant political influence, leading to the formation of a ruling corporate class with great economic and political power. The power these leaders possessed allowed them to defy market pricing rules and exploit shareholders. These socially irresponsible behaviours contributed to the collapse of the economic system leading to the Great Depression of 1929 with mass unemployment and business failures. The post-depression period ushered in a new phase of corporate social relations. While it is difficult to distinctly summarise how CSR developed in developed economies before the 1960s, Table 3.1 provides a summary of the key features. Though there is some degree of overlap, this phase can be divided into three key points of time.

The progressive and shifting perspective of businesses and society regarding CSR before the 1960s is depicted in Table 3.1. Businesses moved from focusing inwards in terms of making social contribution decisions towards a wider and more inclusive perspective that encompassed actions which benefited the community they operated in. Likewise, society began to place more demands on businesses to respond to the needs of a wider section of the community, especially social service communities. Accordingly, businesses began responding to these demands, though in varying dimensions. The period 1920 – 1930 ushered in the stakeholder perspective on CSR as managers were increasingly seen as both agents of the company, and trustees for the various stakeholders in relation with the business. However, these ideas were not developed in academic circles until the 1970s. The increasing diffusion of share ownership and the growing diversity of society were the two main factors that brought about this new perspective (Hay and Gray, 1974). Though philanthropy and corporate contributions to society continued into the 1960s, it was an ad hoc practice, subject to the preferences of executives, and was primarily in response to requests from beneficiary organisations (Muirhead, 1999). The next section discusses how CSR practices evolved during the 1960s – 1990s.

Phase	Features	Examples of CSR activities
1850-1890s		
Profit maximizing management	CSR practices were focused on activities that had direct business consequences, e.g. employee welfare	In 1893, John Patterson deviated from the predominant 'sweatshop' factory system by building factories with floor to ceiling glass walls and windows allowing natural light and fresh air to flow into the production floor, with large green lawns surrounding them (Le Calvez and Lees, 2015).
1890 – 1930		
Pre-legalization period/ trusteeship management phase	CSR activities included actions that maximized shareholder wealth as well as other competing claims from customers, employees and the community, but they were largely voluntary.	Opening of Cadbury factory in a Greenfield at Bournville in 1879, and new product and factory innovations in 1899, leading to improved employee welfare and products and services to customers. The establishment of Bournville village in 1900 to promote housing reforms and green environment in Birmingham. Setting up of work committees with equal numbers of management and worker representatives elected by secret ballot in 1905 to discuss all issues affecting employees (Katsoulakos, Koutsodimou and William, 2004).
1930 – 1950s		
Corporate period/ legalization of corporate philanthropy	Business were seen as social institutions having obligations to the communities they operated in.	Johnson and Johnson credo announcing the company's responsibility to the wider section of society in 1940.

Table 3.1: Main stages of CSR practices before the 1960s

Source: Adapted from Hay and Gray (1974), Muirhead, (1999) and Le Calvez and Lees, (2015)

■ Social activism and state regulations (1960s – 1990s)

The post-1950s phase of CSR development was primarily influenced by social activism from individuals and groups, environmental issues and government regulations. These activities emerged due to concerns about environmental abuse, and the safety of products and workers. Corporate contributions and philanthropy also expanded during the 1960s through to the mid-1980s with more groups benefiting from it (e.g. health and human services groups, culture and arts and civic community groups) (Muirhead, 1999). However, these philanthropic practices were still on the terms and at the convenience of business executives and did not really cost the business much (Carroll and Shabana, 2010). Modern activism emerged in the US during the mid-1950s and throughout the 1960s with the publication of several books and articles, as well as court decisions on social equality and business activities. Cochran (2007), argues that the court's ruling on Brown v. Board of Education in 1954 regarding racial segregation in school enrolments boosted the civil rights movement, while Rachel Carson's 1962 book *Silent Spring*, which criticised the practices of chemical industries, stimulated the environmental movement. The modern consumer movement is similarly traced to Ralph Nader's 1965 publication *Unsafe at any Speed*, written in response to General Motors' safety record.

3

The US war with Vietnam in the 1960s and early 1970s coupled with various emerging social movements transformed the business environment in the US and globally. Group activists and NGOs concerned about unethical and irresponsible business practices were prominent during this era. They mobilised the media in pressuring businesses to be socially responsible. Due to the power of the media in creating unwanted consequences for businesses, many businesses responded by modifying products, policies and practices (Cochran, 2007). However, the range of appropriate responses evolved considerably. By the 1970s, the debate on CSR practices was increasingly referred to as corporate social responsiveness because most corporate social practices were direct responses to social activism and government regulations.

■ Socially responsible investments (SRI)

The concept of socially responsible investment also emerged during this phase, particularly, from churches holding shares in corporate organisations (Katsoulaska *et al.*, 2004; Cohran, 2007). Group activism during the 1960s, 1970s and early 1980s focused more on mobilising market mechanisms, such as selling off or not purchasing the shares of firms which they considered to be socially irresponsible. This compelled firms to respond appropriately to social issues in the communities in which they operated. Notable examples were found amongst the boycotts and campaigns by shareholders, in collaboration with civil societies, against many firms, especially European and US banks that were associated with apartheid in South Africa (Katsoulaska *et al.* 2004; Carroll, 2008). Through collective efforts, shareholders could mobilise market mechanisms to influence corporate social behaviour, policies and practices. There were many other forms in which groups, communities, individuals, educational institutions and so on responded to social issues and corporate practices within their communities during this phase. They include, social entrepreneurship, social venture capital fund and CSR education (Cochran, 2007). Thus, this phase witnessed an increased awareness about CSR and it became a wider social issue as more stakeholders became involved in ensuring that businesses balanced their economic activities with necessary social actions beneficial to host communities and stakeholders.

The concept of SRI is discussed further in Chapter 6 of this book.

■ Environmental and social issues and regulations

The period from 1960-1990 also featured an increased attention to issues originating from environmental catastrophes primarily triggered by the activities of businesses, such as carbon emission, deforestation, waste dumping and the burning of fossil fuels (Cochran, 2007; Carroll, 2008). Several national environmental agencies were established during this period, as well as the United Nations Environment Programme (UNEP), to monitor the impact of industrial activities on the environment. Some companies started providing reports on their environmental impact, but in a limited capacity. By the 1970s, many countries were promoting environmental and social reporting as global issues shifted towards women's rights, racial equality and world peace. Social reporting integrated employee-relations and human resource activities with all other social activities carried out by companies. For example, in France the law required companies with more than 300 employees to produce employee reports. In the US, the Council on Economic priorities started to rate companies publicly, based on their social and environmental impact (Katsoulaska *et al.*, 2004).

An important event during this phase was the 1969 Cleveland fire catastrophe, caused by industrial wastes dumped into the Cuyahoga River by waterfront industries. This incident caused the US government to issue the Clean Air Act in 1970 and Clean Water Act in 1972 (Soderstrom, 2013). In Canada, the Canadian Chemical Producers Association launched the 'Responsible Care' programme in 1985, hoping that their voluntary action would prevent government regulations like that of the US. Therefore, this period witnessed increased environmental regulations from various governments, pressuring companies to provide information about their environmental practices, and the impact of their activities on the environment, to get them to think about ways of minimising these impacts. Likewise, companies took proactive steps regarding environmental issues to minimise the attention of government on their environmental practices.

The 1970s through to the 1990s witnessed the involvement of international and national organisations, such as the Committee for Economic Development (CED), in pressuring companies to maintain a balance between their social and economic impacts, by going beyond philanthropic actions and donations that were done simply to legitimize their activities. Another notable advancement was the establishment of the UN World Commission on Environment and Development (WCED) in 1983. The WCED ratified the Brundtland Report[1] also known as *'Our Common Future'* in 1987, to preserve a sustainable and balanced development. It

---

1 The Brundtland report was put together based on the findings and consultations of the WCED. It outlines that sustainability encompasses environmental, economic and social aspects and provides an overview of the major global environmental issues and recommendations for change. It succeeded in bringing environmental issues to the fore of political discourse globally. However, it was criticised for overemphasising the environmental side of sustainability and ignoring its social aspects. Nevertheless, the concept of sustainability as presented by the Brundtland report has influenced environmental laws and planning in many countries of the world. Sustainability issues are discussed in more detail in Chapter 5.

aimed to by get companies to consciously integrate into their economic strategies the main common problems that impact society daily, such as environmental contamination (pollution, non-renewable energy, lack of recycling etc.) and social inequalities (poverty, hunger, underdevelopment within countries etc.) (Matinez *et al.*, 2016). This phase in CSR development involved reactions from various stakeholders (government, shareholders, companies, NGOs etc.) and the enactment of several state legislations mandating organisations to incorporate social and environmental issues, especially pollution, workers' safety, product safety and employment discrimination, into their business strategy. In 1976, The Organisation for Economic Co-operation and Development (OECD) established guidelines for multinational companies to encourage them to make positive economic and social contributions to the world (Ernst and Young, 2013).

The 1980s ushered in the modern form of CSR reporting (Baue, 2004), though it is increasingly being described as sustainability reporting in the 21st century. Much of the non-financial reporting by businesses was motivated by state regulations, and social pressure from civic societies and NGOs, as well as by environmental catastrophes. However, there are companies that, as part of their business objectives, pursued an environmentally and socially responsible profile, hence they regularly provided social and environmental reports, as well as social audits, to the public. Examples of these companies include the Body Shop, Ben and Jerry's Ice cream, Esprit de Corp and Aveda (Katsoulaska *et al.*, 2004). CSR reporting practices varied from country to country, depending on the political and legal framework of each country and the accounting reporting standards, but they typically contained the social and environmental practices of business organisations.

The 1980s also witnessed several ethical scandals that exposed the irresponsible practices of managers and companies to the public. Notable among them is the Nestle infant milk formula controversy that spanned most of the 1970s and early 1980s, the Bhopal chemical plant disaster in India which killed thousands of people in 1984, and the Ivan Boesky insider trading scandal of the mid to late 1980s (Carroll, 2008). Thus, CSR practices and policies during this phase were influenced by various stakeholders and events in the global business environment. Companies could no longer engage in CSR activities on a voluntary basis only, rather they were compelled to respond appropriately to a range of social, ethical and environmental issues that were primarily caused by their own activities. However, many companies responded by engaging in a practice known as '*greenwashing*' to give the impression that they were environmentally friendly. Likewise, a lot of the corporate and academic discourse on CSR was more talk than action, and several frameworks on CSR only highlighted what companies should be doing, to be seen as socially and environmentally responsible, but did not specify how they should implement these. By the 1990s companies were conceptualised as corporate citizens having the same obligations as human beings to demonstrate respect for the environment, society and other human beings.

■   ## Strategic corporate philanthropy

This phase also featured academic debates regarding corporate philanthropy, which ushered in a new form of the practice – strategic corporate philanthropy. Porter and Kramer, (2002) are proponents of this new perspective. They argued that for businesses to maximise their social impact, they should engage in philanthropic activities that have both social and economic benefits, because in the long run social and economic goals are interconnected. Economic investments have social returns and social investments have economic returns, therefore, these goals should not be separated. Rather, firms should pursue business decisions that have considerably significant financial and social returns. Additionally, businesses should search for social causes that align with their expertise and invest in them, because such investments are more likely to produce optimum social impact. They cited the Cisco Networking Academy deployed to schools around the world as an important strategic philanthropic activity. The initiative by Cisco Systems trains computer network administrators, thereby providing well-trained network administrators for its customers. However, this approach to CSR is criticised for being too self-serving as philanthropy is meant to be purely a matter of the heart and not overly influenced by business objectives. Strategic corporate philanthropy is discussed in more detail in Chapter 4. Other academic debates during this period also focused on distinguishing the legal responsibilities of businesses to shareholders from social responsibilities, and ethical practices for businesses to align their strategies towards a more holistic goal. On the other hand, it is argued that CSR manifested and developed in a different way in developing economies, this is discussed in the next section.

History of CSR in developing countries

As in developed economies, CSR is not a modern concept or practice in developing economies; rather, it evolves from deep-rooted cultural and religious traditions of philanthropy, business ethics and community embeddedness (Visser 2008). For example, developing countries with deep-rooted religious belief systems have historically condemned extortionist business practices and encouraged business practices founded on moral principles of justice and fairness. Additionally, communalism has been an important characteristic of developing countries and it is the major form in which CSR has manifested and is conceptualised in many parts of these regions (Amaeshi *et al.*, 2006). These ancient practices underpin the historical and modern approach to CSR in these regions. Though research on CSR in developing countries is relatively scarce, available studies and debate reveals that the manifestation and conceptualisation of CSR differs remarkably from Western conceptualisations; particularly because of the differences in culture, political and socio-economic needs (Visser, 2008; Jamali, 2014). Although the central concept of ensuring that businesses are socially sensitive to the needs of the communities in which they operate is present, the main historical drivers of CSR in these regions differ, as well as their mode of deployment. Additionally, the development and state of the political and social infrastructures in these regions have shaped the development, conceptualisation and manifestation of CSR in these regions.

Countries in Asia, Africa and South America are usually classified as developing countries by international organisations, and the level and mode of CSR development in these regions is diverse. CSR, especially in Africa and South America has historically been framed around the ethics of colonialism and apartheid, and the prevalence of corruption and fraud (Visser, 2008). Importantly, globalisation, culture, religion, political infrastructure and the socio-economic needs of the larger part of the population are the key drivers in the development of CSR in developing countries. In Asia, CSR evolved with much involvement from the communities themselves; thus, community involvement is the most established form of CSR in Asia (Visser, 2008). On the other hand, business ethics and the economic and philanthropic aspects of CSR seems to dominate the manifestation and conceptualisation of CSR in Africa.

■ Drivers of CSR development in developing countries

The historical nature and manifestation of CSR practices in developing countries has focused more on meeting their pressing social, political, economic and infrastructural needs. These needs include poverty alleviation, job creation, provision of goods and services, HIV/AIDS, education, health care, electricity, roads, and so on (Jamali, 2014). CSR is therefore argued to have developed primarily as a direct response to governance gaps, hence society looks to business organisations to fill the gaps created by poor governance (Frynas, 2005), corruption and political irresponsibility. Accordingly, rather than CSR practices focusing on consumer protection, employee welfare, climate change, or socially responsible investments as seen in developed countries, its primary focus has been to provide basic infrastructure for the larger part of the population (Amaeshi *et al.*, 2006). CSR in these regions has, therefore, developed as an alternative to government and these activities are more likely to be seen as developmental aids, rather than CSR. On the other hand, the overreliance on businesses to fill the gaps created by poor governance may lead to divestments in the long-term as business costs may be too high in such regions (Visser, 2008), and governments may overlook ethical failures of businesses to preserve their investments. A prime example of this is the lack of government intervention to deal with the excessive pollution and environmental degradation caused by the activities of Shell in Nigeria, which negatively affects thousands of citizens in the area (Ite, 2004).

Historically and even in modern times, philanthropy has been an important manifestation of CSR in developing countries, because of their cultural and religious settings, as well as the fact that they have been the main recipients of global aid (Frynas, 2006; Visser, 2008 Jamali, 2014). Hence philanthropy appears to be the norm, rather than the exception (Jamali, 2014), and is much appreciated in developing countries. Due to a historical lack of development, the socio-economic needs of these regions are enormous, and philanthropy is essential to improve the prospects of the communities where companies operate. These activities are not necessarily based on issues that are of direct economic interest to the business, such as employee welfare, rather they are essentially philanthropic practices. An important example of these philanthropic practices is companies' contributions towards the eradication of HIV/AIDS, malaria, polio, maternal mortality and so on. Though these practices have the tendency to bring economic gains to the business in the long-term, it is not the primary motivation for these contributions. The cultural and religious practices in these regions encourage philanthropic practices, hence, business entrepreneurs tend to contribute towards the welfare of society. Interestingly, due to the developmental needs of less developed countries, the economic impact of businesses is seen as social impact (Visser, 2008). Thus, the creation of jobs, goods and services, although primarily economic in character, are seen as positive social impacts of business, while in developed countries, such economic impacts of business tend to be overlooked.

Political events and weak institutional controls over the social, environmental and ethical practices of businesses operating in developing countries, particularly multinationals, also shaped the development of CSR. For example, the political changes towards democracy in South Africa and the redressing of the injustices of the past has been an important event shaping CSR there since the mid-1990s, especially through the practice of improved corporate governance, black economic empowerment and business ethics (Visser, 2005). Weak institutional controls have also necessitated the emergence of stakeholder activism, pressuring businesses to respond to social and environmental hazards created by their economic activities (Dobers and Halme, 2009; Jamali, 2014). According to Visser, (2008) there are four stakeholder groups, in collaboration with local NGOs, that are actively involved in social and environmental activism in developing countries: development agencies, trade unions, international NGOs and business associations. These groups have deployed several means to achieve their goals including civil regulation, litigation against erring companies and international legal instruments. The media is also emerging as an important key stakeholder group in developing countries.

CSR in developing countries has also been motivated by environmental catastrophes and social or health crises, especially the philanthropic kind of CSR. Climate change and HIV/AIDS are important examples of the kind of crises driving the CSR movement in developing countries. Several organisations in the private, public and third sectors have been involved in the health crises in developing countries. For example, Pfizer in collaboration with the Edna McConnell Clark foundation, World Health Organisation, Bill and Melinda Gates Foundation and the British government have contributed to providing medical treatment for the prevention of trachoma in many developing countries (Porter and Kramer, 2002).

It should be observed that CSR in developing countries is still largely infor-mal and is not yet institutionalised locally (Amaeshi *et al.*, 2006). There is also little or no local social and environmental legislation in many of the developing countries, except around some high profile, usually multinational, companies. However, the drive for foreign direct investment and international trade is com-pelling many local companies to embrace international CSR standards and codes. Likewise, local subsidiaries of multinational companies are compelled by their headquarters to implement global standards and codes on social, environmental and ethical business practices (Visser, 2008; Jamali, 2010). For example, Baskin, (2006) conducted a survey of CSR practices in emerging markets and found that local companies are increasingly adopting ISO 14001 and the Global Reporting Initiative's Sustainability reporting guidelines. Likewise, businesses in India that are part of a global supply chain and those in the export-led sectors are increas-ingly pressured into complying with global CSR codes and standards.

The next section briefly discusses how CSR has developed into the 21st century.

Corporate social responsibility in the 2000s

By the turn of the 21st century CSR had become an important aspect of organi-zational goals globally. Several international, intergovernmental and national organisations have become more actively involved in pressuring businesses to integrate CSR practices and reporting into their business strategies. Likewise, CSR has become one of the most important topics in academic, political and corporate debates; especially around the issues of climate change and labour practices. For example, the G8 summit of world leaders in 2007 clearly included CSR as a primary global concern and the leaders committed to promoting and strengthening corporate and other forms of social responsibility as one of the four priority areas for action through internationally agreed CSR and labour standards (G8 Summit Declaration, 2007). It is argued however, that CSR prac-tices and regulations are most evident in Europe, but that globally, they are still predominantly voluntary. Nevertheless, businesses are embracing CSR more than they did in previous centuries. For example, by the start of the 21st century, almost 90% of Fortune 500 firms embraced CSR as an essential element of their organisational goals and actively promoted CSR activities in their annual reports (Boli and Hartsuiker, 2001). Likewise, the views of shareholders regarding CSR practices changed significantly in the 21st century as they began to embrace it and view its relationship with the bottom line performance of the organisation more seriously (Lee, 2008). However, empirical evidence of the impact of CSR on the bottom line is inconclusive (Margolis and Walsh, 2003). The conceptualisa-tion of CSR has equally moved into a rationalisation stage, whereby academic and corporate debates are approaching CSR from the perspective of doing busi-ness to create value, but in a manner that is respectful and proactive towards stakeholders (Carrol, 2008; Lee, 2008). Likewise, many other concepts relevant to CSR emerged more strongly in the 21st century such as triple bottom line and corporate sustainability practices and reporting[2].

The 21st century has also witnessed an increased level of government regulation of CSR practices and reporting, both in developed and developing economies, and companies are increasingly disclosing more information about their environmental and social practices. For example, in 2007, the Malaysian government issued a regulation requiring all publicly listed companies to publish their CSR initiatives on a 'comply or explain' basis. Similarly, the Danish government in 2009 mandated all state-owned companies, with total assets and revenues exceeding 19 million Euros and 38 million Euros respectively and more than 250 employees, to report their social initiatives annually. This century has also seen the increased involvement of international and national organisations and NGOs in ensuring that businesses are accountable to both shareholders and stakeholders, and that they are operating in a socially and environmentally responsible manner, especially with respect to climate change and labour practices (Ernst and Young, 2013). However, there is diversity in the commitment and practices of companies and countries to social and environmental practices even in narrow areas of application, such as labour standards, the environment, human rights and bribery and corruption (OECD, 2001). Additionally, some CSR practices are voluntary while others are mandatory, because some companies are being compelled by regulations and legal decisions to adopt them. CSR in developing economies is still predominantly philanthropy because of the level of socio-economic development and poor institutional structures.

The level and effectiveness of CSR initiatives in various regions of the world in the 21st century is still very much dependent on the political structures prevalent in each region. For example, the effectiveness of CSR initiatives in Europe is attributed to the effectiveness of broader systems of private and public governance (OECD, 2009). On the other hand, the poor level of CSR initiatives and practices in the African region is largely attributed to the poor governance structures and high levels of bribery and corruption within public and private governance structures (Dobers and Halme, 2009). Further, in the 21st century, there has been an increasing alignment and integration of corporate law and regulations, especially international and comparative laws with aspects of CSR's wider vision of corporate responsibility and governance. For example, the UK corporate law of (2006) has produced reforms of directors' duties, business reviews and corporate reporting that explicitly factors in non-shareholder interests (OECD, 2009). These corporate laws regulating the obligations and reporting requirements of company directors have been an important motivator for socially responsible business behaviours in the 21st century.

---

2 These are covered in detail in Chapter 5.

■ Private and intergovernmental initiatives relevant to CSR

Corporate reporting on CSR and environmental practices has been on the increase in the 21st century, but reliable socio-ethical standard-setting still lags. Various private initiatives with their own codes, or standards and principles providing guidance on social and environmental issues exist. Though the focus, membership, usage and structures of these initiatives varies widely, their common aim is to enable businesses to contribute to the improvement of social and environmental conditions (OECD, 2009). In the global scene, there have been various initiatives produced by intergovernmental agreements of which the International Labour Organisation (ILO) declaration, the OECD Guidelines for Multinational Enterprises and the UN Global Compact are most prominent. These initiatives complement private initiatives and provide a wider framework from which the private initiatives emerge. As CSR issues evolve, and society and the business environment changes, new initiatives emerge, and previous ones are modified. It may be difficult to provide a comprehensive listing of the various CSR initiatives, but Table 3.2 attempts to summarise some of the international initiatives that emerged in the 21st century based on an OECD report.

The various intergovernmental and privately developed initiatives in table 3.2 are in no way exhaustive. These initiatives provide guidance to businesses as to how and what to do to ensure that the needs of both shareholders and stakeholders are met and that they balance their economic, social and environmental goals. Some of these initiatives are industry specific (e.g. EITI principles and Electronic Industry Code of Conduct), while some are designed for all organisations, whether private or public (e.g. GRI Sustainability Reporting Guidelines, or the UN Global Compact Series). These initiatives reveal the extent to which a wider range of stakeholders are contributing to ensuring that businesses pursue an ethical and socially responsible business strategy.

Table 3.2: Examples of global and private initiatives relevant to CSR

Intergovernmental and private initiatives relevant to CSR	Brief description
Universal Declaration on Human Rights (UNDHR)	The UNDHR was adopted by the United Nations Assembly in December 1948. It articulates the rights and freedoms to which every human being is equally and inalienably entitled to (www.un.org).
UN Framework Convention on Climate Change (UNFCCC)	The UNFCCC is one of the three conventions adopted at the 'Rio Earth Summit' in 1992. It aims to stabilise greenhouse gas concentrations in the atmosphere at a level that would prevent dangerous anthropogenic interference with the climate system (www.un.org).
ILO Declaration on Fundamental Principles and Rights at Work	Initiated by the ILO in 1998 to commit member countries to respect and promote principles and rights in four categories 1. Freedom of association and the effective recognition of the right to collective bargaining. 2. Elimination of forced or compulsory labour. 3. Abolition of child labour and 4. Elimination of discrimination in respect of employment and occupation (www.ilo.org).
UN Millennium Development Goal	The UN MDG originates from the UN Millennium declaration, and it was signed in 2000. It articulates eight goals focused on alleviating poverty, improving healthcare, especially eradicating the spread of HIV/AIDS and providing basic education to all. These goals were set to be achieved in 2015. In 2016, the Sustainability Development Goals replaced the MDG.
World Summit on Sustainable Development Plan of Implementation	A UN initiative developed at the 'Earth Summit' in 2002. It focuses on improving the lives of people and conserving the Earth's natural resources in the face of increased demand and pressure on the world's resources.
OECD Convention on Combating Bribery of Foreign Officials in International Business Transactions	Initiated by the OECD in 1997 to provide standards for the criminalisation of public officers involved in bribery and corruption relating to international business transactions.
ILO MNE Declaration	Provides guidelines for multinationals, governments, and employers' and workers' organisations in such areas such as training, working conditions, employment and industrial relations. It was issued in 2000 and revised in March 2017

OECD MNE Guidelines	Adopted by the OECD in 1976. These are recommendations and guidelines to promote responsible business conduct by multinational companies doing business in, or operating from participating countries.
UN Global Compact Principles	A UN initiative which seeks to encourage companies to align their strategies and operations with universal principles on human rights, environment, labour and anti-corruption, and take actions that advance society's interest. It was adopted in 2000. It has ten principles derived from other UN initiatives.
International Finance Corporation Performance Standards	An IFC initiative which sets out the responsibilities of its clients towards managing their social and environmental risks. It was adopted in 2006 and revised in 2012.
Extractive Industries Transparency Initiative (EITI) Principles	An agreement initiated by a diverse group of countries, companies and civil society organisations in 2003. It aims to increase transparency over payments and revenues in the extractive sector.
ISO standards (e.g. 14000 series)	An initiative of the International Organisation for Standardisation issued in 1987. These standards are issued to help companies implement quality management in their operations and products. The main areas covered by these standards include audit quality management and environmental management.
GRI Sustainability Reporting Guidelines	Guidelines issued by the GRI to help businesses understand and communicate their most critical impacts on the environment, society and economy. The first full version of reporting guidelines was issued in 2000.
Responsible Care Guidelines	Launched in Canada in 1985 by chemical producing companies to address the concern of the public about the manufacture, distribution and use of chemicals. It is adopted in over 60 countries and includes improved guidelines on the safe use and handling of products along the chemical industry value chain.
ICMM Sustainable Development Principles	Issued in 2003 by the International Council of Mining and Metals to provide a best practice framework on sustainable development for the mining and metal industry.
Electronic Industry Code of Conduct	Founded in 2004 by eight companies operating in the electronic industry. It outlines a set of standards on social, environmental and ethical issues in the electronics industry supply chain.

3

Summary

This chapter provides a historical development of CSR practices over the last two centuries; highlighting the key players and main events in the development process. It is obvious that CSR did not develop in a vacuum, but several factors and social actors influenced its development and shaped what it is today in both developed and developing economies. CSR practices in developed countries and developing economies differ in significant ways. Though the broad aim of CSR in developed and developing economies is the same, the manifestation, progression and conceptualisation of CSR between these two broad economic categories differ. Globally, CSR developed mainly from philanthropic practices and social movements, and in recent times, it has progressed to a wider range of issues and practices such as fair trade, environmental protection, corporate governance and SRI. In developing economies CSR is still very much at the philanthropic phase because of poor governance and weak institutional structures. However, it is clear from the analysis in the chapter, that the CSR decisions and practices of businesses are no longer only motivated by economic benefits but also by response to wider social issues and the changing needs and opinions of a wider section of society.

Discussion questions

1   What was the major way in which CSR manifested itself in the early years of its development in developed and developing economies?

2   Discuss five main drivers of CSR practices and reporting in developed and developing economies.

3   Identify and discuss the main differences in the development of CSR in developing and developed economies.

4   Critically discuss five private and intergovernmental initiatives relevant to CSR.

References and further reading

Amaeshi, K.M., Adi, B.C., Ogbechie, C. and Amao, O.O. (2006). Corporate social responsibility in Nigeria: Western mimicry or indigenous influences? *Journal of Corporate Citizenship*, **24**, 83–99.

Avi-Yonah, R.S. (2005). The cyclical transformations of the corporate form: a historical perspective on corporate social responsibility. *Delaware Journal of Corporate Law*, **30**(3), 767–818.

Baskin, J. (2006). Corporate responsibility in emerging markets. *The Journal of Corporate Citizenship*, **24**, 29–47.

Baue, W. (2004). A brief history of sustainability reporting. Social Funds. Available at: http://www.socialfunds.com/news/print.cgi?sfArticleId=1459, accessed 22/05/2017.

Boli, J. and Hartsuijker, D. (2001). World Culture and Transnational Corporations: Sketch of a project. International Conference on Effects of and Responses to Globalization.

Le Calvez, M. and Lees, L. (2015). History of corporate social responsibility where to next? Sustainable Advantage Group Australia. Available at: www. sustainableadvantage.com.au/blog/history-of-corporate-social-responsibility -where-to-next.

Carroll, A.B. (1979). A three-dimensional conceptual model of corporate performance. *Academy of Management Review*, **4**(4), 497–505.

Carroll, A.B. (1999). Corporate social responsibility: evolution of a definitional construct. *Business and Society*, **38**(3), 268–295.

Carroll, A.B. (2008). A history of corporate social responsibility: concepts and practices. In A. Crane, A. McWilliams, D. Matten, J. Moon and D. Siegel (eds.), *The Oxford Handbook of Corporate Social Responsibility*. Oxford: Oxford University Press, pp.19–46.

Carroll, A.B. and Shabana, K. M. (2010). The business case for corporate social responsibility: a review of concepts, research and practice. *International Journal of Management Reviews*, **12**(1),85–105.

Cochran, P.L. (2007). The evolution of corporate social responsibility. *Business Horizons*, **50**(6), 449–454.

Davis, K. (1960). Can business afford to ignore social responsibilities? *California Management Review*, **2**(3), 70–76.

Dobers, P. and Halme, M. (2009). Editorial corporate social responsibility and developing countries. *Corporate Social Responsibility and Environmental Management*, 249(August), pp.237–249.

E. Ite, U. (2004). Multinationals and corporate social responsibility in developing countries: a case study of Nigeria. *Corporate Social Responsibility and Environmental Management*, **11**(1), 1–11.

Ernst and Young (2013). Corporate Social Responsibility in India: Potential to contribute towards inclusive social development.

Frynas, J.G. (2005). The false developmental promise of corporate social responsibility: evidence from multinational oil companies. *International Affairs*, **81**(3), 581–598.

Frynas, J.G. (2006). Corporate social responsibility in emerging economies. *Journal of Corporate Citizenship*, **24**, 16–19.

G8 Summit (2007). *Growth and Responsibility in the World Economy*. G8 Summit Declaration. Heiligendamm.

Hay, R. and Gray, E. (1974). Social responsibilities of business managers. *Academy of Management Journal*, **17**(1), 135–143.

3

Heald, M. (1970). *The Social Responsibilities of Business: Company and Community 1900-1960.* Cleveland: Press of Case Western Reserve University.

Jamali, D. (2010). The CSR of MNC subsidiaries in developing countries: global, local, substantive or diluted? *Journal of Business Ethics*, 93(Suppl. 2), 181–200.

Jamali, D. (2014). CSR in developing countries through an institutional lens. In: G. Eweje (ed.) *Corporate Social Responsibility and Sustainability: Emerging Trends in Developing Economies.* Emerald Group Publishing, pp.21–44.

Katsoulakos, P., Koutsodimou, M., Matraga, A. and Williams, L. (2004). *A Historic Perspective of the CSR Movement.* CSR Quest Sustainability Framework.

Lee, M.D.P. (2008). A review of the theories of corporate social responsibility: Its evolutionary path and the road ahead. *International Journal of Management Reviews*, 10(1), 53–73.

Margolis, J.D. and Walsh, J.R. (2003). Misery loves rethinking companies: social initiatives. *Administrative Science Quarterly*, 48(2), 268–305.

Martínez, J.B., Fernández, M.L., Miguel, P. and Fernández, R. (2016). Corporate social responsibility: Evolution through institutional and stakeholder perspectives. *European Journal of Management and Business Economics*, 25, 8–14.

Muirhead, S.A. (1999). Corporate Contributions: The View from 50 Years. Conference Board report. Conference Board.

OECD (2001). *Corporate Responsibility: Private Initiatives and Public Goals.* Paris: OECD Publishing.

OECD (2009). *Overview of Selected Initiatives and Instruments Relevant to Corporate Social Responsibility.* Annual Report on the OECD Guidelines for Multinational Enterprises 2008: Employment and Industrial Relations, pp. 235–261.

Porter, M.E. and Kramer, M.R. (2002). The competitive advantage of corporate philanthropy. *Harvard Business Review*, 80(12), 413–436.

Soderstrom, N. (2013), Sustainability reporting: past, present, and trends for the future. Insights, Faculty of Business and Economics, The University of Melbourne, pp.1–7. Available at: www.insights.unimelb.edu.au/vol13/04_Soderstrom.html

Visser, W. (2005). Corporate Citizenship in South Africa. *Journal of Corporate Citizenship*, 18, 29–38.

Visser, W. (2008). Corporate social responsibility in developing countries. In A. Crane, D. Matten, A. McWilliams, J. Moon, and D.S. Siegel(eds) *Oxford Handbook on Corporate Social Responsibility,* Oxford: Oxford University Press.

Wren, D.A. (2005). *The History of Management Thought.* Wiley.

■   ## Some useful web links

https://unfccc.int/resource/docs/convkp/conveng.pdf

http://www.ilo.org/declaration/thedeclaration/lang--en/index.htm

http://www.un.org/en/udhrbook/pdf/udhr_booklet_en_web.pdf

http://www.un.org/millenniumgoals/bkgd.shtml

http://www.un.org/sustainabledevelopment/

https://sustainabledevelopment.un.org/milesstones/wssd

http://www.oecd.org/corruption/oecdantibriberyconvention.htm

http://www.ilo.org/empent/Publications/WCMS_094386/lang--en/index.htm

http://www.oecd.org/corporate/mne/

http://mneguidelines.oecd.org/about.htm

https://www.unglobalcompact.org/what-is-gc/mission/principles

www.ifc.org/performancestandards

https://eiti.org/sites/default/files/documents/english-eiti-standard_0.pdf

https://www.globalreporting.org/information/news-and-press-center/press-resources/
    Pages/default.aspx

http://www.cefic.org/Responsible-Care/

https://www.icmm.com/en-gb/about-us/our-organisation/vision-and-values

3

4 Corporate Social Responsibility

Abdelrhman Yusuf, Zayyad Abdul-Baki,
Bridget Ogharanduku and Yasser Barghathi

Introduction

The traditional objective of business organisations has been to maximise the wealth of capital providers (shareholders). Opponents of this notion have, however, argued that an organisation's activities impact on other parties that are directly or indirectly related to the organisation. Similarly, the achievement of an organisation's objective can be constrained by these parties. For example, the quality of an organisation's product affects its customers while the decision of customers to buy or not to buy from an organisation equally affects the profit maximisation potential of the organisation. The proponents of this alternative view of an organisation's objectives argue that the interests of all of these parties must be considered in the decision making of the organisation for it to be financially viable in the long run. This notion gave momentum to the concept of corporate social responsibility (CSR). With an increase in man-made disasters to the environment (e.g. the Exxon Valdez oil spill in Alaska in March 1989), with consequent threats to human and animals' lives and with increasing workplace disasters (e.g. the Rana Factory collapse in Bangladesh in April 2013), CSR has become a major issue for organisations in recent times. Virtually all organisations now reflect how they are socially responsible in their websites or in a report.

In contrast to private sector organisations, public and third sector organisations do not follow a profit or wealth capitalising motive. Rather, the main objectives of public and third sector organisations is to provide a universal and equitable service through non-market mechanisms to all citizens to maintain and ensure their welfare. Thus, the public and third sector ethos reflects society's full humanity in that it recognises that society can be driven by ethical and moral principles rather than simply the pursuit of profit. However, such organisations have also fallen foul of unethical and questionable moral practices. For example, the Charity Commission[1], which registers and regulates charities in England and Wales to ensure public confidence and support in charities, reported that in 2015/16, one charity alone lost more than £1m to fraudulent activities. Within the public sector, the Department of the Prime Minister and Cabinet in Australia in a speech to the Institute of Public Administration stated that the public sector was responsible for 'some incredible high-profile failures'[2] during 2016 and needed to improve. In the UK, Transparency International UK[3] (TI-UK) highlighted corruption vulnerabilities in some of Britain's key public sector organisations. Recent scandals such as phone hacking, and the debate over the ethics of political party funding are two such examples. Other examples include high-profile crisis cases in public services, such as the mistreatment of patients at the Mid Staffordshire NHS Foundation Trust, and the Rotherham Children's Services scandal, which revealed severe abuse of children under the council's care. Such examples emphasise a lack of corporate social responsibility and reinforce the need for action to be taken.

Despite the call for widespread adoption of more robust CSR systems, the meaning of CSR and the argument for how organisations should engage in it is still not clear. Following on from the foundations on the CSR concept discussed in Chapter 3, the essence of this chapter is to discuss the meaning of CSR, its theoretical justifications and practical implementation in organisations today. To further our understanding and knowledge of CSR issues, debates and ways forward, stakeholder engagement, CSR reporting and procedures for soliciting necessary information about CSR engagement with society are discussed.

CSR and organisations

The general idea of CSR is that organisations do not exist in isolation. They interact with the larger society in which they operate. These groups or individuals within the larger society in which a business operates are called stakeholders. Stakeholders are groups or individuals that can affect or be affected by the achievement of an organisation's objectives (Freeman, 1984). There are many categorisations of stakeholders thus making it somewhat difficult to pick out a universal categorisation. Stakeholders can be internal or external. Internal stakeholders include employees, shareholders, and management while external stakeholders include competitors, customers and creditors. According to Clarkson (1995), primary stakeholders are stakeholders whose continuing involvement is crucial for an organisation's going concern, e.g. customers, shareholders, employees,

1 See: http://www.managementtoday.co.uk/why-weve-lost-faith-charities/reputation-matters/article/1369094

2 See: http://www.abc.net.au/news/2016-12-07/public-sector-responsible-for-high-profile-failures/8100382

3 See: http://www.transparency.org.uk/our-work/uk-corruption/#.WeoKFGhSwuU

government, and the community. Conversely, secondary stakeholders do not engage in any transactions with the business and the survival of the business does not directly depend on them, e.g. the media and NGOs. Freeman and Reed (1983) consider primary stakeholders as *narrow* stakeholders and secondary as *wide* stakeholders. One other categorisation worthy of a mention is *legitimate* and *illegitimate* stakeholders. 'Legitimacy refers to the extent to which a group has justifiable right to be making its claims' (Carroll, 1991, p. 43). This last categorisation is broad and could encompass different stakeholder groups.

Organisations make decisions at different points in time which may affect their stakeholder groups, but stakeholders do not necessarily have congruent interests in the organisation. For example, employees demand higher pay while shareholders demand higher returns. Hence, management will often make a trade-off regarding which stakeholder group(s) they should consider in their decision making. This is usually done by looking at the stakeholder's power or ability to exert pressure on the management and the legitimacy of their claim (Carroll, 1991).

As noted in Chapter 3, there is no universally accepted definition of the concept of CSR. This makes it a difficult task to really say what CSR is and what CSR is not. Many definitions of CSR abound, for example, Dahlsrud (2008) analysed 37 definitions of CSR. However, what is common to the various definitions of CSR is that they can be summarised into five broad themes; environmental, social, economic, stakeholder and voluntary dimensions (Dahlsrud, 2008). The environmental dimension deals with how business activities affect the natural environment; social focuses on the impact of business activities on society; economic examines how business activities contribute to economic development; stakeholder prescribes that business practices should take into consideration all relevant stakeholders of the business; and voluntary implies CSR should be an activity not prescribed by the law.

In general then, corporate social responsibility refers to "organisation activities – voluntary by definition – demonstrating the inclusion of social and environmental concerns in business operations and in interactions with stakeholders" (Van Marrewijk, 2003:102). According to Davis (1973, p. 312) "CSR is the firm's considerations of, and response to, issues beyond the narrow economic, technical, and legal requirements of the firm to accomplish social [and environmental] benefits." These definitions combine all the four dimensions of CSR as discussed above.

Carroll (1991) developed a CSR pyramid that shows various levels of an organisation's CSR activities (see Figure 4.1). It begins with the basic level, moving up to a more inclusive CSR at the peak.

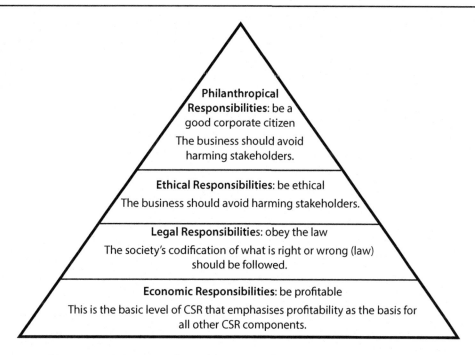

Figure 4.1: CSR pyramid. Source: Adapted from Carroll (1991)

At the basic level, the organisation is concerned about making profits as it is responsible to shareholders. At the next level, the survival of the organisation hinges on it following what is considered right by society and avoiding what is considered wrong. Then, in recognition of other stakeholders, the organisation is expected to carry out its activities in a way that does not negatively affect those stakeholders. At the peak of the CSR pyramid is the notion that businesses should not only do what is expected of them, but should further contribute to improving the lives of citizens and their community through philanthropic contributions.

Corporate citizenship

A common theme that arises in CSR debates relates to how we view organisations and delineate responsibility. For example, can we treat an organisation as a person? Likewise, should we expect organisations to behave according to human ethics and morals? If yes, how can an organisation that is composed of many people with diverse backgrounds do so? This then leads us to ask what set of social norms should an organisation adhere to? Is it those that are defined by its shareholders, the government, or social activists? While these are important and valid questions, remains elusive. Indeed, while the notion of CSR, by definition, is built on the assumption that organisations have a responsibility to pursue other objectives besides profit maximisation, this prime assumption remains controversial. There are two main schools of thoughts regarding corporate citizenship;

the first perceives the organisation as an 'instrument', while the second treats organisations as a 'citizen' of society. We discuss these views below, however, it is important to understand these as opposite ends of a spectrum, with other views of the organisation – society relationship in between.

■ Milton Friedman vs. Charles Handy

The main proponents of the first school of thought are the instrumental theorists who view organisations as an instrument for maximising shareholders' wealth. Theodore Levitt (1958) described CSR as "a happy new orthodoxy, a prevailing vogue, a new tyranny of fad and fancy" (Levitt, 1958:42). The Nobel Prize winning economist, Milton Friedman, claimed that social responsibility was a subversive doctrine in a free society (as cited in Carroll, 1979). Friedman (1970) believes that an organisation's number one duty to society is to maximize returns to its shareholders, and any attempts to spend money on social/environmental donations, or attempt to satisfy stakeholders other than shareholders, are at best misguided (Solomon, 2007).

Friedman, like many other neoclassical economists and agency theorists, believes that money invested in CSR activities is an agency problem as it is a 'theft' of shareholder-owned resources that should instead have been used to maximize shareholders' wealth. Similarly, David Henderson (2001) argues that the obligations suggested by CSR proponents have more harmful effects than good. One of Henderson's most important observations is that acting in a socially responsible way has unfavourable consequences in the developing world, where it is supposed to be most useful. Moreover, he claims that many CEOs, in developed countries, found that making their operations sustainable, which can be costly, puts them at a disadvantage compared to competitors in developing countries who do not face the same pressures.

On the other hand, Charles Handy, an influential British commentator, disagrees with Friedman's view of the role of organisations in society. In Handy's view, organisations are expected to do something valuable to the "whole of society" and to do it "better, or more useful than anyone else" (Handy, 2002:5). Organisations need more than profit generation to justify their existence, and their profits should be just "the means to that larger end" (Handy, 2002:5). Handy's view, like some other theories (e.g. the common good, and stewardship theory[4]), takes public morality as a starting point for CSR and focuses on the moral imperative embedded in the organisation – society relationship. Here,

---

4 The common good is a concept "of social and political ethics developed centuries ago … and identified with some form of common interest shared by the members of a community" (Argandoña, 1998:2). Stewardship theory, unlike the agency theory, suggests that individuals (e.g. managers) are not opportunistic and can be trusted with the resources they manage (Davis, 1997). It claims there are "situations in which managers are not motivated by individual goals, but rather are stewards whose motives are aligned with the objectives of their principals" (Davis *et al.*, 1997).

organisations are committed to bear social responsibilities as an ethical obligation, regardless of any other financial consequences (Garriga and Melé, 2004).

While Friedman's and Handy's positions represent two opposite ends of a
spectrum, there is a growing perception that these two views are reconcilable; that
is, organisations with good CSR agenda do perform well financially (Solomon,
2007). For example, Innovest Strategic Value Advisors, one of the CSR rating
agencies, found that firms with the best CSR ratings do have the best performing shares. However, the link between firms' CSR activities and performance
could be explained differently; profitable companies are the only ones who can
afford CSR activities, as suggested by McGuire *et al.* (1988). In the accounting and
finance literature, several theories are used to explain the positive relationship
between CSR and corporate financial performance. Most of these theories and
perspectives are pragmatic; dealing with eco-social issues as an opportunity for
increasing wealth. For instance, the cause-related marketing perspective[5] con-
tends that an organisation's profits can be boosted by establishing a distinctive
brand and reputation which are associated with eco-social dimensions (Garriga
and Melé, 2004).

In addition, socio-political theories, including institutional theory and stakeholder theory[6], advocate the necessity of CSR activities to business survival.
Institutional theory represents the theoretical lens used by researchers to account
for the effect of culture, regulations and traditions (Bruton *et al.*, 2010). However,
the concept of institutionalisation has been used differently in the literature
(Scott, 1987). One of the main institutional theory versions, probably the most
influential, is concerned with how organizations could adopt new practices to
get legitimacy, rather than improving their efficiency (DiMaggio and Powell,
1983). Adoption of these new practices infused with value can take the form of
conforming to the institutional environment's regulations and norms (Bruton *et
al.*, 2010; Scott, 1987). According to this view, institutionalisation is a process that
the organisation undergoes over time; institutionalisation is viewed as a means
of instilling values (Scott, 1987).

Such theorists challenge the conventional shareholder-based model of the
organisation, arguing that it ignores the complexity of an organisation's sur-
roundings. They propose a stakeholder-based theory of the firm that extends the
role of organisations to include other external and internal players apart from
shareholders (Banerjee, 2007; Freeman, 1984). As far as CSR is concerned, these
two overlapping theories suggest that CSR disclosure is a means for facing social
and political pressures. In this view, organisations that perform badly in the
eco-social domain jeopardise their legitimacy, hence, they attempt to change the

---

5 Cause-related marketing is defined as "the process of formulating and implementing marketing
activities that are characterised by an offer from the firm to contribute a specified amount to
a designated cause when customers engage in a revenue-providing exchanges that satisfy
organizational and individual objectives" (Varadarajan and Menon, 1988, p.60).

6 Stakeholder theory was discussed briefly in earlier chapters.

perceptions of stakeholders by engaging in sustainable activities and social disclosure (Clarkson *et al.*, 2008). This legitimacy-seeking notion stems from the fact that each organisation needs explicit, or implicit, approval from the community, government, and many other stakeholders to operate (Porter and Kramer, 2006).

Limitations of the current approaches to CSR

Although the preceding theories offered different justifications for CSR, they all suffer from one crucial limitation; there is no clear political or legal framework that defines the rights and responsibilities of organisations. Banerjee (2007), argues that the universality of a normative approach (e.g. Whose norms? Why those norms and not any other?), and lack of monitoring and accountability underpinning most of these theories, may have created a distorted situation in which organisations are responsible for everything but are not accountable for anything. While one may argue that lawsuits can be a powerful disciplinary tool for organisations involved in social misconducts, the cost of bringing such lawsuits against wealthy organisations is normally beyond the capacity of the affected communities and activists. Furthermore, organisations usually "escape any punitive action or liability for complicity with repressive regimes involving human rights violations" (Banerjee, 2007). The absence of accountability systems where organisations are sanctioned for their misconduct, eventually encourages the use of CSR activities for mere 'greenwashing' purposes.

Michael E. Porter, one of the founding fathers of strategic management, also argues that while the prevailing theories and concepts of CSR have "advanced thinking in the field, none offers sufficient guidance for the difficult choices corporate leaders must make" (Porter and Kramer, 2006:4). In addition, they tend to discuss business and society as two competing parties, when the two should be regarded as interdependent. Porter believes that there is a need to consider the practical limitations of each approach to CSR and to develop a more practical approach that seizes many of the greatest opportunities for organisations to help their society. Indeed, these practical constraints vary from one approach to another. For instance, the moral or ethical obligation approach to CSR entails considerable limitations, such as the absence of the base on which organisations can weigh social benefits against each other, the financial cost of CSR activities, and how to meet stakeholders' competing demands. There were, however, some attempts to develop more pragmatic approaches to overcome some of these practical difficulties. Elkington's (1998) triple bottom line approach, for instance, directs organisations to identify activities and operate at the intersection of environmental, social, and economic domains (Carter and Easton, 2011; Seuring and Muller, 2008). However, this approach does not offer guidance on how organisations can do that; how to balance long term aims with short term costs; and how to identify these activities (Porter and Kramer, 2006).

This lack of clarity is reflected in empirical studies on CSR. Unsurprisingly, the results range from a negative (e.g. Vance, 1975, cited in Salzmann *et al.*, 2005) to positive relations between corporate sustainability and firm performance (e.g. Lo and Sheu, 2007a, 2010b). On the other hand, the impact of an organisation's sustainability on society becomes:

> *diffused among numerous unrelated efforts, each responding to a different stakeholder group or corporate pressure point. The consequence of this fragmentation is a tremendous lost opportunity. The power of organisations to create social benefit is dissipated, and so is the potential for organisations to take actions that would support both their communities and their business goals.*
> (Porter and Kramer, 2006:5).

The insufficient impact of traditional CSR on both levels (i.e. firm and society) can be attributed to its disconnection from business and strategy. That is, an eco-social initiative which does not relate to the firm's functions will be ineffective and inefficient due to the lack of related expertise and capabilities available in the firm (Bhattacharyya, *et al.*, 2008).

The next section discusses a more practical approach to CSR implementation that connects CSR to the business' operations and objectives; namely strategic CSR.

4

A strategic approach to CSR implementation

In today's business dominated society, organisations are expected to play a role towards eco-social issues (Bhattacharyya, *et al.*, 2008). These expectations coincide with an increased global demand for transparency, especially after successive global scandals such as Exxon Mobil, Enron and WorldCom (Carter and Easton, 2011). Hence, corporate social reporting has emerged as an inescapable priority for organisations all over the world, with multinational companies (MNCs) standing at its heart; due to their greater potential impact on society and the environment[7]. However, the impact that CSR has on both organisations and society is not satisfactory. Most organisations' responses are cosmetic, defensive, and fragmented (e.g. media campaigns, public relations, and philanthropy), which eventually have no meaningful social impact or organisational benefits (Porter and Kramer, 2006). As mentioned above, the results of empirical research on the relationship between an organisation's sustainability and performance are inconclusive.[8] This renders CSR programs vulnerable, and liable to be affected by management change and the business cycle fluctuation.

---

7 Recent studies showed an increasing percentage of sustainability reporting among MNCs from 35% to 45% to 64% in 2001, 2003 and 2008 respectively (Crespy and Miller, 2011).

8 There was evidence of a negative, positive, and no relation between corporate sustainability and firm performance (Lourenço, *et al.*, 2012; Lo and Sheu, 2010; Salzmann *et al.*, 2005; McWilliams and Siegel, 2001).

Several authors have suggested that a strategic approach to CSR will avoid the pitfalls of traditional/philanthropic CSR, which was neither sufficiently benefiting the organisation, or society (McWilliams *et al.*, 2006; Porter and Kramer, 2006; Bhattacharyya *et al.*, 2008). According to Porter and Kramer (2006), strategic CSR goes beyond responsive CSR to mount a small number of initiatives that largely and distinctively benefit both society and organisations. In other words, strategic CSR is about rooting CSR in the strategies of specific organisations, hence, organisations should engage only in eco-social activities that are related to their core business. The more closely tied an eco-social issue is to an organisation's core activity, the greater the chance to benefit both society and the organisation (Bhattacharyya, *et al.*, 2008). Porter and Kramer (2006), suggest that to create a strategic CSR agenda, organisations may follow the steps laid out below.

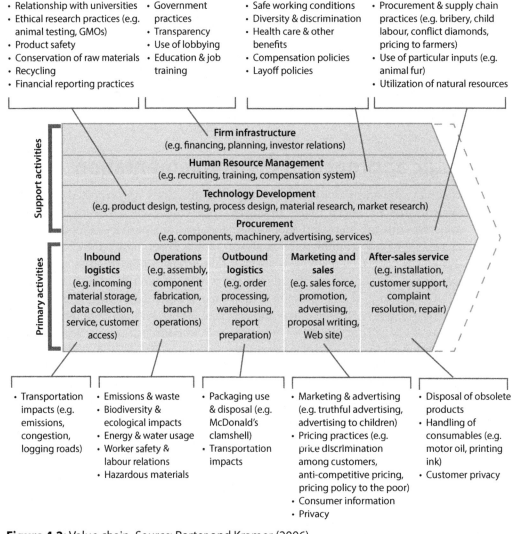

Figure 4.2: Value chain. *Source*: Porter and Kramer (2006)

1   Identify the points of intersection between an organisation and society

Organisations influence society through their day to day operations (i.e. *inside-out linkages*). An analysis of how each part in the organisation's *value chain* (Figure 4.2) interacts and affects the surrounding communities should be the first step in adopting a strategic approach to CSR. A value chain is the chain of activities by which an organisation adds value to its products or services. Due to their dynamic nature, organisations should continuously assess the positive or negative social impact of these activities. Having a diligent process in place for identifying these evolving social impacts of tomorrow is crucial for the organisation's survival.

The organisation-society interaction is a two-way process; the organisation's operations affect society, while the external social conditions also impact upon the organisations' activities (i.e. *outside-in linkages*). Specifically, all organisations, regardless of their industry, operate within a *competitive context* of which the social conditions are an important part. The context offers threats and opportunities that can significantly affect the organisation's ability to prosper. For instance, the quantity and quality of local workers, the size of local demand, and the availability of supporting industry and infrastructure can all be targets for CSR activities. Figure 4.3 shows how firm's value chain and competitive context interacts with the eco-social issues.

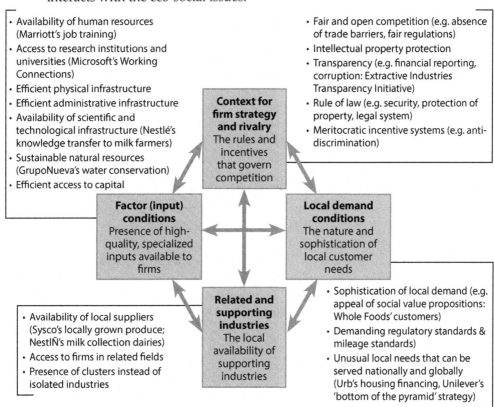

Figure 4.3: Competitive context. *Source*: Porter and Kramer (2006)

2 Choose which social issues to address

By the end of stage one, the firm should have a list of the potential social issues that relate to its core activities, however, solving all of these issues is beyond a single firm's capacity. Therefore, organisations should only choose the social issues that pass the test of 'strategy fitness' or 'shared value'; that is, does this social issue have the potential to create a considerable benefit for both the society and the organisation or not? Porter and Kramer (2006) mention three categories in which any social issue belongs; generic social issues, value chain social impacts, and social dimensions of competitive context (see Table 4.1). Each organisation is then invited to place their social issues into one of these three categories and order them according to their potential impact.

Table 4.1: Prioritizing social issues. *Source*: Porter and Kramer (2006)

Generic social issues	Value chain social impacts	Social dimensions of competitive context
Social issues that are not significantly affected by an organisation's operations nor materially affect its long-term competitiveness.	Social issues that are significantly affected by an organisation's activities in the ordinary course of business.	Social issues in the external environment that significantly affect the underlying drivers of an organisation's competitiveness in the locations where it operates.

3 Create a corporate social agenda

In this stage, the organisation should have a categorised and ranked the social issues that can be used to create a CSR agenda. While such an agenda should be responsive to the different needs of stakeholders (i.e. responsive CSR), the vast majority of the firm's resources should be devoted to the strategic CSR activities that go beyond what stakeholders expect. Table 4.2 compares between strategic CSR and responsive, or traditional, CSR.

4 Integrate inside-out and outside-in practices

While value chain-based social innovations and those targeting a competitive context have the potential to significantly benefit both society and the organisation, the impact is even greater if they are combined. That is, "when value chain practices and investments in a competitive context are fully integrated, CSR becomes hard to distinguish from the day-to-day business of the organisation" (Porter and Kramer, 2006:11). An organisation, for instance, can focus on a CSR activity that helps its main operations (value chain) while enhancing its input quality (competitive context).

Table 4.2: Comparison between strategic CSR and responsive CSR.
Source: Adapted from Porter and Kramer (2006)

	Strategic CSR	Responsive CSR
Managerial Look to CSR (Culture)	CSR is a source of opportunity, innovation, and competitive advantage. Emphasis on the substance not the image. Shared value managerial mindset. It is about corporate social integration.	CSR is a cost, constraint, and charitable deed. Emphasis on the image not the substance. Us vs them managerial mindset. It is about corporate social responsibility.
Purpose of CSR	Creating a shared value; that is, a meaningful benefit for society that is also valuable to the business.	Neither strategic nor operational but cosmetic in forms of public relation, media campaigns, glossy CSR report.
CSR Activities	Moves beyond good corporate citizenship to work according to an agenda composed of a small number of initiatives that have large and unique social and business benefits. Pioneer innovations (both tangible and intangible) to benefit both society and an organisation's own competitiveness (e.g. product offering, and the value chain).	Aggregation of 'anecdotes about uncoordinated initiatives' for greenwashing purposes. Philanthropic activities described in monetary value, or volunteer hours 'but almost never in terms of social impacts.' Activities disconnected from firm's strategy that do not make a noticeable impact on the society, and with no benefit to the business's long-term success and competitiveness
Approach to CSR	Having a clear strategy for CSR. Coherent framework. Forward looking commitments to reach explicit performance targets.	A generic responsive rationale that is not connected to either the business's strategy and core activities or its place of operation.
CSR issues - selection process	Operation management participate in the process of prioritizing CSR issues.	Responding to external pressure. Accommodating to the evolving social concern of stakeholders.
CSR issues - materiality	Belong to 'social dimensions of competitive context'. Investing in social aspects of context that strengthen organisation competitiveness Value chain social impacts: Transform value chain activities to benefit society while reinforcing strategy. Adding social dimension to its value proposition.	Belong to 'Generic social issues' (i.e. may be important to society but are neither significantly affected by the organisation's operations nor influence the organisation's long-term competitiveness). Value Chain Social Impacts: Mitigating existing/anticipated adverse effects from business activities.

4

5 Create a social dimension to the value proposition

A unique value proposition is the cornerstone of any strategy. The value proposition is defined as the set of needs that a firm attempts to fulfil better than anyone else. The best strategic CSR activity is the one that is built on adding a social dimension to the organisation's unique value proposition, achieving the ultimate integration between social component and strategy. One example for such integration would be a grocery store (e.g. Planet Organic, the UK's largest fully certified organic supermarket), selling only organic food products to a special group of customers who are looking for high quality food without compromising on environmental issues. Or, an organisation like Ecover, a Belgium-based organisation, that manufactures ecologically sound cleaning products. While it can be a real challenge to tailor the organisation's entire value proposition to accommodate social issues, adding a social aspect to the value proposition can competitively reposition the firm among its rivals and considerably help its communities.

Within the public sector, Williams and Lewis (2008) demonstrated the applicability and effectiveness of the value chain and stakeholder analyses in their study of seven public sector strategic consultancy projects. Their research demonstrates a strong defence for the use of these strategic management models, when used both independently and in conjunction with each other. Indeed, when used in conjunction they were found to provide a powerful strategic analytical framework that can encourage and illuminate strategic discourses that can facilitate improved CSR in public sector organisations.

Stakeholder engagement and CSR/sustainability reporting

According to Tiron-Tudor and Bota-Avram (2015), sustainability is another term for CSR. However, Finch (2005) explains that CSR is a subset of sustainability; sustainability is the long-term focus of CSR. "Achieving sustainability requires balancing the complex relationships between current economic, environmental, and social needs in a manner that does not compromise future needs." (Global Reporting Initiative, 2002:9) A major distinction between sustainability and CSR is that the former requires carrying out CSR activities with a future orientation, hence, CSR is sustainability in the short-term. Sustainability typically involves integrating the triple bottom line into business strategies and processes. The triple bottom line includes economic (profit), social and environmental issues, but the way in which these issues are integrated is often not defined and is somewhat complex for small organisations (Gao and Zhang, 2006).

Triple bottom line (Elkington, 1998) reporting (or sustainability reporting) refers to the provision of information for accountability and/or decision making against the three broad aspects of sustainability, that is, economic, environmental and social aspects. Accordingly, sustainability reporting "must consist of statements about the extent to which organisations are reducing (or increasing) the options available to future generations" (Gray *et al.*, 2001:308). An important step in sustainability reporting would involve engaging with stakeholders to understand their demands and interests.

Stakeholder engagement is "the process of seeking stakeholder views on their relationship with an organisation in a way that may realistically be expected to elicit them" (Integrated Strategic Environmental Assessment (ISEA), 1999:91). As stakeholders are diverse groups with conflicting interests in and influence on organisations, incorporating their interests into organisational decision-making is a very complex process. More so, stakeholders themselves are not fixed and their interests are not static. Hence, organisations must engage with stakeholders to identify, evaluate and balance these stakes or interests.

Stakeholder engagement is an important part of sustainability as the identification and balancing of conflicting interests is dependent on it. The way and levels of engaging stakeholders vary, and stakeholder engagement can mean different things in different contexts (Gao and Zhang, 2001). According to ISEA (1999), cited in Gao and Zhang (2001, p. 21), stakeholder engagement should have the following features as laid out in Box 4.1.

Box 4.1: Stakeholder engagement

☐ The engagement process should be capable of assisting stakeholders to identify other stakeholders.

☐ The engagement should ensure that the social and ethical accountant (internal or external) involved in the engagement process is trusted by stakeholders.

☐ Dialogue in the engagement process should be two-way and not a one-way information feed.

☐ To ensure parties involved in the engagement process are equipped with well thought out opinions and decisions, there should be sufficient preparation and briefing given to these parties.

☐ Stakeholders should be engaged while drafting the engagement terms. Such terms could include the methods and techniques to be adopted in the engagement, the questions to be asked, how the responses to questions will be analysed and how feedback will be given to stakeholders.

☐ Stakeholders should be allowed to voice their concern without fear or restrictions.

☐ The outcome of the engagement process should be disclosed to the public for the assessment of involved and non-involved stakeholders.

Source: ISEA (1999), cited in Gao and Zhang (2001, p. 21)

There are four levels of stakeholder engagement (See Table 4.3). An organisation may engage stakeholders passively, in which case they are merely provided with information, but do not contribute to the engagement process. At a level above this, information is sought from stakeholders, but no feedback is given to them. Next, stakeholders can be listened to and given feedback on how management has taken care of their concerns in a two-way process. Finally, in a proactive stakeholder engagement, stakeholders are engaged in management decision making.

Table 4.3: Levels of stakeholder engagement. *Source*: Gao and Zhang (2001)

Level of engagement	Stakeholders are merely given Information (passive)	Stakeholders are consulted (listening)	Stakeholders engage in dialogue with organisation (2-way process)	Management is driven by stakeholder (proactive)
Stakeholder engagement approach	Inform stakeholders via public media. Publish reports Policy and product documents.	Listen to stakeholders through formal meetings or suggestion boxes. Hear stakeholders' views through questionnaires and interviews. Have a complaint process	Hold focus group discussions. Provide feedback to stakeholders. Use stakeholder-driven performance measures and reports.	Set up a stakeholder council. Allow stakeholder representatives in management. Ask for stakeholder verification of social report.
Number of stakeholder participants	Mass stakeholders and wide society	Selected stakeholders	Limited number of key stakeholders	Very limited number of key stakeholder (e.g. stakeholder representatives)

CSR reporting

There is no universal standard for reporting organisations' CSR activities. That is, the details about the content and structure of a CSR report does not have a universal framework. Islam (2015:15) defines CSR reporting as a function of:

> *reporting deals with the disclosure of information by an organisation about product and consumer interests, employee interests, community activities and environmental impacts—this disclosure of information is deemed to be a part of an organisation's responsibility to its stakeholders or a response to stakeholder expectations.*

Further, Deegan (2007) defines [CSR] reporting as

> *"the provision of information about the performance of an organisation in relation to its interaction with its physical and social environment and includes, but is not limited to interaction with the local community; level of support for community projects; level of support for developing countries; health and safety record; training, employment and education programs; and environmental performance" (p. 1265).*

Organisations often report their CSR activities together with their financial statements in their annual reports or through a standalone report. The CSR section in the annual reports or the standalone report often has different titles such as: sustainability report, corporate responsibility report, corporate social responsibility report, sustainable development report, environmental and social report (Del Baldo, 2015). It is worth mentioning that most CSR reports are narrative-based with limited financial details. Notwithstanding the non-existence of a universal framework or standard on the content and structure of CSR reports, there are some international initiatives that have been widely adopted by organisations globally for reporting their CSR activities. The Global Reporting Initiatives (GRI) guidelines; the AccountAbility (AA) 1000 for managing and reporting sustainability performance; Social Accountability (SA) 8000 for managing labour practices; and the International Standards Organization (ISO) 26000 on sustainability management are some examples of these standards.

Due to this proliferation of standards for the reporting of an organisations' CSR activities, the Institute of Chartered Accountants of England and Wales (2010) argues that organisations may exploit this opportunity to only report good information, while neglecting bad information about their organisations. For example, Liao, Lin and Zhang (2016) argue that some organisations in China hide negative material information from their CSR report. Thus, like the financial statements audit, there has been calls for CSR report audits. Across the globe, there are three major international standards that are often followed for conducting assurance on CSR reports. According to Liao, Lin and Zhang (2016), these standards include: AA1000 Assurance Standard (AA1000AS) issued by AccountAbility in 2008, International Standard on Assurance Engagements (ISAE3000) developed by the International Auditing and Assurance Standard Board (IAASB) in 2013 and Sustainability Reporting Guidelines, issued by the Global Reporting Initiative in 2006. Out of the three initiatives, the GRI is considered the most comprehensive.

Arguably, the global orientation of the GRI guidelines makes this an attractive tool for organisations in their delivery of CSR reports. However, it must be recognised that GRI while being a guideline and not a standard, has a section on assurance which is summarised in Box 4.2. There is continuing debate on whether the current assurance of CSR and sustainability reports should become mandated as an audit. This will be discussed in more detail in Chapters 5 and 7.

GRI guidelines on assurance

☐ The use of external assurance is recommended by GRI.

☐ External assurance should be conducted by groups or individuals, external to the organisation, who have requisite knowledge and experience in the assurance process.

☐ The manner of preparing the assurance report should be systematic, documented, evidence-based, and blended with defined procedures.

☐ External reports should provide a reasonable and balanced presentation of performance, considering the data accuracy and overall content selection.

☐ The external groups or individuals to conduct the assurance should not be unduly limited by their relationship with the organisation or its stakeholders (i.e. no conflict of interests), to reach and publish an independent and impartial conclusion on the report.

☐ The external report should assess the extent to which the report preparer has applied the GRI Reporting Framework (including the reporting principles) while reaching its conclusions.

☐ The assurance should provide a set of conclusions, publicly available in written form, and a statement from the assurance provider on their relationship to the report preparer.

Box 2: GRI guidelines on assurance Source: Liao, Lin and Zhang (2016, p. 140)

Summary

Whilst CSR has, over the years, attracted attention from practitioners and academics from different disciplines, the whole idea is yet to be put together into a cohesive whole. Indeed, when investigating this concept, it becomes clear that there is no universal agreement on what CSR is, the rationale behind it, or the strategies required for achieving it. However, the existing literature provides a solid foundation with which to explore and integrate these widely divergent viewpoints on CSR. The chapter defines CSR by exploiting four major dimensions (environmental, social, economic, stakeholder and voluntary). It demonstrates that CSR activities are carried out by organisations from the most basic (economic responsibility) to the most developed level (philanthropical responsibility). It further provides an overview of the divergent theoretical arguments regarding the ethics and morality of organisational behaviour. Due to the changing economic and business landscape, a discussion on the need for organisations to take a strategic approach to CSR implementation, which assumes that they should absorb CSR as a key business issue rather than an ad hoc response to corporate social and economic failures is put forward.

The importance of stakeholder engagement in embedding a strategic approach to CSR in organisations has also been shown to offer strategic advantages in the delivery and interpretation of organisational CSR activity. The chapter concludes with a discussion of CSR reporting and the frameworks often employed by organisations in communicating their CSR activities.

Discussion questions:

1 What do we mean by corporate citizenship? Do you think that organisations in the UK are 'good citizens'?

2 Discuss the differences between the responsive and the strategic approaches to CSR.

3 Organisations have stakeholders with conflicting demands. How do organisations blend these conflicting interests?

4 What is stakeholder engagement and discuss the levels of stakeholder engagement.

References and further reading

Argandoña, A. (1998). The stakeholder theory and the common good. *Journal of Business Ethics*, **17**(9), 1093-1102.

Banerjee, S.B. (2007). *Corporate Social Responsibility: The Good, the Bad and the Ugly*. Edward Elgar Publishing.

Carroll, A. B. (1979). A three-dimensional conceptual model of corporate performance. *Academy of Management Review*, 4, 497-505.

Carroll, A. B. (1991). The pyramid of corporate social responsibility: Toward the moral management of organizational stakeholders. *Business Horizons*, **34**(4), 39-48.

Carter, C.R. and Liane Easton, P. (2011). Sustainable supply chain management: evolution and future directions. *International Journal of Physical Distribution and Logistics Management*, 41(1), 46-62.

Clarkson, M. E. (1995). A stakeholder framework for analyzing and evaluating corporate social performance. *Academy of Management Review*, **20**(1), 92-117.

Clarkson, P.M., Li, Y., Richardson, G.D. and Vasvari, F.P. (2008). Revisiting the relation between environmental performance and environmental disclosure: An empirical analysis. *Accounting, Organizations and Society*, **33**(4), 303-327.

Crespy, C.T. and Miller, V.V. (2011). Sustainability reporting: A comparative study of NGOs and MNCs. *Corporate Social Responsibility and Environmental Management*, **18**(5), 275-284.

Dahlsrud, A. (2008). How corporate social responsibility is defined: an analysis of 37 definitions. *Corporate Social Responsibility and Environmental Management*, **15**(1), 1-13.

Davis, J.H., Schoorman, F.D. and Donaldson, L. (1997). Toward a stewardship theory of management. *Academy of Management Review*, **22**(1), 20-47.

Davis, K. (1973)., The case for and against business assumption of social responsibilities. *Academy of Management Journal*, **16**(2), 312-322.

Deegan, C. (2007). *Australian Financial Accounting*, 5th ed. Sydney, McGraw-Hill

Del Baldo, M. (2015). Is it time for integrated reporting in small and medium-sized enterprises? Reflections on an Italian experience. In Idowu, S. O. and Mermod, A. Y. (eds.). *Corporate Social Responsibility and Governance* (pp. 183-209). London: Springer International Publishing.

Elkington, J. (1998). Partnerships from cannibals with forks: The triple bottom line of 21st-century business. *Environmental Quality Management*, **8**(1), 37-51.

Finch, N. (2005). Sustainability Reporting Frameworks. Available at SSRN: https://ssrn.com/abstract=902783 or http://dx.doi.org/10.2139/ssrn.902783

Freeman, R. E. (1984). *Strategic Management: A stakeholder approach*. Boston: Pitman

Freeman, R. E., and Reed, D. L. (1983). Stockholders and stakeholders: A new perspective on corporate governance. *California Management Review*, **25**(3), 88-106.

Gao, S. S., and Zhang, J. J. (2006). Stakeholder engagement, social auditing and corporate sustainability. *Business Process Management Journal*, **12**(6), 722-740.

Garriga, E. and Melé, D. (2004). Corporate social responsibility theories: Mapping the territory. *Journal of Business Ethics*, **53**(1), 51-71.

Gray, R., and Bebbington, J. (2001). *Accounting for the Environment*. Sage.

GRI (2002). *Sustainability Reporting Guidelines*, Global Reporting Initiative, Boston, MA.

Handy, C. (2002). What is a Business for? *Harvard Business Review*, **12**, 1-9.

Henderson, D. (2001). *Misguided Virtue: False notions of corporate social responsibility*. New Zealand Business Roundtable.

ISEA (1999). AccountAbility 1000 (AA1000): Standard. Guidelines and Professional Qualification, Institute of Social and Ethical AccountAbility, London

Islam, M. A. (2015). *Social Compliance Accounting: Managing Legitimacy in Global Supply Chains*. London: Springer International Publishing.

Levitt, T. (1958). The dangers of social responsibility. *Harvard Business Review*, **36**(3), 41-50.

Liao, L., Lin, T. P., and Zhang, Y. (2016). Corporate board and corporate social responsibility assurance: Evidence from China. *Journal of Business Ethics*, 1-15.

Lo, S.F. and Sheu, H.J. (2007). Is corporate sustainability a value-increasing strategy for business? *Corporate Governance: An International Review*, **15**(2), 345-358.

McGuire, J.B., Sundgren, A. and Schneeweis, T. (1988). Corporate social responsibility and firm financial performance. *Academy of Management Journal*, **31**(4), 854-872.

McWilliams, A., Siegel, D.S. and Wright, P.M. (2006). Corporate social responsibility: Strategic implications. *Journal of Management Studies*, **43**(1), 1-18.

Porter, M. and Kramer, M.R. (2006). Strategy and society: the link between competitive advantage and corporate social responsibility. *Harvard Business Review*, **84**(12), 42-56.

Salzmann, O., Ionescu-Somers, A. and Steger, U. (2005). The business case for corporate sustainability: literature review and research options. *European Management Journal*, **23**(1), 27-36.

Sekhar Bhattacharyya, S., Sahay, A., Pratap Arora, A. and Chaturvedi, A. (2008). A toolkit for designing firm level strategic corporate social responsibility (CSR) initiatives. *Social Responsibility Journal*, **4**(3), 265-282.

Seuring, S. and Müller, M. (2008). From a literature review to a conceptual framework for sustainable supply chain management. *Journal of Cleaner Production*, **16**(15), 1699-1710.

Solomon, J. (2007). *Corporate Governance and Accountability*. John Wiley and Sons.

Tiron-Tudor, A., and Bota-Avram, C. (2015). New challenges for internal audit: corporate social responsibility aspects. In Rahim, M. M. and Idowu, S. O., *Social Audit Regulation*, pp. 15-31, Springer International Publishing.

Van Marrewijk, M. (2003). Concepts and definitions of CSR and corporate sustainability: Between agency and communion. *Journal of Business Ethics*, **44**(2), 95-105.

Varadarajan, P.R. and Menon, A. (1988). Cause-related marketing: A coalignment of marketing strategy and corporate philanthropy. *The Journal of Marketing*, 58-74.

Williams, W. and Duncan, L. (2008), Strategic management tools and public-sector management, *Public Management Review*, **10**(5), 653-671.

4

5 Social Accounting and Sustainability

Konstantinos Ritos, Akira Yonekura,
Stephen Rae, Oluwagbenga Adamolekun
and Mohamed Elshinawy.

Introduction

For over four decades, social accounting has been under the scope of accounting study, as well as a concern for major organisations (Milne and Gray, 2012). However, when looking back at annual reports, particularly before the 1970s there was very little that could be identified as a social account. During the 1970s, a few organisations were ahead of their time by disclosing social information in their annual reports and even fewer created a separate social report (Kolk, 2010). During the late 1980s, there was an intense focus on environmental issues (Hahn and Kuhnen, 2013), specifically, how organisations and certain industries are responsible for climate change and what actions could be taken to protect the planet and provide a sustainable environment for society (Hahn and Kuhnen, 2013). Thus, the environmental aspect became included as part of corporate social responsibility. This was the period in which non-governmental organisations concerned with corporate environmental impacts were formed, for example Ceres (1989) (formerly known as Coalition for Environmentally Responsible Economies) and SustainAbility (1987). Following this, the International Organisation for Standardisation (ISO) opened the discussion for ISO 14001 in 1991, which was finally published in 1996. The standard had a clear environmental focus, which was received positively by a wide range of organisations, especially those with environmental concerns and those trying to be viewed as socially and environmentally friendly. It was not until the end of the 2000s that an integrated reporting of both social and environmental aspects was developed. This was mainly because of John Elkington's influential work in the field in the 1990s and his work on the *triple bottom line* (TBL). The TBL opened new horizons in understanding corporate social responsibility (CSR) and allowed for progression in social accounting and sustainability practices and theory (Elkington, 1997).

Capitalising on Elkington's framework and his definition of sustainability, as well as how corporate reporting should evolve, Ceres formed the Global Reporting Initiative (GRI). Before becoming an independent organisation, the GRI issued its guidelines for CSR reporting, which were the first with an integrated economic, environmental and social focus. The GRI guidelines quickly became popular and, within a few years, allowed for sustainability reporting to rise in reputation (Fifka, 2012; Hahn and Kuhnen, 2013). The GRI came to be the most used set of guidelines in major organisations (KPMG, 2015), and were the only integrated guidelines available until 2010, after which the ISO 26000 was released. Despite the ISO having worldwide recognition, the ISO 26000 still lags in its adoption by large organisations. Delay also exists in governmental guidelines; very few nations have issued or mandated any environmental reporting rules, and fewer have issued social reporting requirements (e.g. Japan, UK). Only the Ministry of Corporate Affairs (MCA) of the Government of India (2011) issued and later mandated integrated reporting guidelines in the form of National Voluntary Guidelines for the Social, Environmental and Economic Responsibility of Business (NVG-SEE). The effects of mandating social and environmental reporting (SER), or their separate reports are not yet clear (Lock and Seele, 2016), but the EU Commission has mandated CSR reporting for entities employing over 500 people, encouraging them to use established guidelines, such as the GRI and the ISO 26000.

Given the importance of social accounting and sustainability for both current and future generations, this chapter takes a closer look at the developments outlined above. It begins with a discussion of the triple bottom line (TBL), a key concept influencing the development and practice of social and sustainability reporting. The emphasis is on both the positive aspects of the TBL as well as its limitations. This is followed by a discussion of major initiatives in the context of concern with CSR and sustainability, including attempts by not-for-profit organisations as well as local governments and the EU. The chapter then takes a closer look at some of the key organisations involved in initiatives on CSR and sustainability reporting before briefly discussing key reporting guidelines. Having outlined some key initiatives and the organisations behind them, the chapter then moves on to a discussion of two key concepts in social and sustainability accounting, namely *sustainability* and *accountability*. Some attempts at defining sustainability and examples of sustainability reports, including their relevance to the public sector, are discussed. The concept of accountability and socially and environmentally responsible actions as well as the need for transparency and disclosure are then presented.

The triple bottom line

The triple bottom line (TBL), also referred to as the 3Ps (profit, planet, people), was a concept formed by John Elkington in 1997. The focus was to allow organisations to consider closely not only their economic aspects, but equally their environmental and social impacts. Elkington contended that the modern organisation is held accountable for far more than just its economic performance and, therefore, needs to report on social and environmental aspects to survive competitively and maintain its intellectual capital. The assumptions that TBL reporting would become important were confirmed as more and more organisations started reporting their social and environmental aspects in the late 1990s; a trend which has continued until today. According to a report by KPMG in 2015, 92% of the world's 250 biggest organisations reported their corporate responsibility in 2015, compared to a mere 35% in 1999. It is important to identify the reasons behind this trend and understand the importance of reporting and acting under the TBL.

The environmental performance of an organisation may attract environmentally aware customers (Sridhar, 2012) or suppliers, which can create a competitive advantage. Modern organisations are not only accountable for their CO^2 emissions and their water wastes, but also for the effect of their actions on the fauna and flora in other parts of the local or global environment. Also, some governments have specific environmental requirements from organisations, such as the UK environmental key performance indicators (KPI). Certain governments mandate such measures and others publish them as optional. Whichever the case might be, larger organisations endeavour to comply to legitimise their position towards the government and society. Additionally, environmental non-governmental organisations are actively searching to report organisational misconduct on environmental issues, which can have a major negative impact on the reputation of an organisation. One such example of environmental misconduct that resulted in reputational and financial loss is the 2015 Volkswagen emission scandal, which cost the organisation $18bn.

Social aspects are important for stakeholder groups both inside and outside of the organisation (Elkington, 1997). According to social contract theory (formed in Rousseau's 1762 book *The Social Contract*), society allows organisations to function, use resources and provide products and services if the general costs (financial and non-financial) and waste created in this process do not exceed the total social gain (Mathews, 1993). Demonstrating the organisation's engagement with society, as well as its approach to human rights and the treatment of employees, is not only expected, but also sometimes required from large organisations by stakeholder groups. Such social activity and disclosure may attract investors and employees, thus strengthening an organisation's financial capital by receiving both additional funds and intellectual capital (through attracting better and more experienced employees). Furthermore, taking action, and being transparent connects the organisation with its local community (Sridhar, 2012) which allows for further societal support. Thus, following social contract theory enables the organisation to utilise more resources (Mathews, 1993).

There are, however, more ways to attract capital to an organisation than solely focusing on the economic/financial aspects of it. Through adopting an environmental and social focus, the modern organisation can attract various forms of capital other than just economic. It is argued that this allows the organisation to have long-term planning and extend its survivability (Elkington, 1997). Thus, the TBL slowly became synonymous with sustainability. For example, Glavas and Mish (2014:625) refer to the TBL as 'the practice of sustainability'. Many researchers, professionals and influential organisations, as well as guidelines such as the GRI, depend on these three dimensions to define and develop their sustainability frameworks. Rogers and Ryan (2001), for example, explain how every aspect of the TBL can help create a sustainable future of a local community. Their research shows that the TBL and generally the sustainability concept applies to more than just business entities. However, there is a heated debate in the literature, as to what sustainability is (White, 1999; Milne and Gray, 2012). Indeed, Milne and Gray (2012:18) argue that "even 'ideal' TBL disclosure does not speak to sustainability".

Apart from questions over its connection to sustainability, the TBL has been criticised for certain other issues. Sherman (2012) argues that the TBL, despite providing three different aspects of reporting (profit, people and planet), is lacking integration and comparability. The three aspects do not interact with each other, so organisations report all three different aspects without linking how the lack of one aspect might hinder the other two (Sridhar and Jones, 2013). Also, the way they are presented is different for each organisation, so that the users of the reports cannot tell which organisation is better performing (Sherman, 2012; Sridhar, 2012). Furthermore, this variation in reporting creates an imbalance between reports that are overburdened with either images or tables and those that rely on numbers. It is unclear for organisations which report using the TBL if their reports should be user friendly (usually accused of 'greenwashing') or analytical with hard data. Sridhar (2012) argues that this confusion is created due to interpretation of language; i.e. the human factor in managers. In a later paper Sridhar and Jones (2013) argue that this inconsistency appears because of lack of mandatory regulation. However, as mentioned earlier, the results of mandatory regulation are not yet clear due to a lack of evidence (Lock and Seele, 2016). Finally, the complexity of measurement and representation and lack of standardised reporting of TBL aspects allows for opportunistic management to report only what is easy and positive for the organisation to attract investors, while creatively concealing any negative realities. To solve these issues a TBL-based audit has been suggested. Interestingly, this idea appeared in the debate before Elkington's contributions (1997), but to this day the matter is still discussed, and organisations seek legitimacy of their sustainability and CSR reports through professional accounting or consulting body assurance rather than a TBL audit.

Some of the above criticisms aim directly at the heart of the TBL, but most major criticisms are made against TBL reporting, which, as will be shown in the next section, has yet to be finalised despite being 20 years in development and constantly updated. Nevertheless, the fundamentals of the TBL have influenced many organisations in determining their framework for integrated reporting.

Global initiatives

In the late 1980s and early 1990s the concern for a sustainable environment began to be transferred into business strategies. Along with the foundation of Elkington's SustainAbility consultancy and Ceres, mentioned earlier, the Business for Social Responsibility (BSR) organisation was created with an aim to raise awareness for 'a just and sustainable world.' The World Business Council for Sustainable Development (WBCSD) was formed from the CEOs of 200 international organisations, taking initiative from the first United Nations Conference on Environmental Development (UNCED), also called the Earth Summit, held in Rio De Janeiro, Brazil, in 1992. In the second half of the 1990s these initiatives bore fruit. Large organisations followed sustainable strategies by adopting the 1996 ISO14001 for environmental management, which very quickly became popular, while the markets became friendlier to organisations which strove for a better environment for a sustainably society. In 1999 and 2001 the Dow Jones Sustainability Index (DJSI) and the FTSE4GOOD were, respectively, launched to help investors find environmentally and socially responsible organisations to invest in. This action is a form of socially responsible investment as discussed in detail in Chapter 6. Finally, and arguably most importantly, Ceres formed the Global Reporting Initiative in 1997, which later released the first ever reporting guidelines for integrated reporting, the GRI G1, connecting the three aspects of the TBL in one report. Evidently, the past 30 years have been very influential and important towards the future of organisational sustainability.

■ National initiatives

Apart from individual non-profit organisations, some national governments have made attempts to regulate the environmental, or even integrated, performance and reporting of the organisations operating inside their borders. In 2000, the Japanese Ministry of Environment (MOE) issued one of the first governmental environmental reporting guidelines which had a wide reception and influenced the reporting practice in Japan (Bennett et al., 2003). Initially, the guidelines were only environmentally focused, providing reporting guidelines and addressing environmental Key Performance Indicators (KPIs) that the organisations should use (MOE, 2003). However, in the introduction of the most recent guidelines document (MOE, 2012), the Ministry states that to build a sustainable future, the 'so-called' triple bottom line must be considered. Changes were made to the guidelines, including a more holistic approach to integrated reporting.

In 2006, the UK government issued a document covering Environmental KPIs. In these guidelines, it is stated that the purpose of the guidelines is sustainable development and to secure the future. It is also argued that the KPIs are the best way to regulate organisations' environmental action, since they provide hard data on their performance. However, the guidelines have a strictly environmental focus. The CSR in the UK is regulated through the Corporate Governance Code, the latest version of which dates to 2012.

A stricter approach to promoting integrated reporting was adopted by the government of India, when they mandated the National Voluntary Guidelines on Social Environmental and Economic Responsibilities of Business, (NVG-SEE) in 2012. Initially released in 2009, with a mission for sustainable development and applicability in all entities, regardless of activities, size or location (MCA, 2011), the NVG-SEE also embraced the TBL framework and worked in its three aspects. The developers of the guidelines adopted concepts based on other guidelines such as the ISO26000 and the GRI.

In 2014 the EU commission voted in the mandatory reporting of social and environmental aspects for all large public-interest entities with more than 500 employees. The Commission also encourages these entities to include other relevant matters, prepare a stand-alone report, and/or use the established guidelines (ISO26000, UNGC, OECD and others). This mandate unites a whole continent in sustainability. Both the examples of India and the EU Commission has influenced other governments or regulators to adopt integrated reporting. Ultimately this should provide positive results towards the effect of mandating sustainability reports and result in sustainable organisations on a large scale.

Key organisations in the context of CSR and sustainability

All the aforementioned organisations (SustainAbility, Ceres, BSR and WBCSD) have two main characteristics in common. They are non-profit organisations, acting as consultants for other large or small, profit or non-profit organisations, with an aim to make them aware of their environmental and social contributions and create more sustainable strategies in all three aspects. *Sustainable* here is conceived under the context of doing business in a way that the future of society and the environment is preserved (Elkington, 1997). However, despite these major similar points, these organisations are different in various ways. SustainAbility was formed by two activists and remained an entity that not only does business by consulting, but is also heavily involved with other activist organisations in the world. Ceres and BSR, on the other hand, were founded by entrepreneurs. This creates a reasonable focus to these organisations of seeking to raise the sustainability awareness of investors, organisations and capital markets. These target groups are very influential, since they hold a large stake in the economy, society and the environment. Thus, the mission undertaken by the consultancy organisations is of major importance for the future of sustainable development.

Different from the above organisations, the WBCSD is a coalition of organisations, which work together under its flag to make a more sustainable world. This network creation allows the exchange of knowledge and strategy, while also making support amongst otherwise unrelated organisations feasible. A major difference of WBCSD from the other organisations is the use of a framework. SustainAbility, BSR and Ceres consultations are based on the TBL framework and promote it, whilst separating that framework into its three aspects. WBCSD, on the other hand, has created a separate framework working on Energy, Food and Land-use, Cities and Mobility, and Redefining Value. However, since it is an organisation constituted by profit-making organisations, its mission has a bias towards economic sustainability and profit making.

In the early years of the millennium, many of the above organisations received broad recognition caused by the popularity of sustainability and integrated reporting, and all of them started their global expansion during that decade. However, the lack of regulation, uniformity, and standardisation in reporting was a major problem and remains so today. Furthermore, the globalisation of the consultancies meant that different principles of sustainability would start conflicting with one another on a large scale. So, in 2009, the UK's Prince of Wales assembled a meeting of groups and organisations relevant to sustainability and formed the International Integrated Reporting Council (IIRC), with a mission to promote integrated reporting and thinking in business under its international integrated reporting (IR) framework. The IIRC released a strategic report for global adoption, calling the three years between 2014 and 2017 the breakthrough phase. During that phase, they explained their engagement with various groups, such as shareholders, stakeholders, regulators and other organisations to promote integrated thinking.

In 2011, another similar initiative was launched in the US, following the concept of the Financial Accounting Standards Board (FASB), without being affiliated with it. The Sustainability Accounting Standards Board (SASB) was meant to create a set of standards like the financial ones, but with a focus on sustainability. However, the sustainability described in the standards created by SASB is mostly focused on the economic impact of an organisation's actions, while the aim of the standards seems to mainly enable investors to make long-term financially profitable sustainable investments. This is achieved by ensuring that organisations make extensive reports, which are more transparent, by disclosing more information.

■ Reporting guidelines

After ISO 14001 received wide adoption from organisations around the world, the next step for sustainability reporting was to create a set of guidelines for reporting all three aspects in a standardised manner. This was achieved by the GRI guidelines. The KPMG annual survey of 2015 indicates that 60% of the surveyed organisations refer to the GRI in their reports, while 72% of the standalone reports that are produced use the GRI. However, the survey states that the use of the guidelines has decreased within the G250 (the 250 largest organisations in the world) in the past few years. This could be an indication that the criticisms discussed in the previous section are influencing the use of the standards, or that the most recent generation of the guidelines (generation four) no longer satisfies the reporting needs of these organisations. Despite this decrease of usage, the GRI remains the most popular set of guidelines for reporting and has pioneered integrated reporting, not only for large entities, with the original set, but also for SME, with a specific set of guidelines being developed for them in 2014. In contrast to SASB's mission to empower investors, the GRI aims to empower decision makers. Additionally, the GRI aims to establish a broad stakeholder network to help create a more sustainable world. The organisation also adopts a global perspective and supports the idea that global change is necessary. The SASB standards, on the other hand, are designed to fit the 10-K and 20-K Form, which are mandatory reports for US organisations. Arguably, the global applicability of the GRI guidelines is what makes them the most popular.

During the global expansion of integrated reporting, the ISO released the ISO 26000. The standard has many similarities to the GRI guidelines, as it provides guidance globally, to all organisations. It can be applied to both large entities and SMEs. However, due to the late release (10 years after the release of the GRI-G1), the standard has not yet received wide adoption. It is important to note here that there is no competition between the GRI guidelines and the ISO 26000, since they can both be used for the annual report or a stand-alone sustainability report (Global Reporting Initiative, 2011). Furthermore, researchers argue that the use of both guidelines and adopting a single way of reporting sustainability will be highly beneficial for the quality of the reports (Habek and Wolniak, 2013; Lock and Seele, 2016). As mentioned earlier, voluntary compliance with the standards allows the preparers of the reports to only present a single, positive, picture of the organisation. Additionally, reports show that, even if both the GRI guidelines and the ISO 26000 are being used together, valuable information and hard data might be missing. To avoid that practice and increase the quality of the reports, Lock and Seele (2016) argue that the current assurance of the reports should be secured by a mandatory audit, such as that conducted on the financial statements (more about the audit of social reports will be given in Chapter 7).

Sustainability: definition and debates

It is argued in the sustainability reporting literature that there are many different approaches to and definitions of sustainability. This lack of clarity on the matter has caused problems in the past, especially for stakeholders and users of these reports. Due to the large number of definitions, the various organisations and reporting initiatives could claim at least some relevance to sustainability, even if they were only partly or not at all connected to the term. Thus, the organisations that reported under them, even though only slightly connected to sustainability, could also claim that they employed a sustainable strategy (van Marrewijk, 2003; White, 1999).

In the search for a clear, unbiased definition of the term, the Oxford Dictionary defines sustainability as either "the ability to be maintained at a certain level", or "the avoidance of the depletion of natural resources to maintain an ecological balance". The definition, most commonly found in the business and accounting literature, however, is the one by Elkington (1997, p. 20). "Sustainability is the principle of ensuring that our actions today do not limit the range of economic, social, and environmental options open to the future generations." This definition is inspired by the World Commission on Environment and Development report *Our Common Future* (WCED 1987:16) (also referred to as the Brundtland Report), which gave a very similar definition for sustainable development.

Humanity has the ability to make development sustainable to ensure that it meets the needs of the present without compromising the ability of future generations to meet their own needs.

Bebbington and Larrinaga (2014) present the argument of Cohen *et al.* (1998), that this definition is neither scientifically correct, nor radical, as it leaves matters of poverty, inequity and basic human needs relatively unaddressed. A similar approach to that of the WCED is followed by Gray (1994), who stated that sustainability reporting is the practice of showing how organisations activities are providing, or reducing, the options of future generations; so being sustainable is to provide these options. For Pirages (1994), on the other hand, sustainability means to provide equilibrium between societal demands upon the environment and the capability of the environment to satisfy them. This definition, despite acknowledging the presence of society in sustainability, does not consider the interactions between humans. It neglects important issues, such as human rights, education and many more. Kates *et al.*, (2005) argue that even after the Johannesburg Declaration in 2002, which advanced the WCED (1987) definition on sustainable development, it remained unclear what the details of sustainable development were, even though the three aspects of the TBL were widely adopted as a practice by organisations all over the world.

White (1999), a founding member of the GRI, shows that the dispute on the definition of sustainability is reasonable as there are many ways one can perceive it. Apart from the two definitions given above, White presents the argument that corporate sustainability is an oxymoron because, with the progress of time, organisations and their people become more short-term focused. Even though White does not support a specific definition, he argues that corporate sustainability definitely relates to the three dimensions of the TBL. On a similar note to White's last argument, it has also been asserted that "there is no standard recipe: corporate sustainability is a custom-made progress" (Jacques Schraven, chairman of the Dutch Employees Association, in van Marrewijk, 2003:96). This means that every organisation can pursue sustainability according to its circumstances.

That brings the discussion back to the argument of standardisation and stakeholder communication. If every organisation perceives CSR and sustainability differently, then stakeholders cannot tell if the organisation is good or bad for the environment and society, because there is no benchmark. It would also be helpful if the various definitions defined who the stakeholders are and who is supposed to use the reports, because different organisations and initiatives might consider different groups as important (Spence, 2009). We can see then that most of the definitions, despite emerging from the accounting and business communities, do not define sustainability in a way that can easily be applied by organisations.

There is also a persistent debate in the literature around whether being socially and environmentally responsible creates value for the organisation and its shareholders. Windsor (2001) shows that the results in the literature, at that time, were mixed. However, more recently, Windsor (2013) argues that being socially responsible creates short term value loss for the shareholders, but generates more value in the long-term. Windsor (2013) also observes that the CSR and sustainability literature rarely considers the costs that an organisation must bear to adopt a sustainable policy and strategy, and report on the outcomes. These costs can be high, because significant organisational change and education are often required. The significance of these costs, combined with a general lack of resources, and lower pressure from stakeholders, means that small to medium sized enterprises (SMEs) typically lag behind in adopting a sustainable strategy (Shields and Shelleman, 2015), despite specific guidelines and focus given by several initiatives (e.g. GRI, ISO, IIRC, NVG-SEE).

■ Reporting for a sustainable economy, society and environment

Sustainability reporting has become a very popular practice over the past 20 years, despite being an issue first referenced for multinational organisations over 40 years ago (Kolk, 2010). The academic literature looking at this phenomenon has grown recently, as the matter has become more widely recognised and more organisations are engaging, both with its reporting and regulation (Kolk, 2010). This spread of sustainability reporting is now moving into developing and emerging economies, which were previously lagging behind (Fifka, 2012). During this popularisation phase, different terms of reporting have been used to describe the same reporting practice by both the literature and by organisations. Thus, corporate reports and research with similar or identical focus might be found under various titles, such as, sustainability or CSR reporting, social reporting, environmental reporting, or SER (Fifka, 2012). Since there is such a great diversity in the definitions of sustainability and CSR, it was a natural consequence that the definitions of sustainability and CSR reporting would be mixed as well. However, that does not mean that the terms are the same, despite being related (Bebbington and Larrinaga, 2014). Reporting the actions and performance of social and environmental aspects does not necessarily mean that the long-term sustainability, of any aspect of the entity, is reported and *vice versa*.

As explained previously in this chapter, the TBL is frequently connected with sustainability reporting, but the above criticism questions that connection. Milne and Gray (2012) criticise the TBL reporting objectives for providing organisations with a short-term focus. They conclude that there is a false assumption, made by almost the entire sustainability reporting community today: that they are either sustainable or are moving towards it. Considering the popularity of TBL thinking, since it is embedded in the GRI (the most popular guidelines for reporting), the current standing of sustainability and SER is indeed questionable.

Van Marrewijk (2003) offered three main reasons why any organisation might get involved in the practice of sustainability reporting: they are reacting to external pressure by stakeholders or competitors; they are reacting to a new mandate or regulation (e.g. EU commission mandate); or they simply decided to do it on a voluntary basis. All of these reasons connect in some way with the organisations' stakeholders; be it either cause or effect, directly or indirectly. However, Spence (2009) argues that sustainability reporting, apart from its role in signalling to investors, is mainly for internal communication. This might explain why large multinational organisations are more active in reporting (Perego and Kolk, 2012), since they are larger and find it more difficult to communicate both internally and with their subsidiaries. Likewise, Gray (2013) argues that sustainability (and especially environmental) reports do not have any material connection to accountability. He also criticises the fact that the reports are of poor quality and require great effort to be prepared, while ironically, they also demonstrate the great potential of reporting practices. On the other hand, there is a large part of the literature which argues that multinational organisations report sustainability because they affect the environment and society much more and are held accountable by a wider range of stakeholders than SMEs.

◼ Sustainability reporting in the public sector

In 2013, Her Majesty's Treasury (HMT) in the UK published guidelines for sustainability reporting in the public sector. The document details the minimum reporting requirements which include statements on emissions, waste and resource consumption, while also proposing further voluntary reporting guidelines. These minimum requirements will help to ensure that the reports are comparable between sectors and accounting periods. The legitimisation of government actions in the public sector and the apparent internal regulation between government controlled organisations has become more prevalent since 2010. Following on from this, the GRI have issued specific guidelines for sustainability reporting in the Australian public sector. However, the framework was based on the previous generation of guidelines and has yet to be updated for the new fourth generation. The Australian public sector was chosen due to the increasing demand by stakeholder groups to report their sustainability. However, legitimacy pressures in the public sector exist all over the world and, where there are no standards set, organisations look to independent third parties (Farneti and Rammal, 2013; Marx and van Dyk, 2011).

Public sector sustainability reports are not as widely adopted as their private sector equivalents (Marx and van Dyk, 2011). Figure 5.1 describes the main reasons that sustainability reporting is required in the public sector, as determined by the GRI. Despite being a new area of research and focus, there is an incrementally growing requirement from an increasing number of governments (e.g. UK, Australia, South Africa, Italy) to provide reports. This is mostly due to pressure being applied by stakeholder groups alongside an increasing need for public sector organisations to legitimise their actions, since they rely on taxpayers' money. The GRI document for Australia provides six reasons sustainability reporting is important in the public sector.

Six good reasons why sustainability reporting is needed in the public sector:

- **The changing landscape of society** – organisations today face heightened expectations around their wider role in society.

- **The role of government** – agencies have a civic responsibility to properly manage public goods, resources and/or facilities in a way that supports sustainable development objectives and promotes the public interest.

- **The need for transparency** – public sector sustainability reporting provides a framework to link financial performance to the organisation's use of, and impact on, the significant resources and relationships upon which it depends. It also guides the governance and ethical conduct of an agency, offering transparency and accountability benefits by requiring the reporting of the organisation's key performance information.

- **The need for global alignment** – regulators globally are starting to talk about sustainability reporting and there is a growing list of national policies mandating sustainability reporting. GRI is the globally-recognised framework for voluntary reporting of sustainability performance – it provides an independent reporting framework that provides transparency, accountability and comparability amongst reporting organisations.

- **The value of integrated thinking** – integrating sustainability factors into an organisation's decision making is an emerging trend internationally for both government and corporations. The International Integrated Reporting Council (IIRC), established by the Global reporting Initiative, the Prince of Wales's Accounting for Sustainability and the International Federation of Accountants, is developing an integrated reporting framework that will help to bring together data that is relevant to the performance and impact of an organisation in a way that will create a more profound and comprehensive picture of the risks and opportunities an organisation faces, specifically in the context of the drive towards a more sustainable economy.

- **The need to reduce reporting complexity and burden** – sustainability reporting is not about adding more information for public reporting; it's about making connections and holistic thinking, thereby removing the clutter and reducing the reporting burden.

Figure 5.1: Reasons for public sector sustainability reporting.
Source: Global Reporting Initiative Focal Point Australia (2012)

Despite the need for public sector reporting and communication with stakeholders, the voluntary nature of the disclosure still allows organisations to present a rosy picture, rather than a clear statement of the hard and sometimes unpleasant facts. Guthrie and Farneti (2008) found that Australian public sector organisations were only reporting the most positive indicators from the GRI framework, while concealing the negative ones. Farneti and Rammal (2013) did similar research in Italian public sector organisations and had similar findings.

The reason given for such actions, is the reluctance of organisations to present difficult truths to the various stakeholder groups. In the UK, sustainability reporting regulation is step towards overcoming such behaviours, not only for public sector, but for sustainability reporting in general. Establishing mandatory minimum requirements and a standard reporting format that organisations must comply with, while still allowing additional voluntary disclosures, is a major step towards transparency and comparability.

Research into public sector sustainability reporting is still relatively new, but future work will no doubt provide more insight into what can be done to improve and develop effective reporting practices. It might also improve our understanding of how to make sustainability reporting work in the private sector, despite the differences in the stakeholder groups and the factors driving accountability.

Accountability

As explained above, all business and other organisations are social constructs, since they exist in a community and are composed of people. It is to this community and these people that the organisation will turn to sell products or services in exchange for resources. Under social contract theory (Mathews, 1993), these people need to have awareness of the actions of the organisation and the effects and the costs of the products and services it provides, to assess if they are willing to allow this organisation to continue to operate. In this way the organisation is held accountable for its actions by its people and the community. It becomes obvious that the larger the organisation, the wider is its sphere of effect. As it covers more territory, it affects more of the natural environment, it employs more personnel, it affects more of society and it transfers more resources in and out, and thereby influences more of the economy.

■ ## Socially and environmentally responsible actions

Specific stakeholder groups keep the organisation accountable for different aspects of organisational activity according to their interests. For example, the financial performance, profitability and economic sustainability of an organisation is being monitored by the shareholders, or other owners, employees, and the government. Each group has a different incentive for holding the organisation accountable for providing informa tion on these demands. Shareholders want to increase their wealth, employees seek secure employment and working conditions (or they may seek employment elsewhere), and governments want to monitor for tax purposes. Governments also require organisations operating within their borders to protect society and the environment. To legitimise their position, therefore, organisations publish their accounts in annual reports, which are subjected to audit to show that the information provided is a 'true and fair' reflection of reality.

The environmental performance of an organisation is obviously very important. Sustaining the environment and providing a better, healthier future for future generations is a matter that concerns everyone. Most major governments have already implemented laws limiting emissions and waste production, promoting and maintaining a clean atmosphere, ensuring the quality of water, and placing constraints on land use. Furthermore, organisations in specific sectors regulate one another for environmental sustainability, while environmental activists and the media hold organisations accountable for their environmental performance. This forces most organisations, regardless of the economic sector in which they are placed, to be not only socially and environmentally responsible within the bounds of the law, but also, to voluntarily promote the cleansing, renewal and protection of their local environment.

As we have seen, the organisation is inextricably linked to the society in which it is located and is accountable to the citizens for its continued existence. It is, therefore, important for the organisations to give back to the local society, either financially, or through other actions. Providing funds for common-use establishments (e.g. parks, libraries, hospitals, etc.) and funds or volunteers for education, entertainment, or health, are just some of the actions which organisations undertake to engage with their local community. Also, high profile, or historical organisations can contribute to their local community by attracting visitors and tourists, whose expenditure can create a positive impact on the local economy and community.

■ Transparency and disclosures

Increasingly, for the organisation to maintain the continued support of its local community it needs to provide an enhanced information stream, which is arguably most effectively done through better disclosure in its reports. However, the more information they provide, be it financial or non-financial, the more transparent they become. This might have both positive and negative consequences. Greater transparency results in improved trust from shareholders and other stakeholders, while on the other hand, the organisation's operations are more exposed to the scrutiny of its competitors, with the attendant risk of losing some competitive advantage. These arguments are consistent with theories of political economy, as well as stakeholder theory and legitimacy theory (Gray *et al.*, 1995).

Under stakeholder theory, the organisation acts and reports according to stakeholder pressures and needs. The more power and influence the stakeholders possess, the more the organisation will be forced to disclose in its reports and be more transparent. Lindblom (1994, in Gray *et al.*, 1995) develops the framework for legitimacy theory, stating that organisations report to close the legitimacy gap between them and their stakeholders. To achieve that, they can either adopt a high transparency approach and disclose their actual actions and results, or, less transparently, they may seek to change the perception of what is legitimate (perhaps by questioning who are the affected stakeholders), or they may simply

imply that the expectations of the stakeholders were too high to begin with. Gray *et al.* (1995) argues that these two theories are overlapping: the more power the stakeholders have, the more legitimacy practices the management will be forced to adopt to close the legitimacy gap. Whatever their motivations, SER and CSR reporting provide more tools for organisations to legitimise their position, by providing accounts to their stakeholders. These practices provide a framework to either extend the annual report, or produce separate reports with more information for all the interested parties.

Summary

This chapter offered a brief overview of the development of SER, CSR, and sustainability reporting. It provided an historical background of the roots of the concern for socially and environmentally responsible business. The first attempts on reporting and the trends of each period were shown. The fundamentals of the very influential TBL were laid out. It has been shown how the TBL has changed, not only accounting and reporting, but also corporate strategies and thinking. The initiatives promoting integrated thinking and sustainability strategies as well as the organisations promoting them were outlined. The suggested voluntary, or mandatory, guidelines, were formed as a natural response to the increasing concerns for social issues in the 1970s and the environment during the 1980s. Today, these initiatives play a major role, affecting mainly large organisations. Despite their wide influence, there are many theoretical problems associated with the fundamentals of both the TBL and sustainability reporting, and, consequently, the initiatives. Additionally, there are major criticisms of the TBL and reporting practice that reflects the TBL. Controversy over the definitions of sustainability is also still ongoing.

It was argued that because all organisations are accountable to their stakeholders, they feel pressure and are obliged to act and be transparent about their actions through increased reporting mechanisms. The increase in the popularity of these forms of reporting is positive. However, it is not clear if the activities and actions discussed in the chapter are sufficient to safeguard the economy, people and the environment. It will be interesting to see if the EU Commission's mandate for corporate social responsibility will have an impact on enhancing sustainability. There is agreement that more research and education is needed to better understand the challenges and solutions in the context of social accounting and sustainability. The concept of sustainability is currently highly debated, which is indicative of its importance. Providing students (the next generation and inheritors of the future) with knowledge about sustainability can have a positive effect on the future of both its practice and the possibility of a more sustainable world. As de Aguiar and Paterson (2017) show, it is positively received by both students and academics in higher education. Additionally, the subject creates valuable knowledge and skills for both these groups.

Discussion questions

1 Discuss the impact of the triple bottom line in social and environmental accounting.

2 National and mandatory guidelines for reporting are still underdeveloped. What are the positive and negative impacts of their development?

3 How would you define a sustainable organisation?

4 Major organisations argue that more disclosures are hurting their accountability. Discuss the role of disclosures and transparency in the future of Social Accounting.

References and further reading

Bebbington, J. and Larrinaga, C. (2014). Accounting and sustainable development: An exploration. *Accounting, Organizations and Society*, **39**(6), 395-413.

Bennett, M., Rikhardsson, P. and Schaltegger, S. (2003). *Environmental Management Accounting*. (1st ed.) Boston: Kluwer, pp.89-113.

de Aguiar, T. and Paterson, A. (2017). Sustainability on campus: knowledge creation through social and environmental reporting. *Studies in Higher Education*, pp.1-13.

Elkington, J. (1997). *Cannibals with Forks*. Oxford: Capstone.

Farneti, F. and Rammal, H. (2013). *Sustainability Reporting in the Italian Public Sector: Motives and Influences*. Kobe, Japan, pp.1-22.

Fifka, M. (2012). The development and state of research on social and environmental reporting in global comparison. *Journal für Betriebswirtschaft*, **62**(1), 45-84.

Glavas, A. and Mish, J. (2014). Resources and capabilities of triple bottom line firms: going over old or breaking new ground? *Journal of Business Ethics*, **127**(3), 623-642.

Global Reporting Initiative (2011). GRI and ISO 26000: *How to Use the GRI Guidelines in Combination with ISO 26000*. GRI's Research and Development Publication Series. Amsterdam, the Netherlands: Global Reporting Initiative.

Global Reporting Initiative Focal Point Australia (2012) *Integrating Sustainability into Reporting - An Australian Public Sector Perspective*, GRI Focal Point Australia, Sydney

Gray, R. (1994). Corporate reporting for sustainable development: accounting for sustainability in 2000AD. *Environmental Values*, **3**(1), 17-45.

Gray, R. (2013). Back to basics: What do we mean by environmental (and social) accounting and what is it for? A reaction to Thornton. *Critical Perspectives on Accounting*, **24**(6), 459-468.

Gray, R., Kouhy, R. and Lavers, S. (1995). Corporate social and environmental reporting, a review of the literature and a longitudinal study of UK disclosure. *Accounting, Auditing and Accountability Journal*, **8**(2), 47-77.

5

Guthrie, J. and Farneti, F. (2008). GRI Sustainability Reporting by Australian Public Sector Organizations. *Public Money and Management*, **28**(6), 361-366.

Hąbek, P. and Wolniak, R. (2016). Assessing the quality of corporate social responsibility reports: the case of reporting practices in selected European Union member states. *Quality and Quantity*, 50(1), 399-420.

Hahn, R. and Kühnen, M. (2013). Determinants of sustainability reporting: a review of results, trends, theory, and opportunities in an expanding field of research. *Journal of Cleaner Production*, **59**, 5-21.

Her Majesty's Treasury (2013). *Public Sector Annual Reports: Sustainability Reporting.* London, United Kingdom: HM Treasury, pp.1-78.

Kates, R., Parris, T., and Leiserowitz, A. (2005). What is sustainable development? Goals, indicators, values, and practice. *Environment* (Washington DC) 47(3), 8-21.

Kolk, A. (2010). Trajectories of sustainability reporting by MNCs. *Journal of World Business*, **45**(4), 367-374.

KPMG, (2015). *Currents of Change. The KPMG Survey of Corporate Responsibility Reporting.* Amsterdam, Netherlands: Haymarket Network Ltd.

Lindblom, C. (1994). The implications of organizational legitimacy for corporate social performance and disclosure. Critical Perspectives on Accounting Conference, New York. Vol. 120.

Lock, I. and Seele, P. (2016). The credibility of CSR (corporate social responsibility) reports in Europe. Evidence from a quantitative content analysis in 11 countries. *Journal of Cleaner Production*, **122**, 186-200.

Marx, B. and van Dyk, V. (2011). Sustainability reporting at large public-sector entities in South Africa. *South African Journal of Accounting Research*, **25**(1), 103-127.

Mathews, M. (1993). *Socially Responsible Accounting.* London: Chapman and Hall.

Milne, M. and Gray, R. (2012). W(h)ither ecology? The triple bottom line, the global reporting initiative, and corporate sustainability reporting. *Journal of Business Ethics*, **118**(1), 13-29.

Ministry of Corporate Affairs, (2011). *National Voluntary Guidelines on Social, Environmental and Economic Responsibilities of Business.* New Delhi: Ministry of Corporate Affairs, Government of India.

Ministry of the Environment (2003). *Environmental Reporting Guidelines.* Tokyo: Japan Government.

Ministry of the Environment (2012). *Environmental Reporting Guidelines.* Tokyo: Japan Government.

Perego, P. and Kolk, A. (2012). Multinationals' accountability on sustainability: The evolution of third-party assurance of sustainability reports. *Journal of Business Ethics*, **110**(2), 173-190.

Pirages, D. (1994). Sustainability as an evolving process. *Futures*, **26**(2), 197-205.

Rogers, M. and Ryan, R. (2001). The triple bottom line for sustainable community development. *Local Environment*, **6**(3), 279-289.

Sherman, W. (2012). The triple bottom line: The reporting of doing well and doing good. *Journal of Applied Business Research*, **28**(4), 673.

Shields, J. and Shelleman, J. (2015). Integrating sustainability into SME strategy. *Journal of Small Business Strategy*, **25**(2), 59-75.

Spence, C. (2009). Social and environmental reporting and the corporate ego. *Business Strategy and the Environment*, **18**(4), 254-265.

Sridhar, K. (2012). Corporate conceptions of triple bottom line reporting: an empirical analysis into the signs and symbols driving this fashionable framework. *Social Responsibility Journal*, **8**(3), 312-326.

Sridhar, K., and Jones, G. (2013). The three fundamental criticisms of the Triple Bottom Line approach: An empirical study to link sustainability reports in organisations based in the Asia-Pacific region and TBL shortcomings. *Asian Journal of Business Ethics*, **2**(1), 91-111.

van Marrewijk, M. (2003). Concepts and definitions of CSR and corporate sustainability: between agency and communion. *Journal of Business Ethics*, 44(2), 95-105.

White, A. (1999). Sustainability and the accountable corporation. *Environment: Science and Policy for Sustainable Development*, **41**(8), 30-43.

Windsor, D. (2001). The future of corporate social responsibility. *The International Journal of Organizational Analysis*, **9**(3), 225-256.

Windsor, D. (2013). Corporate social responsibility and irresponsibility: A positive theory approach. *Journal of Business Research*, **66**(10), 1937-1944.

World Commission on Environment and Development (WCED) (1987). *Our Common Future*. New York: Oxford University Press.

■ Some useful web links

Business for Social Responsibility: https://www.bsr.org/en/

Ceres: https://www.ceres.org/

Dow Jones Sustainability Index: http://www.sustainability-indices.com/

European Commission Non-Financial Reporting: http://ec.europa.eu/finance/organisation-reporting/non-financial_reporting/

FTSE4GOOD: http://www.ftse.com/products/indices/FTSE4Good

Global Reporting Initiative: https://www.globalreporting.org/

International Integrated Reporting Council: http://integratedreporting.org/

International Organisation for Standardisation: https://www.iso.org/

Sustainability Accounting Standards Board: https://www.sasb.org/

SustainAbility: http://sustainability.com/

World Business Council for Sustainable Development: http://www.wbcsd.org/

6 Socially Responsible Investment

Mohamed Elshinawy, Oluwagbenga Adamolekun,
Audrey Paterson, Mohamed Sherif and Stephen Rae

Introduction

So far, we have considered various issues and aspects of social accounting and their applications such as in corporate social responsibility (CSR). We now turn our attention to another important aspect of business, which is how organisations attract and maintain financial investment to support and grow. Businesses require investment; without it, they have no financing for operations that foster growth. Some investors have their own set of priorities when committing cash to an organisation and these can encompass their personal concerns about the social responsibility activities of the prospective investment. These concerns have led to a practice known as *socially responsible investment* (SRI). This can loosely be defined as shareholders making investments with a desire for socially beneficial outcomes, in addition to the obvious desire for financial returns.

SRI can be viewed as investors responding to an organisation's CSR actions. It can act to control, or mediate, corporate behaviour. For example, investors may reward a particular behaviour, e.g. by buying shares only in organisations that have a dedicated commitment to Fair Trade sourcing. Alternatively, investors may refrain from investing in organisations that have taken actions that are not within their social preference, e.g. not investing in an organisation that is known to use sweatshop labour. By choosing where to invest their wealth, investors have the power to grant or deny funding to organisations. In turn, organisations must follow expected social standards, or face lower investment, higher capital costs and potential financial failure. However, selecting where to invest is not a straightforward matter for investors when non-financial concerns are present. For example, it leads to questions over which actions are to be rewarded or penalised and the extent to which the investor values social results over financial returns.

SRI serves as a means to find suitable investment opportunities when faced with these and similar concerns.

The concept of SRI has grown considerably in recent years, particularly in response to the media raising awareness of the ruthlessness of corporate activity and social inequality across the globe. In this chapter, we begin with a discussion of the SRI concept and provide a brief outline of its evolution and its continuing importance to the present day. Following this, we discuss the legitimacy of SRI in the 21st century and the influence of the United Nations sustainable development goals and principles on SRI and the impact of these on investors' behaviour. Approaches to SRI decision making are then introduced in the form of *environmental social governance* (ESG) a vital tool in selecting investments based on a combination of financial returns, social responsibility, and personal ethics. The importance of non-financial outcomes to investors is also discussed. This is then followed by a discussion of some investment options that are available to investors before moving on to consider the performance of SRI investments.

The socially responsible investment concept

Socially responsible investment (SRI) refers to an investment type that prioritises ethical and social concerns in addition to the traditional financial activities of selecting securities and building portfolios (Weigand *et al.*, 1996). SRI is also known as ethical investment, green investment, or sustainable investment and seeks to achieve financial returns within the context of social, environmental, and ethical considerations (Hutton *et al.*, 1998; Lowry 1993). Overall, it identifies and indicates the manner in which potential investments or organisations are either included or excluded according to an ethical screening of their activities and products. Thus, investors select investments based on values that reflect their desire for ethical action toward positive social change.

The SRI concept is not new but has been around in various forms and guises for centuries. History suggests that the Islamic, Jewish and Christian religions embraced economic actions that aligned with their beliefs. In the middle ages, the Catholic Church forbade loans that had very high rates of interest (usury). This position has also been held in other religious beliefs. Some of the first instances of social responsibility investment are argued to have been influenced by religious tenets such as the old Jewish tradition (i.e. Talmud) and the Religious Society of Friends (Quakers). Indeed, the Quakers in the US colonies became involved in the early custom of social investing by focusing on their principles. There is also evidence of socially responsible investment within the Methodist faith dating back more than 200 years. Some historians suggest the foundations of SRI can be traced back at least to the ideology of Islamic Sharia investing and perhaps even before that. Each religion developed and applied their own value principles to investment, e.g. the Muslim faith did not permit investment in banks. The

Methodists favoured investments that aligned with their faith's social principles such as the right to organise and bargain collectively, avoid discrimination (age, race, gender etc.) and be allowed human rights.

It can therefore be argued that SRI has been a part of business decisions for centuries and this tradition has continued to influence it in more modern times. In the UK, ethical funds have strong roots in Victorian social reforms and have historically tended to focus on employee welfare, or the development of a local area. In the 19th century for example, the church became very active in investing in public health and non-university education. In the 1920s churches encouraged members not to invest in organisations that made money from gambling, tobacco, and alcohol. In other parts of Europe, the emergence of specific investment funds has been more of a contemporary phenomenon. The first recognised ethical fund in continental Europe was the Ansvar Aktiefond Sverige, created by the Church of Sweden in 1965. Similar funds addressing societal needs have since appeared elsewhere.

From the above, we can see that the concepts of social accountability and responsible investment have a long tradition. However, the examples seen in Chapter 2 demonstrate that social responsibility was not a significant concern for the vast majority of businesses. Rather, their focus was on profit maximisation, in which social responsibility concerns held little or no weight. It was the reporting of large profits, executives' bonuses, evidence of environmental damage and social inequality in the mid-20th century that led to increasing attention being turned onto the activities of organisations and the impact that they have had on the natural environment and wider society. This has led to the worldwide establishment of many SRI activist groups seeking greater social and environmental responsibility from organisations and governments. Some of these and their attitudes to SRI were identified by the OECD in 2007 and are laid out in Box 6.1.

Other issues that have increased calls for more social accountability and SRI include civil unrest, political instability and war. For example, in the US, the unprecedented media coverage of the Vietnam War began to turn a large section of public opinion against armed conflict, with attendant effects on investments in the arms industry. Around the same time, the Civil Rights Movement led to wide changes in societal norms in respect of fairness, equality and human rights. Increased attention was also drawn to environmental considerations as emergent environmental science began to show the effects of unrestrained pollution and consumption of limited resources. In the early 1970s, a number of funds that focussed on socially responsible investment were launched in the US and they increased significantly after the EXXON Valdez Alaskan oil spill incident of 1989, which caused huge environmental damage (Brown and Braddock, 1990).

Box 6.1: Sample worldwide SRI groups

Australia: The Australian Ethical Investment Association defines SRI as 'the integration of personal values with investment decisions. It is an approach to investing that considers both the profit potential and the investment's impact on society and the environment.'

Canada: The Social Investment Organisation alternatively defines SRI as 'the process of selecting or managing investments according to social or environmental criteria.'

Sweden: The Forum for Sustainable Development states that SRI 'is investment that in addition to financial criteria, also takes social, ecological, and ethical factors into investment decision-making processes.'

UK: The Social Investment Forum says that 'Socially Responsible Investment (SRI) combines investors' financial objectives with their concerns about social, environmental and ethical (SEE) issues.'

USA: The Social Investment Forum argues that 'Integrating personal values and societal concerns with investment decisions is called Socially Responsible Investing (SRI). SRI considers both the investor's financial needs and an investment's impact on society. With SRI, you can put your money to work to build a better tomorrow while earning competitive returns today.'

Europe: The European Social Investment Forum (Eurosif) offers a detailed explanation of the concepts: 'Socially Responsible Investment (SRI) combines investors' financial objectives with their concerns about social, environmental, ethical (SEE) and corporate governance issues. SRI is an evolving movement and even the terminology is still very much in the evolving phase. Some SRI investors refer only to the SEE risks while others refer to ESG issues (Environmental, Social, and Governance). Eurosif believes both are relevant to SRI. SRI is based on a growing awareness among investors, companies and governments about the impact that these risks may have on long-term issues ranging from sustainable development to long-term corporate performance.'

Asia: The Association for Sustainable and Responsible Investment in Asia (ASrIA)'s view is that 'Sustainable and Responsible Investment (SRI), also known as Socially Responsible Investment, is investment which allows investors to take into account wider concerns, such as social justice, economic development, peace or a healthy environment, as well as conventional financial considerations.'

Source: OECD (2007:5)

6

By the 21st century, SRI had become very popular, and a number of indices had been created that specifically tracked 'socially acceptable' market constituents. Examples include:

Natur Aktien Index; DJSI STOXX; ASPI Eurozone; 400 Social; Impax ET500; Dow Jones Global Sustainability Index; FTSE4Good World Social Index; FTSE 4 Good indices; Ethical Index Euro; Ethical Index Global; Ethical Index Europe small cap; and KLD NASDAQ. (Ballestero *et al.*, 2015:10).

Such indices are useful to investors seeking to identify socially responsible organisations to invest in and to organisations themselves when seeking to attract new investors.

SRI legitimacy in the 21st century

The influence of SRI in the 21st century has increased dramatically. The OECD has offered the following reasons for its rise (OECD, 2007:13):

- The concern over the ability of public policy (national governments and international organisations) to address issues such as environmental degradation and human right abuses, especially in developing countries, coupled with an acknowledgement that (international) business has the responsibility and financial resources to address these issues.

- Empirical research showing that investors can increase their portfolio risk-adjusted rates of returns by considering ESG issues.

- The perception in some countries that fiduciary responsibility may and should include wider concerns than financial returns.

- Public opinion favouring SRI, largely as a result of intense advocacy by lobbying groups.

Figure 6.1: Social responsibility dimensions.
Source: Szelagowske, A. and Marek Bryx.M (2015) in CeDeWu

There are several government and research institutes whose primary concerns relate to solving world sustainability and social equity issues (Statman, 2014). One such is the UN Sustainable Development Summit which meets annually to discuss and debate issues such as environmental crisis, sustainable development, social equity, and justice. The primary aim of the UN Sustainable Development Summit is for all countries to improve the lives of people regardless of age, ethnicity, religion, gender, or where they are located in the world. Its mission is universal, inclusive, and indivisible. It calls to action governments, businesses, and civil society to work together with the UN to mobilise efforts to achieve sustainable development, equality, and social justice. In 2006, the UN developed a set of ten principles for responsible investment (Table 6.1). These principles state the minimum fundamental responsibilities for businesses in the areas of human rights, labour, the environment and the fight against corruption. These principles are intended to counter the relative lack of consideration of ethics and the environment in global business practice and investment decision making.

Area	Principle
Human rights	Principle 1: Businesses should support and respect the protection of internationally proclaimed human rights; and
	Principle 2: make sure that they are not complicit in human rights abuses.
Labour	Principle 3: Businesses should uphold the freedom of association and the effective recognition of the right to collective bargaining;
	Principle 4: the elimination of all forms of forced and compulsory labour;
	Principle 5: the effective abolition of child labour; and
	Principle 6: the elimination of discrimination in respect of employment and occupation.
Environment	Principle 7: Businesses should support a precautionary approach to environmental challenges;
	Principle 8: undertake initiatives to promote greater environmental responsibility; and
	Principle 9: encourage the development and diffusion of environmentally friendly technologies.
Anti-corruption	Principle 10: Businesses should work against corruption in all its forms, including extortion and bribery.

Table 6.1: The UN 10 principles for responsible investment.
Source: https://www.unglobalcompact.org/what-is-gc/mission/principles

Accordingly, businesses are required to take positive action to satisfy government-led initiatives towards sustainable development and social responsibility goals. Advances in this area are evident in the increasing volumes of SRI investments appearing in global financial markets. If we take the US as an example, we can see that the growth of SRI funds over the last two decades has been remarkable. In their 2016 report, the US Sustainable Investment Forum reported that US domiciled assets invested using SRI strategies had grown to $8.72 trillion at the start of 2016. This is the result of a compound growth rate of 13.25% since 1995, the year in which they first began to measure the market. There is also some suggestion that the trend is accelerating with the combined growth from 2014-16 reaching 33%. This rapid level of growth over the last two decades means that "these assets now account for more than one out of every five dollars under professional management in the United States" (US SIF 2016:12). Similar trends have been seen in the other foremost SRI markets in Japan, Canada, Australia and New Zealand. The extent of this growth demonstrates that, in the developed world at least, there is a real appetite amongst investors for investment linked to social improvement.

To advance their global societal initiatives, the UN in September 2015 developed a set of Sustainable Development Goals (SDGs) which are embedded in the 2030 Agenda for Sustainable Development. The UN's Global Compact principles are aimed at mobilising a global movement of sustainable, socially responsible businesses and stakeholders by supporting organisations to operate responsibly by aligning their operations and activities with the ten principles mentioned above and take strategic actions toward advancing sustainable development.

Figure 6.2: The UN 17 societal goals for responsible business and investment.
Source: https://www.unglobalcompact.org/sdgs/17-global-goals

Adopting these principles and the global societal goals laid out in Figure 6.3 arguably enables investors and businesses to improve their capacity to receive funds and align more effectively with the ethical, social, and environmental requirements and standards. These principles are also designed to encourage organisations to take more positive actions toward sustainable investing and support organisations that have already started their responsible investing strategies (Hutton *et al.* 1998). The statements underlying the UN's goals are listed below:

- *End poverty in all its forms everywhere.*
- *End hunger, achieve food security and improved nutrition, and promote sustainable agriculture.*
- *Ensure healthy lives and promote well-being for all at all ages.*
- *Ensure inclusive and equitable quality education and promote lifelong learning opportunities for all.*
- *Achieve gender equality and empower all women and girls.*
- *Ensure availability and sustainable management of water and sanitation for all.*
- *Promote sustained, inclusive and sustainable economic growth, full and productive employment and decent work for all.*
- *Build resilient infrastructure, promote inclusive and sustainable industrialization, and foster innovation.*
- *Reduce inequality within and among countries.*
- *Make cities and human settlements inclusive, safe, resilient, and sustainable*
- *Ensure sustainable consumption and production patterns.*
- *Take urgent action to combat climate change and its impacts.*
- *Conserve and sustainably use the oceans, seas and marine resources for sustainable development.*
- *Protect, restore and promote sustainable use of terrestrial ecosystems, sustainably manage forests, combat desertification, and halt and reverse land degradation and halt biodiversity loss.*
- *Promote peaceful and inclusive societies for sustainable development, provide access to justice for all and build effective, accountable and inclusive institutions at all levels.*
- *Strengthen the means of implementation and revitalize the global partnership for sustainable development."*

6

Figure 6.3: For more information, see https://sustainabledevelopment.un.org/?menu=1300

A specific remit of the UN is to achieve broader engagement worldwide to lift 767 million people above the international poverty line of $1.90 a day and to encourage organisations to engage in more socially responsible and sustainable business practices. The 2017 annual summit met at the UN headquarters in New York in September 2017. Representatives from more than 150 countries attended to discuss, agree and formally adopt an ambitious new sustainable development agenda for the next 15 years. The UN Goals and the targets within this agenda are designed to stimulate action in areas of critical importance for humanity and the planet over the next 15 years. It is to be hoped that the growth of SRI is indicative that genuine progress is being made towards the realisation of this agenda.

Ethical and moral investment

Initiatives such as those of the UN are clearly having an impact on investor behaviour. SRI is both a moral and a financial judgement, but in the past, ethical investors exercised their views by simply avoiding investment in organisations that acted against their moral convictions or ethical beliefs; e.g. organisations involved in tobacco, gambling, military relations, fossil fuels, or organisations that neglected the communities in which they operated (Lusyana and Sherif, 2017). Increasingly, however, investors tend to prioritise investments in organisations that align with their moral values, such as organisations with high standards in governance and responsible environmental and social policies. For example, investing in an infrastructure organisation that provides energy, clean water, or medical facilities is a win-win for both SRI advocates and for those who benefit from the products. At every step of the investment process fund managers now think about the impact of issues such as sustainability, climate change, safety, governance, and human rights. It is logical that these factors should be a part of any long-term investment process. Investors can achieve a good return by taking a long-term view and considering a very broad range of factors that might affect an organisation. Indeed, the Global Sustainable Investment Alliance (GSIA) in 2012 conducted a review of many different studies in Canada, USA, Australia, Japan, Europe, and Africa. They concluded that from a range of investment options available, socially responsible investing is more likely to achieve higher returns.

Some observers believe that since the financial crisis of 2007, there has been a moral crunch in financial capitalism which has increased the level of distrust between the stock market and the people. Landier and Nair (2008) posit that SRI has the potential to reconcile the people with the financial markets by serving as a channel of reassurance and mitigation of market imperfections. Indeed, Wu *et al.* (2017) showed that an SRI portfolio performed better and recovered its value quicker in post-crisis than a comparable non-SRI portfolio. This demonstrates that the SRI portfolio has been found to be more resistant to economic upheaval and market shocks and leads us nicely into a discussion of approaches and strategies adopted when making SRI decisions.

■ ## The environmental, social and governance approach to SRI

As previously discussed, SRI is primarily concerned with investing in activities that combine social purpose, value and financial return. Individual investors will place different weighting on each of these values. With the increase in indices that track the social responsibility of organisations it is clear that there is a growing trend among investors to understand and engage with the broader social values that their investments feed into. We have established that such investors are concerned with understanding the benefits that SRI can accrue from both their own and a wider societal perspective. However, we also need to recognise that SRI can generate societal benefits which are not readily measurable in financial terms. In this section we consider the environmental, social and governance (ESG) approach to SRI.

The ESG approach has become increasing attractive in recent years. It can be used by investors to assess the corporate behaviour of an organisation and forecast the future financial performance of its activities while also considering non-financial aspects. ESG encompasses issues relating to sustainable, ethical and corporate governance, such as the management of an organisation's carbon footprint and ensuring there are systems in place to ensure its accountability. This approach can be particularly useful to investors interested in organisations that deal in energy, water, fossil fuels, etc., as it focuses on the overall carbon footprint of the organisation's activities, including energy usage, pollution, waste, environmental damage, regeneration, and sustainability aspects. For example, the BP oil spill in the Gulf of Mexico in 2010, which caused extreme long-term damage to the ocean and shoreline, caused death and injury to wildlife and affected the living conditions and natural habitat of humans and wild creatures alike, provides a good example of how such disasters can affect investor confidence and trust. The poor health and safety record of BP, were acclaimed to be the principal reason for the fall in share price of BP during 2010. Disasters such as this further strengthen the argument for ESG performance-based indicators.

Indeed, in response to the impact that such disasters can have on the natural environment and consequently society, environmental screening systems that consider hazardous waste disposal, environmental clean ups, pollution, etc., are becoming an increasing part of the decision-making criteria when making SRI. Likewise, concern over climate change and resource depletion has prompted the financial markets to respond to scientific research that demonstrates that the earth is experiencing climate change. Consequently, clear targets regarding climate change and fossil fuel asset management are sought after by shareholders, particularly in the oil industry. Moreover, investors are now more conscious as they screen investments in terms of their potential impact on climate change, with increasing attention being drawn to renewable energy usage, carbon emissions, greenhouse gas emissions, disclosure/measurement and reporting and sustainability factors.

The study of Heinkel *et al.* (2001) revealed that firms might have an inducement to take expensive action to change their technology from a dirty to an environment-friendly one due to the existence of socially responsible investors. Socially responsible investors are likely to avoid firms that use dirty technologies, therefore their risk may be carried by a smaller number of investors, creating challenges for such organisations when they seek finance. Organisations will therefore be motivated to change their technology if the cost of doing so is less than the discount in their market value if they continue to use the old technology. Furthermore, some investments that are perceived as socially irresponsible (e.g. shares of companies involved in the production of alcohol, tobacco, and in activities such as gambling) often have a lower expected return than comparable socially responsible stocks (Hong and Kacperczyk 2009). This is because most institutional investors are being pressured to avoid investing in firms considered socially irresponsible.

The social criteria of the ESG approach aims to evaluate how the firm relates to the community. The community in this context refers to employees, competitors, suppliers, and partners. Some of the areas considered in screening within the social criteria include: diversity (i.e. fostering an all-inclusive working environment), human rights, animal welfare, consumer protection, and predatory lending (such as the UK and US Subprime crisis which led to the collapse of the respective housing markets, leaving thousands of families homeless as their property became repossessed by the lenders). Other factors include, child labour, sweat shops and a fair living wage. Many big brand clothing retailers such as Nike, H&M and Gap have come under attack following allegations of sweat shop working conditions, low wages and use of child labour and as a result have experienced a downturn in revenues as well as investment.

The governance criterion of the ESG approach considers the structure of the organisation's board, its corporate practices, transparency of accounting methods and stakeholder structures. Examples of the areas normally considered within this screening approach include: the managerial structure (the power of the board and the CEO), executive compensation schemes, separation of the Chairman/CEO position, and dual class share structure. Executive compensation regularly hits the headlines when CEOs receive massive bonuses, even during times of financial crisis and organisational scandal. Mylan, producer of the EpiPen, for example, rewarded their CEO a sum of $98m in 2016 despite losses incurred by its investors from serious failures in its corporate governance. The CEO of Wells Fargo and Co also received a large bonus of $12.8m despite an accounts scandal that negatively affected the organisation's investors and employees. Nor are public and third sector organisations exempt from such scandals. In the UK for example, it was revealed that some executives in these sectors were awarded over £400,000 per annum in compensation despite overseeing cuts to essential services.

While financial performance is of the utmost importance, an increasing number of investors in Europe, the UK and other global regions are utilising ESG non-financial performance indicators to assess the long-term sustainability of organisations. Indeed, the ESG movement has increased significantly in recent years and has benefited from organisations such as the Governance and Accountability Institute, which is the knowledge centre for ESG issues and trends. This institute provides ESG information to analysts, corporate leaders, boards, social sector organisations, public sector managers, amongst others and facilitates knowledge and understanding of the key issues that affect organisations. This in turn aids organisations and investors to adopt strategies to address ESG risks and opportunities for their organisations and investments. The ESG movement is also receiving increasing support from major investment management organisations. In 2016,

Laurence Fink (head of Black Rock, the world's largest investment management company) wrote to the CEOs of large companies requesting that they "focus more on long-term value creation, rather than short-term dividend pay-outs; be open and transparent about growth plans; and focus on environmental, social and governance factors because they have 'real and quantifiable financial impacts'." From this we can see the increasing importance that is being attached to approaches such as ESG.

SRI strategies and methods

Having considered the importance of SRI and the ESG approach we now turn our attention to factors that aid investors' decision-making. SRI strategies refer to tactics employed by investors to ensure that the investment undertaken aligns with their social criteria. There are various methods utilised to ensure that investment is not harmful to societal interests. Predominantly, the strategy for SRIs has been through screening, although this practice has changed over the years. When faced with portfolio investment decisions, the managers of ethical funds focus on screening firms based on socially responsible criteria. Three well established approaches to SRI are seen in Figure 6.4 and are discussed in turn.

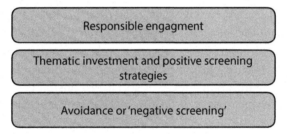

Figure 6.4: Socially responsible investment (SRI) approaches

First, within the responsible engagement approach, organisations use dialogue, voting and responsible shareholder activism to encourage positive change and to help reduce the risk level associated with non-SRI. Second, the thematic investment and positive screening approach focuses on directing investment towards corporations that meet a fund's *positive* SRI objectives. Areas that could be considered include: organisations with a good employee-employer relationship, that have strong environmental practices, that put human rights protection at the forefront of their operations or that make products that are both safe and useful. Examples include the essential necessities of life (food, clothing, electricity, water or housing). Positive screening is a popular method used by most charities seeking to further their investment aims and encourage responsible business practices, with approximately 60% of large charities following an ethical investment policy. Finally, *negative screening* (also known as avoidance, or exclusion screening) involves the fund manager rejecting organisations that engage in activities that are deemed socially unacceptable, or unethical. Socially unacceptable items could include: the provision of goods or services that support political administrations' repressive behaviours, or fuel political unrest (e.g. funding rebellion); that have a negative impact on the environment (e.g. extraction of oil and gas, and mining); and the production of tobacco, alcohol, abortion pills, weapons, or other products that are deemed harmful to health, or human existence (Solomon and Solomon, 2004). Thus, negative screening involves avoiding investments that do not meet the investor's ethical investment policy and can be useful to protect their image and reputation.

A more contemporary approach to screening SRIs includes evaluating firms based on their efforts to improve their social responsibility. This method was referred to as the 'best in class' approach by Mansley (2000). It involves ranking firms in an industry based on a metric that evaluates their compliance to issues of environmental and social responsibility. This approach is prevalent in charitable organisations seeking to become exemplars in their field. The best in class approach is popular in government-controlled funds and with pension fund managers since they are required to provide stable returns whilst also ensuring that portfolios are fully diversified. These techniques demonstrate how, through liberal groups, society, and other change agents, fund managers are pressed to implement investment policies that are not counter to societal values. Funds seeking a positive SRI stance will avoid investing in organisations that are deemed unethical and positively screen for those that promote the rights of employees and society and that work to mitigate environmental concerns.

Having considered some approaches that aid organisations and investors in their pursuit of SRI we turn our attention to the influence that shareholders can have on the organisation's level of social responsibility. A shareholder can be defined as a person, group of people, or an organisation that holds one or more shares in an organisation and in whose name the share certificate is issued. The purchasing of a share gives the investor a voice in the organisation's activities through a shareholder voting system. Shareholder activism is the process of dialogue between shareholders and the organisation's executives. It is through such dialogue that shareholders can log a formal resolution ratifying or requesting a specified action by a corporate board. Such actions generate investor pressure on organisational executives, attract media attention (which adds even more pressure on organisations to improve their behaviour), and educates the public on often-ignored social, environmental, and labour issues. However, the legal framework of the country of listing governs resolutions. In some countries, shareholders often form pressure groups to facilitate the resolution process. For example, Greenpeace successfully lobbied ExxonMobil shareholders to back a resolution that called into question Exxon's track record of denial of the risks of climate change, and questioned its business model, following allegations of it supressing research into the effects of climate change. Shareholder activism can serve as a powerful tool to encourage an organisation to alter its social and environmental policies, which ultimately can lead to a more sustainable company.

The assumption of portfolio theory is that investors are willing to take on a certain level of risk only if they are compensated by an equal or higher reward at that level. A substantial body of literature has argued for the inclusion of other criteria to better specify the preferences of investors (See Aouni *et al.*, 2014). The emergence of non-financial performance indicators among the SRI literature underpins the necessity of broadening the definition of return to investors; a consideration of stock returns at a permissive level of risk, alongside societal returns, indicates the presence of multi-facets of return. Multiple criteria decision making (MCDM) policy helps ensure this criterion reflects on the portfolio of investors, as a bespoke portfolio can be built to suit an investor's moral values and stock return preference. MCDM refers to a group of research methods that focuses on making choices in the presence of multiple conditions, goals or objectives (Ballestero *et al.*, 2015). Furthermore, it assesses multiple conflicts in criteria in decision-making. This approach fosters decision-making where conflicting interests and inconsistent principles are apparent.

■ Investment fund options

Having considered some SRI strategies and methods, we now turn our attention to various types of investments open to investors. Over the past decade, sustainable and responsible investing (SRI) involved investment advisors directing investors in a relatively unstructured way. Today, the area of SRI has developed a much more professional approach, due to the investment community's increased awareness of the importance of the issues, and a consequent growth in fund choice. Accordingly, investors are expecting access to sophisticated funds that fit well with their SRI goals. For example, institutional investors such as pension funds, ISAs and Takaful have been encouraged by green and ethical investments that seek a balance between social and environmental issues and maintaining sound returns. The factors considered by SRI investors can be categorised in three groups as seen in Figure 6.5.

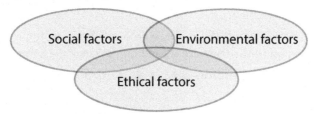

Figure 6.5: Factors considered by SRI investors

A new subset of investors believes that, instead of focusing on buying shares of organisations, greater impact can be achieved by investing directly in institutions such that support the community through poverty alleviation, provision of social goods, or soft loans for education, personal development, and SMEs. This form of investment is commonly known as *municipal investment* and is growing in acceptance in the US and some parts of Europe.

More traditional forms of investment that are also useful for SRI are detailed here.

- *Index investment funds* are prevalent in the US and elsewhere. The index fund is part of an investment portfolio which is constructed to track the components of a market index. It is a passive form of fund management and is a form of mutual fund. Mutual funds are skilfully managed investment funds that pool money from a wide array of investors and purchases securities. This has been an important vehicle for SRI investors in recent years as witnessed by the surge in the number of SRI mutual funds. The main benefits of such funds are professional management and diversification of the portfolio, while their major drawback is the level of fees required to maintain them. Mutual funds can be classified in terms of their structure (closed-end funds, open-end funds, unit investment trusts, and exchange-traded funds) as well as in terms of the type of underlying investment (money market funds, bond funds, stock funds and hybrid funds).

- *Closed-end funds* are normally created through a typical IPO (Initial Public Offering) with the shares then traded on a stock exchange. The fund is not obligated to repurchase shares sold by investors, thus investors are compelled to offer their shares for sale openly on the stock exchange.

- *Open-end funds*, on the other hand, buy back shares when offered for sale at the close of daily business. In addition, unlike the closed end fund, most open-end funds offer shares in their fund for sale on a daily basis.

- A *unit investment trust* (commonly known as a *unit trust*) is generally comprised of a fixed portfolio of stocks and bonds normally redeemable after a fixed time span. However, the shareholder can redeem their shares at any time within that time period. Such investments are designed to provide capital appreciation and/or dividend income. Furthermore, shares in a unit trust can only be offered to the public at commencement. Unlike other funds there is no professional management and constituents of the fund are fixed during the life span of the trust.

- *Exchange traded funds* (ETF) share both attributes of the open-end funds and the close-end fund. They are traded on the stock exchange.

Other major SRI fund forms (Lee *et al.*, 2010; Rayner Spencer Mills Research, 2014) include:

- *Responsible engagement funds* aim to perform more responsible business practices to enhance investor returns with better risk management.

- *Sustainability themed funds* focus on the sustainability agenda when deciding on sources of investments.

- *Balanced ethical funds* are ethically screened funds that balance the positive and negative aspects of company behaviour across a range of ethical, social and environmental issues.

- *Environmentally themed funds* integrate environmental opportunities and risks into their investment decisions.

- *Negative ethical funds* avoid a range of activities that do not meet more traditional, ethical or 'values based' standards.

- *Faith based funds* are limited group of funds that invest in line with a specific set of religious values.

- *Clean technology funds* operate in markets leading clean technology and environmental solutions companies.

- *Specialist funds* include investments which fall within the broad definition of sri but do not fit within any of the above forms of funds.

Further alternatives include stock funds, hybrid funds and bonds.

- *Stock funds* also often referred to as *equity funds*; they focus on a particular area of the stock market. The strategy can be built to focus on a country, region, industry, or type of company.

- An alternative is a *hybrid fund* which consists of stocks, bonds, money market instruments and convertible securities. Money market funds invest in high quality fixed income securities, typically with a short time to maturity.

- *Bond funds* include corporate bonds, government bonds or municipal bonds. A bond is a debt instrument. The bond issuer is obligated to pay a specified amount of money at specified future dates to the investor. Bonds are essentially loan agreements used to raise capital. As such bonds are also known as a fixed-income security. An example of this is government savings bond, the purchase of which renders the purchaser a lender to the government.

■ SRI performance

With respect to tracking the performance of mutual funds, a classic article by Jensen (1968) concluded that the performance of mutual funds, after taking account of expenses, was inferior to the performance of randomly selected portfolios with equivalent risk over the period 1945 through 1964. Two studies conducted by Henriksson (1984) and Chang and Lewellen (1984) respectively of mutual fund performance during the 1970s found that the net returns to fund investors before load fees lie along the Sharpe-Lintner market line (The Sharpe-Lintner line identifies the expected return from the mutual funds). However, by the 1980s mutual fund performance was found to be slightly different. Ippolito (1989), focussed on reviewing the period 1965 to 1984, discovered that returns before loads but net of other expenses are slightly above the Capital Asset Pricing Model (CAPM) market line However, attention needs to be paid to the benchmark adopted. Nevertheless, both individual and institutional investors continue to seek out SRI opportunities. In the US for example, from 1995-2016 SRI investments increased from $639 billion to $8.72 trillion, an almost 14-fold increase. Eurosif, (a pan-European sustainable and responsible investment membership organisation), produced a report in 2016 that assesses SRI in Europe. The findings of the report indicated SRI had increased to €20 trillion with the Netherlands holding the largest market share.

The report also revealed that the UK had overtaken Switzerland becoming the second largest SRI market. A report conducted by Morgan Stanley also revealed a significant growth in SRI themed investments. SRI performance data from 10,228 open-end mutual funds and 2,874 separately managed accounts over a seven-year period (2008-2015) signified that SRI, when considering an absolute and risk adjusted basis, met or significantly exceeded the performance of comparable non-SRI investments. SRI themed assets grew by 11% per year reaching €59bn in 2015, thus signifying this is a long-term trend rather than an investment fad.

Summary

In this chapter we have introduced to the concept of SRI. We have acknowledged that it is not a new concept, but rather has evolved over many centuries and has been influenced by several factors including religion, culture and regional preferences. Over the past two decades, SRI has expanded greatly and has now become mainstream amongst investors. It gives investors the ability to enact social accountability and ethical considerations when considering their investment options, encourages better social and environmental performance by organisations, and improves actual financial performance in a sustainable economy. This indicates that a socially responsible corporation should consider adopting business practices and policies that go beyond basic legal requirements and contribute more effectively to the welfare of the organisation, community, and key stakeholders. Such an approach can facilitate organisations in gaining a more competitive strategic position and turn the corporate social responsibility into a reality by "achieving commercial success in ways that honour ethical values and respect people, communities and the natural environment" (Cunningham and Harney, 2012: 217). Today, many Anglo-Saxon and Scandinavian countries base their policies around issues of environmental and ecological concern, although some like the UK put issues of community development at the forefront of their agendas. Campaigners in favour of SRI argue that screens are more than mere tools to allow the moral standards of investors to be aligned with investment choices; they argue that by investing in firms that demonstrate a high level of social responsibility, SRI lowers the cost of capital of such organisations and thereby encourages the focus on improved CSR performance (Vanwalleghem, 2013). Such attitudes clearly demonstrate that the SRI movement is increasing in strength and is here to stay.

Discussion questions

1 What are the factors that have influenced the development of SRI as we know it today?

2 Describe the environmental, social and governance (ESG) approach to SRI and its relevance to investment decisions.

3 Explain how the multiple criteria decision making (MCDM) approach facilitates SRI. Provide examples to support your argument.

4 Discuss the pros and cons of the various investment screening strategies available to investors.

References and further reading

Ballestero, E., Pérez-Gladish, B. and Garcia-Bernabeu, A. (2015). *Socially Responsible Investment. A multi-criteria decision-making approach*. International series in operations research and management science, Vol. 219, 1st ed. Cham: Springer.

Beal, D.J., Goyen, M. and Philips, P. (2005). Why do we invest ethically? *Journal of Investing*, **14**(3), .66-78.

Bollen, N.P. (2007). Mutual fund attributes and investor behaviour. *Journal of Financial and Quantitative Analysis*, **42**(3), 683-708.

Brill, J.A. and Reder, A. (1993). *Investing from the Heart: The guide to socially responsible investments and money management*. 2nd ed. New York: Crown.

Brown, E.J. and Braddock, J.F. (1990). Sheen screen, a miniaturized most-probable-number method for enumeration of oil-degrading microorganisms. *Applied and Environmental Microbiology*, **56**(12), 3895-3896.

Business for Social Responsibility. (2003). Overview of Corporate Social Responsibility, Available at http://www.bsr.org/BSRResources/IssueBriefDetail. cfm?DocumentID=48809.

CFA Institute. (2008). Environmental, social, and governance factors at listed companies: A manual for investors. Available at www.cfapubs.org/doi/pdf/10.2469/ ccb.v2008.n2.1 [Accessed 8 August 2017].

Chang, E.C. and Lewellen, W.G. (1984). Market timing and mutual fund investment performance. *Journal of Business*, **57**(1), 57-72.

Cunningham, J. and Harney, B. (2012). *Strategy and Strategists*. 1st ed. Oxford: Oxford University Press.

Diara, M., Alilo, M. and McGuire, D. (2004). Corporate social responsibility and public–private partnership: The case of the academy for educational development and ExxonMobil. *Development*, **47**(3), 69-77.

Friedman, A.L. and Miles, S. (2001). Socially responsible investment and corporate social and environmental reporting in the UK: an exploratory study. *British Accounting Review*, **33**(4), pp.523-548.

6

Global Sustainable Investment Alliance (2013). Global sustainable investment review 2012, January. Available at: gsiareview2012.gsi-alliance.org/pubData/source/Global%20Sustainable%20Investement%20Alliance.pdf [Accessed 8 August 2017]

Global Sustainable Investment Alliance (2017). Global sustainable investment review 2016, January. Available at: www.gsi-alliance.org/wp-content/uploads/2017/03/GSIR_Review2016.F.pdf [Accessed 8 August 2017]

Hayat, U. (2015). ESG Issues and Investment Practice. *CFA Institute Magazine*, **26**(5), 50-50.

Heinkel, R., Kraus, A. and Zechner, J. (2001). The effect of green investment on corporate behavior. *Journal of Financial and Quantitative Analysis*, 36(4), 431-449.

Henriksson, R.D. (1984). Market timing and mutual fund performance: An empirical investigation. *Journal of Business*, **57**(1), 73-96.

Hong, H. and Kacperczyk, M. (2009). The price of sin: The effects of social norms on markets. *Journal of Financial Economics*, **93**(1), 15-36.

Hutton, R.B., D'Antonio, L. and Johnsen, T. (1998). Socially responsible investing: Growing issues and new opportunities. *Business and Society*, **37**(3), 281-305.

Ippolito, R.A. (1989). Efficiency with costly information: A study of mutual fund performance, 1965–1984. *Quarterly Journal of Economics*, **104**(1), 1-23.

Jensen, M.C. (1968). The performance of mutual funds in the period 1945–1964. The *Journal of Finance*, **23**(2), pp.389-416.

Knoll, M.S. (2002). Ethical screening in modern financial markets: the conflicting claims underlying socially responsible investment. *The Business Lawyer*, **57**, 681-726.

Knowledge, O.B. (2007). Recent trends and regulatory implications in socially responsible investment for pension funds. Unpublished paper prepared for the 16th Session of the OECD Working Party on Private Pensions, pp.16-17.

Landier, A. and Nair, V. (2008). *Investing for Change*. New York: Oxford University Press.

Lee, D.D., Humphrey, J.E., Benson, K.L. and Ahn, J.Y. (2010). Socially responsible investment fund performance: the impact of screening intensity. *Accounting and Finance*, **50**(2), 351-370.

Lowry, R.P. (1993). *Good Money: A guide to profitable social investing in the '90s.* New York: WW Norton and Company.

Lusyana, D., and Sherif, M. (2017). Shariah-compliant investments and stock returns: evidence from the Indonesian stock market. *Journal of Islamic Accounting and Business Research*, **8**(2), 143-160.

Malkiel, B.G. (1995). Returns from investing in equity mutual funds 1971 to 1991. *Journal of Finance*, **50**(2), 549-572.

Mansley, M. (2000). *Socially Responsible Investment: A guide for pension funds and institutional investors*. London: Monitor Press.

OECD (2007). Recent Trends and Regulatory Implications of Socially Responsible Investment for Pension Fund, OECD roundtable on corporate responsibility the OECD guidelines for multinational enterprises and the financial sector. Available at https://www.oecd.org/corporate/mne/38550550.pdf [Accessed 19 September 2017].

Peifer, J.L. (2010). Morality in the financial market? A look at religiously affiliated mutual funds in the USA. *Socio-Economic Review,* **9**(2), 235-259.

Rayner Spencer Mills Research (2014). A Guide to Sustainable and Responsible Investing, SRI Services.Available at: www.sriservices.co.uk/wp-content/uploads/1404-SRI-Guide-final-Adviser-Guide.pdf. [Accessed 11 August 2017].

Segrado, C. (2005). Case study: Islamic microfinance and socially responsible investment. Italy: MEDA Project. Available at: www.gdrc.org/icm/islamic-microfinance.pdf [Accessed 23 July 2017].

Solomon, J. and Solomon, A. (2004). *Corporate Governance and Accountability.* 1st ed. West Sussex: John Wiley and Sons.

Statman, M. (2014). Behavioral finance: Finance with normal people. *Borsa Istanbul Review,* **14**(2), 65-73.

Szelagowska, A. and Bryx, M. (2015). Eco-innovations in cities, CeDeWu. Available at: http://cedewu.pl/Eco-innovations-in-Cities-p1417.

US Sustainable Investment Forum (2016) Report on US Sustainable, Responsible and Impact Investing Trends, 11th Edition. Available at: http://www.ussif.org/files/SIF_Trends_16_Executive_Summary(1).pdf [Accessed 5th Nov. 2017]

Vanwalleghem, D. (2017). The real effects of sustainable and responsible investing?. *Economics Letters,* **156**, 10-14.

Weigand, E.M., Brown, K.R. and Wilhem, E.M. (1996). Socially principled investing: Caring about ethics and profitability. *Trusts and Estates-Atlanta,* **135**, 36-42.

Wu, J., Lodorfos, G., Dean, A. and Gioulmpaxiotis, G. (2017). The market performance of socially responsible investment during periods of the economic cycle–illustrated using the case of FTSE. *Managerial and Decision Economics,* **38**(2), 238-251.

6

7 Auditing for Social Aspects

Darren Jubb, Konstantinos Ritos, Yasser Eliwa, and Chris Ryan

Introduction

This chapter provides an overview of the main developments within the social audit movement. It is difficult to provide an overarching definition of the term 'social audit', because the nature and purpose of social audit varies across organisations, industries and jurisdictions. Whilst social audit has developed to represent an array of activities and practices, the overall motivation for conducting social audits remains consistent with the ideas put forward when the concept was initially conceived. The origins of the movement can be traced back to 1950s and the pioneering work of social philosopher and reformer George Goyder. Indeed, it is Goyder who is often attributed as being the first person to use the term 'social audit'. Goyder's views grew out of the perceived limitations of conventional financial auditing practices and principles. Financial audit, which is an independent assessment of an organisation's financial reports to ensure that they are accurate, complete and have been prepared in line with the relevant accounting standards, was seen to not only overlook the social in favour of profitability, but also reduce the social to the economic (Geddes, 1992). Goyder believed that financial auditing,

> *is a one-sided state of affairs and belongs to the days when companies were small and public accountability was secured. In an economy of big business, there is clearly as much need for a social audit as for a financial audit.* (Goyder, 1961, cited in Zadek et al., 1997:17)

As an early advocate of social responsibility, Goyder believed that stakeholders in local communities and wider society should demand greater accountability from organisations regarding their social, environmental and ethical impact. Social audit was put forward as a means of delivering such accountability to stakeholders. According to Goyder, if organisations are not willing to take control over their own social and environmental accountability, then society at large must take matters into its own hands. Social audit, therefore, began as an exercise at the level of civil society, carried out by parties external to the organisation being audited. This is the first of three main types of social audit covered in this chapter: the *external social audit*. The chapter highlights the development of external social auditing from its origins, concern for issues relating to labour and the workforce before turning attention to the development of consumer audits.

After considering external social audits, attention is turned to second party audits, with a principal focus on *supply chain audits*. Supply chain audits are driven by external stakeholder pressure and corporate scandals, and consist of organisations carrying out audits of their suppliers against internal codes of conduct or external standards, to ensure that the safety and rights of workers are protected. This section focuses on supply chain audits, including how they are conducted, who conducts them and why they are necessary. It finishes by discussing the effectiveness and impact of supply chain audits.

Finally, the chapter discusses the *self-generated social audit*. This is where organisations conduct an evaluation of their own social, ethical and environmental performance and produce their own social audit reports. The section begins by discussing the pioneering work of Traidcraft plc and New Economics Foundation, which provided the catalyst for the development of self-generated social audit activity, particularly for organisations operating in the public and third sectors, or those whose main objectives were social in nature. The nature and scope of self-generated social audit are discussed, followed by how the data used in self-generated social audits is collected, how it is reported and who is responsible for providing assurance in relation to self-generated social audits.

Early developments in social audit

Despite the early work of Goyder, the theory and practice of social audit did not develop in any significant fashion until the 1970s and the pioneering work of Charles Medawar (1976). A central tenet of Medawar's work is the idea that those in positions of power, who are charged with making decisions on behalf of, and in the interests of, stakeholders should be held accountable for those decisions (Gray *et al.*, 2014). Further to this, Medawar was one of the leading figures in the formation of the influential organisation Social Audit Ltd, a group who led the way in social audit during the 1970s. Social Audit Ltd was important to the development of social audit, as they were one of the first organisations to publish social audit reports. Perhaps the most prominent example of their work is the report produced on the company Avon Rubber. This represented the first detailed social audit report into a single organisational unit. Social Audit Ltd went on to produce several other social audit reports focusing on numerous companies within the corporate sector. The scope of these reports was wide-ranging and covered several social issues including labour relations, health and safety, issues relating to products and services, pollution, waste disposal and energy. The work of Social Audit Ltd paved the way for future social audit organisations and initiatives whereby social auditing was conducted by stakeholders external to the organisation being audited.

Early social audit activity was developed further in the work of Counter Information Services (CIS), particularly in relation to the interests of the workforce (Gray *et al.*, 2014). Throughout the 1970s and 1980s CIS issued several Anti-Reports, that concentrated on those industries and organisations with the largest workforces and included organisations such as Ford (formerly a public-sector industry), Unilever and the NHS. Whilst covering a range of social issues, the CIS reports focused mainly on labour relations, working conditions, redundancy programmes and strikes. The reports were designed to scrutinise the wealth of UK's largest companies, focusing on contrasting profits with wages, work conditions and environmental costs, as well as disclosing the privatisation of the public sector. The reports produced by CIS represented the first steps in the narrowing of focus of social audit reports, with reports produced that looked specifically at issues relating to the workforce, plant closures and the interests of consumers. These are discussed in more detail in the following sections.

The work of Social Audit Ltd and CIS has influenced external social audit, which has spread far beyond the United Kingdom. Indeed, reporting of this nature continues today with external social reports that have a worldwide reach such as those produced by Greenpeace (2005a, 2005b), Friends of the Earth (2003) and other social and environmental organisations. Some of these reports focus on individual organisations (e.g. United National Development Programme, 2010), whilst some have a more societal focus (e.g. Christian Aid, 2003, 2005). The most prominent developments are discussed in the following sections of this chapter.

Government, local authority and NGO audits

Building on the CIS reports' concern with issues relating to the workforce, social audits continued to develop during the 1980s with the work of trade unions and local authorities (Gray *et al.*, 2014). These social audits arose due to the rapidly changing industrial environment in the United Kingdom during the early 1980s. Driven by de-industrialisation and rising unemployment, several local authorities began to conduct social audits looking at the impact of plant closures on local communities. Specifically, these social audits considered the impact that such closures would have on employment levels as well as the wider economic impact on local businesses and other stakeholders. Further to this, macroeconomic assessments of the public cost of closures were also undertaken. Thus, the reports produced by local authorities during this period had an overarching social and financial focus. This continued with social audits of the impact of the steel industry in the county of Cleveland (1983) and the coal industry in Barnsley Metropolitan Council (1984). In the late 1980s, the social auditing activities of local authorities expanded away from focusing on the financial impact of single plant closures towards considering a wider range of social issues evidenced by the wide ranging social audits conducted by Newcastle City Council (1985) and Sheffield City Council (1985). Social audit relating to local authority activity then experienced a hiatus until recently when authorities such as Salford City Council (2016) proposed the embedding of social responsibility and social value into local government activity (Gray *et al.*, 2014).

Outside of the United Kingdom, stakeholders external to governments and NGOs have conducted social audit activities to monitor and assess the performance of organisations. The focus of these audits has often been organisations that are operating in several developing countries, including Bangladesh, India (e.g. Centre for Good Governance, 2005) and Pakistan (Khlaid *et al.*, 2010) as well as several countries on the African continent (e.g. WEMA, 2011). Like the early work conducted by Social Audit Ltd, this type of social audit focused on holding to account those organisations that purport to act in the interests of stakeholders within local communities. For example, social audit has been used as a tool to assess and measure non-financial activities through the monitoring of internal and external consequences of specific government schemes or NGO activity. This type of social audit attempts to evaluate the achievement of the social goals of the government or local authority from the point of view of a wide variety of stakeholders within communities. These social audits exist to counter public audits and parliamentary reviews, which are considered to not go far enough in considering the wider impact and performance of public agencies.

7

Consumer audits

Protecting the rights of consumers has been a central concern of the social audit movement since its inception (Gray *et al.*, 2014). One influential organisation formed in 1957 was the Consumers' Association, who produced the magazine *Which?*, with the primary aim of countering the power of organisations in the interests of the everyday consumer. Since its inception, the Consumers' Association has grown to become the largest consumer body in the United Kingdom. In addition to the publication of the magazine, the organisation has launched numerous campaigns in the interest of consumers, with many of these leading to positive changes in law and behaviour. The association remains active today, with an extensive online presence. In addition to *Which?*, journals such as *New Consumer* and *Ethical Consumer* were also prominent during the 1980s and continued to drive a consumer-focused movement in social audit that still remains today. The journals were short-lived, however, and the Ethical Consumer organisation has turned attention to rating and scoring companies based on their ethical performance. Through their Ethiscore metrics, Ethical Consumer gathers a wealth of information regarding the performance of companies and ranks the organisations based on a range of criteria.

Along similar lines, the Ethical Company Organisation, founded by William Sankey, remains active in the consumer-focused social audit. The Organisation produces external reports that do not focus on one specific organisation but instead evaluate over 30,000 companies, to produce the Ethical Company Index, which gives each company and brand an independent score. These ethical rankings are subsequently used to produce reports, such as *The Good Shopping Guide* and *The Good Nutrition Guide* that can be used by consumers to assess the ethical performance of organisations before making their purchasing choices. Additionally, *The Good Shopping Guide* is designed to encourage poorly performing companies to improve their ethical performance, whilst rewarding those companies with a high level of ethical standard with a higher score.

On a more global scale, Consumers International is an organisation that was founded in 1960 with the aim to fight for a fair and safe future for all consumers within the global marketplace in the face of increasing globalisation. Consumers International currently has over 240 member organisations from 120 countries, made up largely of local consumer groups and consumer government agencies. Like the organisations previously discussed, Consumers International publish numerous reports on a wide range of issues including, but not limited to, ethical trade, health and nutrition, competition and climate change.

The activities of the above enterprises represent the broadest scope of social audit. These organisations seek to gather data from as wide a range of companies and brands as possible to protect consumers and encourage organisations to be more ethically responsible. In reaction to the initial calls for civil society to demand greater accountability from organisations with respect to their social responsibility, the activities of social audit have developed as being broad in nature and scope. Early developments in social audit were driven by stakeholders external to organisations. Because of pressure from stakeholders, organisations began to become increasingly aware of their social, ethical and environmental responsibilities, resulting in social audit activities moving from solely being the remit of external stakeholders towards organisations beginning to take responsibility for social audit themselves. This is discussed in more detail in the following section, where the notion of supply chain audits is introduced.

Supply chain audit

In a similar vein to the early developments in social audits, the increase in the use of supply chain social audit has been driven by pressure from stakeholders external to organisations, including many voices from the public and third sectors. Workers' rights within supply chains have arisen as an important issue because of increasing globalisation during the 1980s. During this period several organisations began to move their operations to countries where wages paid to workers were lower and the social, ethical and environmental legislative environment was weaker (Rahim and Idowu, 2015). Shortly after this occurred, NGOs and journalists began to expose child and 'sweatshop' labour and sub-standard working practices in overseas production sites (Pruett, 2005). This resulted in calls for greater transparency and accountability within global supply chain management, culminating in the introduction of social audit practices that sought to identify, correct and solve environmental and social problems in supply chains.

Supply chain issues gained additional prominence in the mid-1990s after several high-profile companies were further criticised for substandard working conditions in their supply chains. Many these claims originated from countries in Asia including Bangladesh, Cambodia, China, India and Pakistan (Locke and Romis, 2012). For example, the study by Locke and Romis (2012) highlights how, during the 1990s, Nike was criticised for sourcing its products from countries where low wages, human rights issues and poor working conditions were prominent. In response to such criticisms, several large private sector organisations, including Nike, Gap and Levi Strauss, were pressurised by third sector organisations to adopt codes of conduct designed to ensure adequate working hours, wages and working conditions in the supply chain.

The garment and footwear industry began conducting social audits for organisations to monitor performance against their own standards and codes of conduct within their supply chains. Outside of garments and footwear, non-specialise retailers such as supermarkets and department stores have developed less stringent codes of conduct, and they have managed to avoid scrutiny, feeling less pressure to behave in a responsible way towards the workers employed in their supply chain (Pruett, 2005).

Supply chain audits consist of organisations evaluating the working conditions and practices of factories and production sites within their own supply chains. Overall, a supply chain social audit should aim to assess and identify violations of workers' rights within production facilities, to assess and evaluate the performance of suppliers in relation to social standards. Supply chain audits should also encourage improvements at the workplace in line with the codes of conduct that have been developed by organisations, or in relation to external standards.

Codes of conduct and external standards

As stated above, many organisations developed internal codes of conduct that were designed to protect the rights of workers within supply chains. Whilst the development of codes of conduct represented a positive move from organisations, in most instances these codes of conduct have been developed in an ad hoc manner by a range of different stakeholders. This has resulted in questions being raised about the consistency and quality of codes of conduct applied to global suppliers (Jenkins, 2001; O'Rourke, 2003). These issues stem from codes being created for different purposes and from different viewpoints. To overcome this issue, several global standards have been created. The most prominent of these is the SA8000 standard that was established by Social Accountability International in 1997 as a multi-stakeholder initiative. It is a voluntary standard that can be used as third-party verification. The standard sets out the requirements that are to be met by organisations. This includes the establishment or improvement of workers' rights, better workplace conditions and a more effective management system. The standard has since evolved into a framework that is designed to help organisations demonstrate their dedication to the fair treatment of workers across industries and in any country, and covers nine main areas: child labour, forced or compulsory labour, health and safety, freedom of association and right to collective bargaining, discrimination, disciplinary practices, working hours, remuneration and management systems (Social Accountability Internal, 2014).

In addition to the SA8000 standard, the Ethical Trading Initiative (ETI) was established in 1998 with the objective of improving the lives of individuals working within global supply chains. This initiative was designed to ensure that all employers of labour in the supply chain aim to improve the working conditions and lives of the individuals responsible for creating the products that the organisation sells. The 'base code' that underpins the ETI is similar in nature to the nine main areas of the SA8000, with the basic principles being that: employment is freely chosen, freedom of association and the right to collective bargaining are respected, working conditions are safe and hygienic, child labour shall not be used, living wages are paid, working hours are not excessive, no discrimination is practised, regular employment is provided and no harsh or inhumane treatment is allowed (Ethical Trading Initiative, 2014). As supply chain audit has developed further, a range of other standards covering several different areas and industries have been created such as the Business Social Compliance Initiative (BSCI), Worldwide Responsible Accredited Production (WRAP), and the Sedex Members Ethical Trade Audit (SMETA) audit. An important aspect of supply chain audit is the enforcement and assessment of compliance. The parties that are charged with conducting social audits of supply chains are discussed in more detail in the following section.

■   Who conducts supply chain audits?

For supply chain social audits to be most effective, verification of suppliers should be carried out by an independent party who is external to the organisations present in the supply chain. This, however, is not always the case in practice. The reality of the situation is that, broadly speaking, there are two main types of social auditor: the internal social auditor and the external social auditor. As the name suggests, internal social auditors are employed by the organisation who have conducted the activities that are to be audited. The social auditors being employed by the organisation means that they are less likely to be objective and more likely to put the interests of their employers ahead of labour standards and the interests of other stakeholders. External social auditors are more independent than internal social auditors, but they often work for commercial firms whose business models may conflict with delivering a credible social audit as there is a tendency to want to please the clients and suppliers who are paying for their services. Despite these issues, external auditors are preferable to internal auditors.

The desire for independent social auditors has resulted in the creation of an industry of social auditors who are present themselves as self-aligned experts in supply chain audit (Pruett, 2005). There are several types of organisation that are involved in conducting supply chain social audits. These include the global financial auditing firms, and specialised for-profit and not-for-profit social audit organisations. Commercial audit firms took an interest in conducting social audits, particularly during the 1990s. Although making up a small aspect of their business activities, these organisations offer increased resources and expertise. Commercial auditing firms, however, have not been immune from scandal and criticism. To take a specific recent example, the Ernst and Young audit of a Nike supplier in Vietnam illustrates the issues surrounding the independence of auditors. This audit has been criticised because of inconsistency and bias in key areas such as wages, overtime, and health and safety conditions (O'Rourke, 1997). Thus, even where an independent external party is engaged to undertake supply chain audits, it is no guarantee of effectiveness.

For social auditors assessing supply chains, there are three primary means of collecting data when conducting supply chain social audits. The first of these is to conduct interviews with workers, management, local unions and NGOs. When carrying out interviews, it is important that social auditors speak directly to workers about the conditions that they work in, without management present, for workers to feel comfortable enough to speak freely without fear of repercussions. Next, it is common for organisations and social auditors to complement the use of interviews with techniques that are familiar to a financial audit, such as observation and inspection of relevant documentation. In this instance, auditors would conduct a document review of numerous aspects of the suppliers' business including, but not limited to, wages, hours, bonuses and personnel management. Finally, organisations and social auditors may also conduct a site inspection that aims to reveal health and safety problems and information about management-worker relations. The impact and effectiveness of social audit are discussed in more detail in the following section.

■ The impact of supply chain audits

Despite the development detailed above, supply chain social audits have been criticised for being insufficient. They have been criticised for failing to detect important breaches of compliance with labour standards and codes of conduct (e.g. McDougall, 2008; Bunting, 2011; Wilshaw, 2011; Rustin 2014). Indeed, social audit has failed to be effective in several famous cases, including the admission in Nike's 2005 corporate responsibility report which disclosed collusion with its supplier in relation to the falsification of information by Chinese factories throughout the social audit process, including the coaching of workers by management in how to respond to social audit interviews (Nike, 2005). More than problems with detection, however, supply chain audits have also been criticised for rarely leading to improved working conditions and better workers' rights. It has previously been found that the effectiveness of social audit is limited, and social audits cannot produce change by themselves (Pruett, 2005). For the outcomes of social audit to be meaningful, some sort of follow up mechanism is required.

Social auditors often have limited powers to investigate as they can only verify the information that is presented to them. This has been problematic in a range of social audits, particularly with respect to audits of supply chains, where the regularity and pre-existing knowledge of upcoming audits allow suppliers to remove harmful documentation, remove illegal workers and temporarily improve working conditions. Overall, the practices of social auditors currently suffer from being fragmented and variable in nature. Inconsistency in the quality of social audits has led to range of criticisms of social auditors, including variation in the issues being considered to be important, the wide variations in methodology that is employed to collect information, the length of time spent conducting the audit, the level of skill and experience of the social auditors, and the methods of reporting the information that has been collected (Jenkins, 2001; O'Rourke, 2003).

Self-generated social audit

The final type of social audit discussed in this chapter are first-party social audits, which are most prominent in the public and third sectors. In recognition of the increased accountability demands from stakeholders regarding the social activities of organisations, many organisations began to produce self-generated social audit reports. One of the earliest and most prominent examples of self-generated social audit is the work conducted by Traidcraft plc, a fair-trade retail and wholesale organisation based in the UK, in conjunction with the New Economics Foundation in the early 1990s. This marked the first attempt by community organisations to attempt to fully understand their impact on society and to evaluate and report whether they were catering for the needs of all their stakeholders.

Not only did Traidcraft plc. develop a single set of social accounts for the first time, but they also published documentation on the thought process behind the publication, which influenced further developments in this area. This approach saw the first involvement of both internal and external parties in social auditing and was the beginning of an approach that underpins this type of social audit today. Because of this pioneering work, a social audit methodology for use by organisations was developed and refined, eventually becoming a model of good practice that future developments would build upon. One of the main developments to emerge was the practice of conducting a regular, year-end social audit using independent financial auditors in much the same vein as the financial audit.

Following the work done by Traidcraft plc and the New Economics Foundation, developments in social audit continued throughout the 1990s but continued to lack coherence, with a diverse range of groups developing across the United Kingdom. In Scotland, the Strathclyde Community Business Ltd (SCB) built on this work in the 1980s, where they recognised the need to understand, account for and report on the social benefits of the community businesses, to produce *Social Auditing for Small Organisations: The Workbook* (Pearce *et al.*, 1996). This workbook built on the New Economics Foundation's work with Traidcraft plc, and resulted in the creation of the 'Scottish model' of social auditing, which has influenced other social audit initiatives such as the one launched by the CBED Unit (Community-based Economic Development) of Liverpool City Council which ran until 2004 with over 200 people completing the Open College Network approved course.

A similar development took place in England, where a social audit model began to be developed by the Industrial Common Ownership Movement (ICOM) through its Beechwood College near Leeds. The 'Beechwood model' was primarily concerned with worker co-operatives. This model was first used in the early 1980s and was further developed by the Social Enterprise Partnership into the Social Audit Toolkit (Social Enterprise Partnership, 2000) and used within the community sector, especially in the context of several transnational European programmes.

Building on the above, the New Economics Foundation itself ran a pilot social audit programme in association with the Association of Chief Officers of Voluntary Organisations, for 13 voluntary organisations throughout the UK, titled Social Auditing for Voluntary Organisations (SAVO), between 1998 and 2000. Around the same time, development of social audit was continuing in Scotland as the Community Business Scotland Network (CBSN) launched a social audit programme in 2000 with two sets of community organisations undertaking training and preparing social audits.

Perhaps the most significant recent development in social audit in the United Kingdom occurred in 2000 when the Social Audit Network (SAN) was launched at a symposium held in Edinburgh. Starting out as an email network, SAN now manages a register of approved social auditors, runs training courses and publishes a directory of social accounts. SAN were one of the first organisations to produce guidance to parties wishing to carry out social auditing in their Social Accounting and Audit Manual. Despite this, challenges to conducting social audit remained and after consultation with stakeholders, SAN published *Prove, Improve, Account: New Guide to Social Accounting and Audit* (Social Audit Network 2012: 3), which included "reference to other frameworks and tools; placed more emphasis on outcomes (as well as outputs); revised the reporting requirements to make it more accessible to smaller organisations; and revised the audit process". This represented one of the first attempts to bring a level of coherence and professionalisation to the practice of conducting social audit.

7

Further afield, there have been several similar social audit developments. Social audit has been a feature of a growing number of EU funded transnational programmes that have been based on both the Scottish and the Beechwood models. The Scottish model has also been used as the basis for developing several social audit initiatives across the world including, for example, programmes run by COMMACT Aotearoa community organisations in New Zealand. Community organisations in India, Nepal, the Philippines, South Africa and Canada are amongst the many others who have experimented with appropriate forms of social accounting and audit to suit their needs. In India, for example, social auditing was formally introduced into law in the 2005 Mahatma Gandhi National Rural Employment Guarantee Act (Rahim and Idowu, 2015). Because of these developments, self-generated social audit has become an essential aspect of the activities of community and voluntary organisations. More than simply being an accountability tool for these organisations, social audit is one part of a holistic approach to setting, managing and reporting their social mission, values and goals. The following section elaborates further on the nature, purpose and scope of self-generated social audits.

■ The nature and purpose of self-generated social audit

The first-party social audit has become especially useful for organisations whose primary purpose is the maximisation of social, ethical and environmental impact in place of, or alongside, the generation of profit. Social audit is an important means for such organisations to assess if, and how successfully, they are achieving their primary purpose, and the extent to which they are acting in the interests of relevant stakeholders. Indeed, the creation and maintenance of stakeholder dialogue with shareholders is an important and central aspect of social audit. By making social audits available to all stakeholders, organisations can engage in a two-way dialogue with key stakeholders and further increase accountability towards such groups. For these organisations, then, social audit can be a holistic approach to the planning, evaluating and reporting of the impact of organisational activities and acts as:

> a logical and flexible framework that will enable your organisation to build on existing documentation and reporting systems and develop a process whereby you can: account fully for your organisation's social, environmental and economic performance and impact; report on that performance and impact; provide the information essential for planning future action and improving performance; and be accountable to all those you work with and work for. (Kay, 2011:1).

It is important for both organisations and stakeholders to know if objectives are being achieved, to assess the impact that the organisation is having on the community, society and the environment, and to continually assess whether the values and objectives that the organisation is operating from remain relevant and up-to-date. Social audit allows those in charge of managing companies to make themselves more accountable to both internal and external stakeholders, resulting in increases in stakeholder trust and confidence by highlighting that the organisation is sticking to its vision, values and objectives. Thus, a social audit will enhance the organisation's reputation within local communities and wider society.

In addition to helping organisations monitor their social and ethical performance, the reflective nature of social auditing practices can aid management in shaping their strategy in a socially and ethically responsible manner. Doing so will help management identify opportunities and threats before they are incurred and by reflecting on organisational performance in this manner facilitates organisational learning. The holistic approach to social audit means that organisations should develop a set of social, ethical and environmental goals against which their performance can be assessed and evaluated. This approach is based on several key principles which can be summarised as laid out in Box 1.

Box 1: The key principles of self-generated social audit

1 **Inclusive**: Social audit should be for the benefit of stakeholders and include the voices of all relevant stakeholders.

2 **Regular**: Social auditing should be conducted in a regular and continuous cycle, with the outcomes of the social audit process fed back into the organisation.

3 **Engaging**: Stakeholder dialogue is an integral aspect of social auditing. Outcomes of social audit should be disclosed in a meaningful and proactive manner, and aim to reach all relevant stakeholders.

4 **Verifiable**: Social audit reports should be assessed by an independent external party to ensure the validity and reliability of the information produced. More information on this is contained later on in the chapter.

5 **Continuously improving**: As indicated in point 2, social auditing does not end with the production of a social report. Rather, the outcomes from the social auditing process should be re-embedded within the organisation to improve and refine social, ethical and environmental objectives and strategies.

6 **Comparable**: After several social audit cycles have been completed, organisational performance should be compared with the results of previous social audits as well as external benchmarks from other organisations or statutory regulations or societal norms.

Source: Kay (2011).

7

■   # The scope of self-generated social audit

The scope of social audit will vary depending on the organisational mission and objectives. Further, there is a differentiation to be made here between the purpose of different organisations. For corporate sector organisations, their primary purpose is growing share value and increasing returns to shareholders, rather than being interested in being socially, ethically and environmentally responsible. For such organisations, the use of social audit has been questioned as being no more than an exercise to demonstrate corporate social responsibility and to manage stakeholder relations, rather than being completely altruistic. However, several corporate organisations have been influential, including Body Shop, Ben and Jerry's and Shared Earth (Social Audit Network, 2012). On the other hand, organisations whose primary purpose is the maximisation of social, ethical and environmental issues, such as community organisations and charities will have primary goals and areas of interests that are wide-ranging. In this instance, social audit aims to capture information relating to a wide array of issues, the most common of which are detailed in Table 7.1.

Area	Brief description
Ethics	Includes creating ethical policies, checking if these are being upheld by assessing whether organisational activities undermine planned ethical practices.
Staffing	Includes ensuring that organisations reward, train and develop staff in a non-discriminatory, fair and equitable manner.
Environment	Includes policies relating to care for the environment, waste management and disposal, and whether these are adhered to. Organisations should regularly review practices to ensure they are in line with established policies.
Human Rights	Includes how organisations ensure that they do not violate human rights, including making sure they do not deal with, trade with or support organisations that violate human rights.
Community	Includes organisational policies relating to the local community and community involvement. Most commonly this takes the form of community partnerships and projects that are driven by the organisation.
Compliance	Includes how organisations comply with relevant legal requirements, such as health and safety, employment law, environmental law, criminal law and, of course, financial and tax laws. Note that these regulations may create legal obligations in relation to some of the other issues identified within this table.

Table 7.1: the scope of self-generated social audit (Social Audit Network, 2012)

■   # How are self-generated social audits conducted?

In a similar vein to supply chain audits, conducting self-generated social audits mostly involves collecting primary data in the first instance. The processes and procedures of data collection in the production of self-generated social audits are much the same as for supply chain social audits in that most of the information is qualitative in nature. As one of the central tenets of self-generated social audit is the involvement of all stakeholders in the process, one of the most common techniques is carrying out surveys of stakeholders via questionnaires. The content of these will vary depending on the mission, values and objectives of the organisation in question, but are designed to evaluate whether it has performed well in the eyes of stakeholders. The use of questionnaires is often supplemented by focus groups and interviews to investigate the views of stakeholders in greater depth. Organisations may supplement the above data with a review of secondary data such as policy documents, external standards and other regulations to highlight their social and ethical performance through compliance.

Whilst the gathering and presentation of data is an integral aspect of social audit, it is important that the social audit does not become a token exercise for organisations. For social audit to be most effective, it should be used by organisations to continually re-shape their social, ethical and environmental goals, objectives and activities. Stakeholders have an important role in this instance. They should continue dialogue with organisations to hold organisations to account for their actions and to ensure that they are first and foremost sticking to their overarching mission and objectives, as well as continuing to act in the interests of all stakeholders. Once data collection has been completed, the results of the questionnaires and interviews are subsequently analysed and compiled in the social audit report, which is discussed in more detail in the next section.

How are self-generated social audits reported?

The final step in the social audit process is the production and dissemination of the social audit report. Communicating the results of social audit has always been an important aspect of social audit process. In the early stages of the development of social audit, reporting was central to the activities of organisations such as Social Audit Ltd and Counter Information Services. These externally generated reports represented the first attempts to increase transparency and accountability in relation to the activities of organisations and were designed to communicate information to as wide a range of stakeholders within society as possible. Since the early developments in social audit, the creation of a dialogue with stakeholders has become one of the central principles of social audit. As a result, the social audit report is more than simply a document that is made available to stakeholders. Rather it is a process of communication between the organisation and key stakeholders. Reporting the results of social audit allows stakeholders to ascertain whether an organisation has 'listened' to the issues that matter to them and, if so, how they have responded. Stakeholders themselves play an important role, as they have increased demands for transparency and are taking a much more active role in communicating their expectations with respect to accountability, as well as being actively involved in the creation of the social audit report at the data collection stage.

Whilst the social audit report is an important communicative device, the usefulness of social audit reports has been questioned in some instances. Whilst companies could have completely altruistic intentions, it has been found that, in many instances, social audit reports amount to window-dressing designed to improve the organisation's public image and appeal to a wider range of stakeholders. Further, social audit reports have been criticised for being an ineffective strategy for engendering change; rather they are used as a means of limiting the potential liability of organisations (Esbenshade, 2004). Although the main role of social auditing is to measure and assess, and at times to challenge, the activity of organisations in relation to their social objectives, it should also be used to engender positive outcomes in respect of shaping management strategy, facilitating organisational learning and strategic management and informing stakeholders.

■ Who conducts self-generated social audits?

Like financial audit, one of the main aspects of the self-generated social audit is verification. It is the process of reviewing the social accounts of an organisation at the end of each social accounting period to assess and reflect on whether the organisation has conducted social activities in line with the stated mission and objectives. The term 'social audit' is often used interchangeably with the term 'social accounting' to refer to the entire process from social bookkeeping through to the final audit of the social accounts. As with supply chain social audits, once the report has been prepared, these activities should ideally be reviewed by an independent third party who produces a report for circulation to relevant stakeholders, including the public. Thus, social audit allows organisations to report on their achievements based on independently verifiable evidence rather than relying on anecdotes and unsubstantiated claims. The parties that produce and independently review social audit reports will vary from between organisations and jurisdictions with organisations ranging from large commercial audit firms to small independent advisors being involved in the social audit process.

As discussed earlier, within the self-generated social audit movement there has been a range of initiatives and organisations that have been designed to provide advice on how to conduct social accounting and social audit. The most prominent of these organisations, the Social Audit Network, not only provides advice on how to carry out social audits but also helps to connect social auditors and organisations by maintaining a register of social auditors. To be accepted onto this register as an approved social auditor, individuals must complete a relevant training course, attend verification panel meetings and be approved by the Social Audit Network. Additionally, auditors are required to make annual returns to SAN regarding their relevant training and chairing activities.

There is, therefore, a movement towards bringing more coherence to the practice of self-generated social audit. Whilst there is currently no formal or standardised training for social auditors in this area, there have been calls. The AA1000 framework addresses the expectation that social auditors have the required skills and capabilities to undertake a social audit by proposing a professional qualification linked to a training professional development programme (Gao and Zhang, 2006). The recommendations contained within AA1000 cover the competencies and knowledge required of social and ethical accountants and auditors, recommendations of the level of professional training considered necessary to support social auditors in meeting the required standard of competency, and how these standards and levels can be maintained. Ensuring that social audit reports are independently verified is therefore growing in importance within the self-generated social audit community. The main motivating factor behind this move is to increase the effectiveness and impact that social auditing has for organisations, community and society.

Summary

This chapter has presented an overview of the social audit movement. Social audit has been shown here to be multi-faceted in nature and scope and, as a result, this chapter has presented three main types of social audit.

First, a discussion of external social audits that are prepared by parties external to the organisation being audited was presented. By looking at the early developments in social audit, the chapter highlighted the origins of social audit as an external mechanism designed to increase transparency and accountability regarding the impact of organisational activities on an array of stakeholders. As stakeholders began to demand greater levels of accountability, coupled with several corporate scandals, organisations started to take responsibility for assessing and reporting on their social, ethical and environmental impact.

Along these lines, the chapter discussed two further types of social audit: supply chain audits and self-generated audit. The former concerns organisations, mainly from the corporate sector, adopting codes of conduct and external standards to ensure the safety and fair treatments of workers within supply chains. Once adopted, organisations should ensure, through a process of social audit, that these standards are being adhered to by factories and organisations in their supply chains.

Finally, the chapter considered the increased adoption of the holistic process of social audit by organisations designed with social, ethical and environmental goals in mind. The chapter detailed the development of several initiatives in this area that have resulted in moves towards professionalisation of the social audit movement across all economic sectors.

7

Discussion questions

1 Discuss the limitations of financial audit, and why social audit has been put forward as a more effective alternative.

2 Describe the reasons behind the increasing importance of supply chain audit and discuss the effectiveness of such audits.

3 The independence of social auditors is a significant issue in social auditing. Discuss the different options available when choosing a social auditor and comment on which option is most effective to a public sector organisation.

4 Discuss the professionalisation of the self-generated social audit movement.

References and further reading

Barnsley Metropolitan Borough Council (1984). *Coal Mining and Barnsley*. Barnsley: Barnsley Metropolitan Council.

Bunting, M. (2011). Sweatshops are still supplying high street brands. The Guardian, April 28. Retrieved from https://www.theguardian.com/global-development/poverty-matters/2011/apr/28/sweatshops-supplying-high-street-brands

Centre for Good Governance (2005). *Social Audit: A Toolkit A Guide for Performance Improvement and Outcome Measurement*. Hyderabad: Centre for Good Governance.

Christian Aid (2003). *Behind the Mask: The real face of corporate social responsibility*. London: Christian Aid.

Christian Aid (2005). *The Shirts off Their Backs: How tax policies fleece the poor*, London: Christian Aid.

CIS (1972). Anti-Reports. London: Counter Information Services. Available at: http://anti-report.com/

County of Cleveland (1983). *The Economic and Social Importance of the British Steel Corporation in Cleveland*, County of Cleveland.

Esbenshade, J. (2004). *Monitoring Sweatshops: Workers, Consumers and the Global Apparel Industry*. Philadelphia: Temple University Press.

Ethical Trading Initiative (2014). *The ETI Base Code*. London: Ethical Trading Initiative.

Friends of the Earth (2003). *Failing the Challenge: The other Shell report 2002*. London: Friends of the Earth.

Gao, S. and Zhang, J. (2006). Stakeholder engagement, social auditing and corporate sustainability. *Business Process Management Journal*, **12**(6), 722–740. https://doi.org/10.1108/14637150610710891

Geddes, M. (1992). The social audit movement, in Owed D. (ed.) *Green Reporting: Accountancy and the challenge of the nineties*, pp. 215-41. London: Chapman and Hall.

Goyder, G. (1961). *The Responsible Company*. London: Blackwell.

Gray, R., Adams, P.C., Owen, D., (2014). *Accountability, Social Responsibility and Sustainability: Accounting for Society and the Environment.* Pearson, Edinburgh.

Greenpeace (2005a). *Climate Crime File – Land Rover.* London: Greenpeace.

Greenpeace (2005b). *Climate Crime File – Esso.* London: Greenpeace.

Jenkins, R. (2001). Corporate Codes of Conduct: Self-Regulation in a Global Economy. (Last Updated: April 2001). United Nations Research Institute for Social Development (UNRISD). Available at http://www.eldis.org/static/DOC9199.htm.

Kay (2011). *The New Guide to Social Accounting and Audit,* Liverpool: Social Audit Network.

Khalid, Y.M., Mujahid, E., Mehmud, K., Saud, S., Abkar, S.H., and Khan, N.U. (2010). *Social Audit of Local Governance and Delivery of Public Services.* Islamabad: United Nations Development Programmme.

Locke, R. M., and Romis, M. (2012). Improving work conditions in a global supply chain. *MIT Sloan Management Review*, **48**.

McDougall, D. (2008). The hidden face of Primark fashion. *The Guardian*, June 22. Retrieved from www.theguardian.com/world/2008/jun/22/india.humanrights.

Medawar, C. (1976). The social audit – a political view, *Accounting, Organizations and Society*, **1**(4), 389-94.

Newcastle City Council (1985). *Newcastle Upon Tyne Social Audit 1979-1984.* Newcastle upon Tyne: Newcastle City Council.

Nike, Inc. (2005). *FY04 Corporate Responsibility Report.* Nike, Inc.

O'Rourke, D (1997). Smoke from a Hired Gun: A Critique of Nike's Labor and Environmental Auditing in Vietnam as Performed by Ernst and Young. (Last Updated: November 10, 1997). Transnational Resource and Action Center. Available at http://nature.berkeley.edu/orourke/PDF/smoke.pdf.

O'Rourke, D. (2003). Outsourcing regulation: analyzing nongovernmental systems of labor standards and monitoring. *Policy Studies Journal.* **31**(1), 1-30

Pearce, J., Raynard, P., Zadek, S., and New Economics Foundation. (1998). *Social Auditing for Small Organisations: A workbook for trainers and practitioners.* London: New Economic Foundation.

Pruett, D. (2005). Looking for a Quick Fix: How Weak Social Auditing is Keeping Workers in Sweatshops. (Last Updated: November 2005). Clean Clothes Campaign. Available at http://www.cleanclothes.org/ftp/05-quick_fix.pdf.

Rahim, M. M., and Idowu, S. O. (2015). *Social Audit Regulation - Development, Challenges and Opportunities.* London: Springer.

Rustin, S. (2014). This cry for help on a Primark label can't be ignored. *The Guardian*, June 25. Retrieved from https://www.theguardian.com/commentisfree/2014/jun/25/primark-label-swansea-textile-industry-rana-plaza

7

Salford City Council (2016). Final draft of Salford City Council's Social Value and Sustainability Policy, https://www.salford.gov.uk/media/390070/social-value-and-sustainability-policy-full-version.pdf

Sheffield City Council (1985). *Sheffield Jobs Audit*. Sheffield: Sheffield City Council.

Social Accountability International (2014) *Social Accountability 8000 International Standard*. New York: Social Accountability International

Social Audit Network (2012). *Brief History of Social Accounting and Audit*. Liverpool: Social Audit Network.

Social Enterprise Partnership (2000). *Social Audit Toolkit (3rd Ed.)*. Social Enterprise Partnership Ltd

WEMA (2011). *WEMA 2011 Social Audit Report*. Toronto: University Health Network and University of Toronto

Wilshaw, R. (2011). Social audits flawed as a way of driving sustainable change. *The Guardian*, July 12. Retrieved from https://www.theguardian.com/sustainable-business/blog/social-audits-flawed-companies-developing-world

Zadek, S., Evans, R., Pruzan, P., (2013). *Building Corporate Accountability: Emerging Practice in Social and Ethical Accounting and Auditing*. Oxford: Routledge.

8 Social Accounting and the Public Sector

Vasileios Milios, Anees Farrukh, Stelios Kotsias, and Mercy Denedo

Introduction

In modern societies, the public sector is at the heart of democracy as it illustrates the sovereignty of citizens who transfer their power to sovereign governments (Jones and Pendlebury, 2010). The social nature of the public sector is undeniable as it displays fundamental difference when compared to the private sector. The main target of the public sector is not profit maximization but the creation of social value. The definition of assets differs in public sector accounting as they are not expected to bring economic benefits, but they are expected to provide services and goods to the citizens. However, defining social value is problematic. Within the public sector there is a complex framework of interests which derive from differing perspectives. In this context, the role of accounting is very important as it must ensure democratic control over the use of funds (Pallot, 1992).

After the end of WWII, governments in many parts of Europe undertook the responsibility for providing a wide range of services to their citizens focusing on health, education and social insurance. These efforts were labelled as the development of the Welfare State and they illustrated the humanistic direction of Europe. Especially for the period 1945-1975, it constituted a major part of the political agenda and the increase in public expenses reflected this priority (Pierson, 1998). At the beginning of the 1980s, because of the financial crisis which occurred during the late 1970s, the rise of neoliberalism and the globalization of capital markets, the social achievements of these governments, and the UK government in particular, were questioned. There were calls for the reduction of social expenditure, arguing that the cost of social policy was so high, and on occasion wasteful, that it was putting the fiscal sustainability of the public sector in danger. There were also some voices claiming that public sectors should be reformed in a way that could offer a balance between markets, competitiveness and social justice. In response to these calls, a new initiative for the management of public services was put forward in the form of New Public Management (NPM) first coined by Hood in 1985 (Sitala, 2013). NPM has been the main initiative for public sector management reform, although there have been other later initiatives that have tried to rebalance the neo-liberalistic attitude of NPM.

The global financial crisis of 2008 brought to the surface new and strident calls for the restructuring of the public sector. In Europe, the crisis in the countries of the south and the implementation of austerity measures not only forced the reduction of social expenditure, but also had a huge impact on the lives of citizens. Poverty and unemployment increased, inequalities widened, and social achievements were questioned. This then led to greater attention being paid to the role that accounting and improved financial management could play in addressing some of these issues. The call of Hopwood and Tompkins (1984) for researchers to explore the organisational, institutional and social nature of accounting practice thus became more relevant than ever. The rest of this chapter will provide some details regarding the fundamental characteristics of public sector accounting. The debate will be grounded in the examination of the environment in which public sector accounting operates. For this reason, there will be an exploration of the causes of and responsibilities for the public sector crisis, the initiatives that have been undertaken, the heterogeneous challenges that the public sector faces, and how these issues could be addressed.

The nature of public sector accounting

According to Bandy (2011), the traditional techniques of accounting such as recording, measuring and communicating, are the basis for the success of the accounting profession, but within the public sector, they are not sufficient even if they are necessary. The accounting profession has less influence in government than it has in the private sector. Sometimes, in political debates, politicians will observe that they are not accountants, in order to promote their socially responsible image. A key fundamental difference with the private sector is that accounting is much more important for investors and shareholders than it is for voters. Further, accounting information might be very complex for someone who does not have specific knowledge. It is, therefore, a challenge for accounting to provide both comprehensive and comprehensible information to the citizens in a form by which they can evaluate the performance of their government.

Hopwood and Tompkins (1984) argue for the social role of public sector accounting as the public sector is a complex entity which cannot operate in isolation from the wider social, economic, and political environment. They define the three main pillars of public sector accounting: external reporting and accountability, financial planning and control, value for money and performance review. External reporting and accountability information are essential in any decision making and accounting constitutes the basis of that information. Additionally, accounting standards are influenced by organisational and political factors because of the importance that they have. Frequently, institutions within public sectors have conflicting interests regarding standardisation and comparability. With regard to financial planning and control there is a significant interdependency between technical accounting practices and the wider environment of public sector organisations.

The political context of the public sector creates complexities in financial decision making. For example, any change in the political or economic environment will affect cash planning and spending policy. However, periods of uncertainty can be the ideal point of time for technical innovations. With value for money and performance review there must be emphasis on the role of accounting regarding emerging interests in the political rhetoric, as there might be a gap between the accounting mission and the actual accounting practices. In the pursuit of efficiency, the will and commitment of the responsible bodies, as well as the auditing of operations, are highlighted as the most important factors. However, conducting audits within public sector organisations could meet resistance from the political environment. Hopwood and Tompkins (1984) conclude that public sector accounting should not be separated from those social processes, which give rise to the significance of the accounting issues and shape the consequences that accounting developments can have. There are many studies of public sector accounting that do not focus on its technical aspects, but rather examine the wider environment in which the public sector operates. The reason for this is that it is crucial to understand the environment to be able to effectively examine the technical aspects of public sector accounting.

Who is responsible for public sector crisis?

Since 2008, there has been a huge social debate regarding the responsibility for the current public sector crisis. Austerity measures and political changes created a challenging force for existing social institutions and generally for capitalism. Notably in the countries of the European South, there is an intense debate over the reforms that should be made because of the fiscal problems that these countries face. This debate is global. There are extreme voices of neoliberalism that put the blame on governments and citizens, and voices of populism that put the blame on governments and corporations. Are all of them responsible for the crisis?

In capitalism, the banking sector has a crucial role in the function of societies. The great recession of 2008, the greatest since the 1930s, hugely affected the banking sector, especially after the collapse of Lehmann Brothers. Toxic assets emerged, as result of creative accounting, and governments started taking initiatives to rescue failing banks (McDonald and Robinson, 2009). These initiatives included recapitalization, government guarantees to the financial sector and quantitative easing. A total failure of the banking sector would have been disastrous for any national economy and the crisis would inevitably spread to the wider public sector. Banks are vital to the functioning of the economy as they provide finance to both the state and companies. An example of the importance of banks was seen in the UK. In 2009, the assets of UK banks were four times more than UK annual GDP. Consequently, the government decided to rescue the banks, the burden of which came to its citizens in two ways. The first was a direct increase in taxes, for the state to raise more funds, the second was related to substantive cutbacks in public spending, which resulted in a decline in the services that are provided to the citizens (Hodges and Lapsley, 2016).

The rationale of austerity has been at the centre of neoliberal ideology as it is believed that it could lead to reductions of public debts and deficits. There are studies which have argued that the policies of debt reduction can lead to economic growth and that recession could be dealt with through financial conservatism (Reinhart and Rogoff, 2010 and 2011). The positions of Reinhart and Rogoff were challenged by Herndon *et al.* (2013). In countries such as Greece, Spain, and Ireland, huge austerity programs were implemented in collaboration between local governments and institutions like the International Monetary Fund (IMF), European Central Banking (ECB) and the European Commission (EC). These programs imposed significant short-term reductions in public spending. The criticism of these programs is that they overlook any long-term effects that they may have in the economies of these countries.

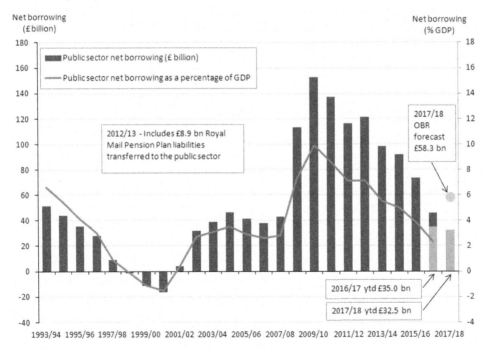

Figure 8.1: Public sector net borrowing (excluding public sector banks) April 1993 to August 2017. *Source*: Office of National Statistics (2017:8)

The effect of the UK government austerity programme for debt reduction on the public sector can be seen in Figure 8.1 from chart in the Office of National Statistics report of 2017. In the financial year ending March 2017 (April 2016 to March 2017), the public sector borrowed £45.7 billion, or 2.3% of gross domestic product (GDP). This was £27.5 billion lower than in the previous full financial year and around one-third of that borrowed in the financial year ending March 2010, when borrowing was £152.5 billion or 9.9% of GDP (ONS, 2017:8). The effects of these debt deficit programme are being felt by public sector service providers. For example, following the government's first comprehensive spending review in 2010, the Avon and Somerset Police Force in response to the austerity programme has made savings of £65m, with 655 fewer police officers. To meet the government austerity targets, it will have to find a further £17m by 2021-22 to balance its budget. Avon and Somerset constabulary has stated "We now face a tipping point. We cannot sustain further funding cuts without extremely serious consequences" (Morris, 2017). Other areas of the public sector face a similar crisis. To help alleviate such problems, KPMG in 2010 proposed an approach which should focus on the long-term rethinking of public services provision and not exclusively on the reduction of fiscal deficits (Hodges and Lapsley, 2016).

In this context, this leads us to ask what is the role of citizens? And do they have any responsibility for the crisis? In Greece for example, some groups claim that society participated in the establishment of a clientelist and unproductive public sector, which undermined the fiscal performance of the country. Globally, there are some voices which argue that huge public spending, through the welfare state, decreased the participation of citizens in political affairs. The eternal responsibility of citizens is grounded in the context of democratic participation. Citizens should be aware of social, political, and economic issues, to develop their critical thinking, behave as responsible citizens and be the guardians of democracy and transparency. Additionally, citizens must constitute a pressure on the state and corporations for more transparency, enhanced accountability, and better use of resources. Steiner *et al.,* (2015) talked about socially responsible citizens who could lead innovation, in periods of crisis, through bottom-up processes. In other words, citizens should be vital assets for the public sector in the efforts of the state to create a democratic, efficient and sustainable public sector.

Public policy

Public policy includes the means through which, the state provides goods and services to the citizens. However, it is a polycentric system of decision making which includes a lot of different stakeholders with different interests and sources of power. Public policy is defined by the constitution or by law and it aims to sustain social order. It is established through political and social processes, so it can have different forms through time and it can express different ideological perspectives. Social policies can be regulatory, distributive, and redistributive and in this way, they set priorities that shape the way in which a state operates. In western societies, social policy has some stable pillars which include health policy, education policy, and legal policy. Public policy includes social policies which have provided fertile ground for the development of the welfare state (Glennerster, 1983). Social policy represents a range of interdisciplinary policies aimed at the development of the quality of life for citizens. As accounting represents the quality of information which is available, it is highly important in social policy, because it is used to support the needs of stakeholders. Thus, in a very complex public sector environment, poor accounting information could constrain any intervention that the stakeholders might attempt.

New Public Management was the main trend that shaped public policies during the 1980s. NPM aimed to improve the involvement of administration in the proper management of the public sector, treat the citizens as 'clients', introduce benchmarking, reduce public spending and control growth, promote privatizations, and establish an international agenda for public sector affairs (Hood, 1991, 1995). Beyond efficiency, NPM also highlighted the role of transparency and accountability as fundamental for good governance. The values of NPM, such as budgets, costing, savings, efficiency, accountability for performance, control systems and productivity, received wide acceptance among Organisation for Economic Co-operation and Development (OECD) countries during the 1980s and the 1990s (Malmose, 2015). Of course, depending on the cultural characteristics of each country, there might be some differences in the implementation of policies. On the other hand, NPM can create social benefits as, according to Pallot (2001), it can it can have positive impact on democratic participation and the decision-making of citizens.

It was crucial for public policy initiatives to focus on the views of citizens. For this reason, an important initiative that aimed to enhance citizens' involvement and participation were the Citizen's Charters at the beginning of the 1990s. This has been a global approach, and, in the context of UK, it tried to combine the ideas of both the left and right. The main goal was to push towards the improvement of public services and to encourage more efficient use of taxpayers' money (Drewry, 2005). The main themes of this initiative were related to the high level of standards, the accessibility and quality of information, the democratization of processes, and value for money. Citizen's Charters attempted to change the public debate of the 1990s in a sense that public expenditure should not be the only means for the policies of a welfare state. In the UK, the next step was to increase citizens' participation in the late 1990s under the government of the Labour party which had succeeded the right-wing agenda. A criticism of Citizen's Charters was that it did not have a constitutional document and it provided a vague framework of principles. In the UK, this resulted in the existence of various sectional charters with merely a consulting role. However, the constant development of European Union and the emphasis on people influenced the mentality of Citizen's Charters towards more humanistic values.

Since the beginning of the century, the role of the Charters has been declining as most of their values have been absorbed by public services, especially by the demands for improved services. Nevertheless, the rationale of the initial Citizen's Charters is considered as an ideal example of citizens' participation as it can combine modernization processes, reforms, and a consumer focus as well as a humanistic approach in both left- and right-wing political contexts.

Pressures to address

The result of the crisis was not only the need for bank recapitalization. The increase in social inequality and concentration of wealth intensified the pressure on public service delivery. Unsurprisingly, since the financial crisis, the pressures have been mounting from varied perspectives. On one hand, the public sector must fulfil its social role and attempt to shorten the inequalities that the crisis has created. On the other hand, the politics of neoliberalism has put immense pressure on the public sector globally due to swelling privatisation. Neoliberalism, which has been a buzzword ever since the 2008 financial crisis both in the developed and developing economies, reshaped the global economy, modes of trading, and financial flows between various governments with concerns on long-term sustainable future.

(i) Neo-liberalism – a modern capitalistic view

The rise of free market capitalism has resulted in a world in which the future will always be more globalised than it was in the past (Bryan and Farrell, 1996). Neoliberalism, according to Jessop (2002), promotes deregulation of markets and institutions throughout the globe under the guise of free market capitalism. These deregulations support privatisation of state-owned public services and push towards a global shift from state welfare to market capitalism, which mirrors a neoliberal belief in the state's failure to deliver public welfare services. Rodrik (2000) notes that international policy makers, mainly the US government and leading international economic organisations, persuaded the global community to soften their political boundaries in order to compete in the global market. Therefore, governments today are competing to earn market confidence and attract trade and capital inflows. Harvey (2007:3) concisely portrays the pervasiveness of this hegemony:

> *Deregulation, privatisation, and the withdrawal of the state from many areas of social provision have been all too common. Almost all governments, from those newly minted after the collapse of the Soviet Union to old-style social democracies and welfare governments such as New Zealand and Sweden, have embraced, sometimes voluntarily and in other instances in response to coercive pressures, some version of neoliberal theory and adjusted at least some policies and practices accordingly… Neoliberalism has, in short, become hegemonic as a mode of discourse.*

8

Noam Chomsky in his popular book *Profit over People*, refers to Neoliberalism as 'capitalism with the gloves off' (1999:7), in which neoliberal policies represent only the interests of the corporations and wealthy investors, who have been given more power than ever before with little or no organised opposition. This has resulted in the exploitation of social and public goals, mostly of developing countries and southern governments, who have less control over the economic outcome of such actions. Most scholars argue that southern governments are reluctant to regulate economic outcomes as they struggle with each other to attract foreign direct investment in this capitalist framework. Supra-national organisations such as the World Trade Organisation (WTO), the World Bank and the IMF promote neo-liberal policies intended to override the existing regulatory frameworks of developing countries, so that they might secure foreign direct investment.

The barriers to free trade are removed through the exploitation of Southern markets by Northern capitalist corporations seeking access to cheaper resources. Kamla *et al.* (2012) note that, in the context of globalisation, powerful global forces and national governments put pressure on less powerful governments, to conform to Western norms and practices. Realistically, most of the emerging economies are compelled to adopt these policies as they are vulnerable to further impoverishment if they resist the change. It is important to ask under what global economic conditions developing countries accept the neo-liberal policies of such institutions. Although this economic system works for developed economies (and in some cases for the interests of a handful of elites), it is important to understand if it works for the general population in an integrated world market. The public sectors of Southern governments are in continuous jeopardy as their public goals are negotiated by a thin spectrum of developed world elites who own the corporations that deliver 'badly needed' goods to a 'target' population (Escobar, 2011). Hence, it is argued that development under the neoliberal regime has become destructive to the Third World, ironically in the name of peoples' interests.

(ii) Declining public sectors and increasing privatisation

The demand for improved and equal public sector services is on the rise, especially in a context of crisis and increased inequality throughout the globe. There is an immense pressure on governments for better utilisation of resources and enhanced provision of public sector services. An efficient and effective public sector will bring multiple benefits as it will contribute to the maintenance of social stability (Hermann, 2015).

As noted earlier in this chapter, most of the reform measures taken by governments since the 2008 financial crisis have been focused on the downsizing of the public sector. Although equal access to healthcare, education, transport and energy has an important role in decreasing social inequalities (Hermann, 2014), little or no attention was paid to the redistributive capabilities of the public sector. Public services, which are used mainly by poor or middle class people, have been taken over by private firms due to neoliberal regime shift. For instance, across the UK, private sector employment has grown faster than public sector employment, which has declined between 2008 and 2014. On the other hand, Southern European governments who have recently opened up their borders to multinational corporations (MNCs) are more vulnerable to both domestic and external shocks under the neoliberal regime.

It is important to note that the labour unions, which play a diminishing role in the private sector, have had a major influence on government policies through their dynamic lobbying efforts. Generally, these unions favour increases in government spending as they personally benefit from expanded programs (Edwards 2010). Since the rise of neoliberal politics and the more recent economic and debt crisis, governments have adopted austerity measures as a mechanism for settling the public sector crisis. Glassner (2010) notes that the severe austerity measures launched by many European governments are based on cuts in social and public sectors. Although mass rallies and demonstrations organised by labour unions in the public sector were more frequent as compared to the private sector in the European countries, such demonstrations have declined tremendously compared to those of the 1970s and 1980s. Citizens of countries like Greece, France, Italy, and Spain now have far less influence on their governments through these organised trade unions, which were previously able to channel powerful protests against such austerity measures. Such settings promote the dissemination of neoliberal politics, as corporations and the private sector dictate wage moderation and hold the power to control the social and employment benefits of the workforce.

It appears that the global public sector will continue to change unless alternative paths of economic, social and political rearrangements are explored. There are voices who claim that inequality cannot be stopped by the policies of privatization and the shrinkage of the public sector that the neo-liberal agenda has imposed. Citizens and taxpayers need to regain control of their governments, which is only possible through the labour unions. It is, however, important to note that some of the public-sector changes are demographic, caused by increasing and ageing populations, while others are political and economic, linked to the opportunities created by technological advancements that are transforming public services. A recent study by the Association of Certified Chartered Accountants (ACCA, 2016) on understanding the changes in the public sector placed economic growth as the top driver of change in the public sector. This is not surprising as it is fundamental for any government to sustain economic growth that would support public services to function effectively.

■ Public private partnership

One way of addressing the growing problems of public sector, it has been argued, is by building a healthy relationship between the public and private sector, known by the popular term Public private partnerships (PPPs). PPPs usually bring together the labour, resources and knowledge of both the public and private sector and although the phenomenon and practice of PPPs has its origins in British and American public policy (Mitchell-Weaver and Manning, 1991), there has been an increasing interest in PPPs in developing countries too. PPPs are used extensively in Western countries, but third world countries have started to experiment with PPP for infrastructure development projects. PPPs have the potential to reduce the burden on strained public resources, and can also provide access to private finance to expand or improve public services. Moreover, PPPs provide an opportunity to rethink existing public service models in a more holistic way.

Though governments worldwide are exploring diversified ways of improving environmental sustainability, PPPs tend to develop a relationship between government and the private sector that continues to explore new and innovative ways to deliver public services. Scholars like Jamali (2004) associate PPPs as an engagement mechanism that will promote direct participation and intervention to an indirect role that increases partnership and assistance. Since many developing countries are often dependent on foreign financial assistance from organisations such as the World Bank, there is an added pressure from the first world to improve the infrastructure and public services delivery which is mostly inspired by the idea of PPPs.

There is a need for a holistic approach from both the government and corporations on the outcome of services to citizens with a long-term sustainable funding of services for an ageing population. An effective state intervention through PPPs could regulate the power relationships between public and private partners. It is important in this regard that governments and private sector organisations devise policies to decentralise their institutions through PPP interventions. Since PPPs tend to bridge the gap between public and private institutions there is also a nagging fear that such interventions could be dominated by the interests of private sector firms, while disregarding the expansion of public institutions.

Therefore, despite their global spread, PPPs also carry risks and can result in failures if not executed properly. There has been a growing debate on the finding uses for the PPP model that best suits its function, as the outcomes from PPPs should promote services for the citizen rather than the organisational unit. It is also important that both public and private parties are involved in joint decision making to further explore and plan the scope of the project. This will allow both parties to interlace their objectives and interests with opportunities to look at problems and solutions from various perspectives.

■ Public sector management initiatives

Due to the introduction of PPPs and the competitive global environment, new initiatives for public sector management have emerged. The importance that PPPs have in modern economies has intensified the pressure on the stakeholders to demonstrate the success of these projects. The co-operation between public and private sector requires specific management and reporting structures that will ensure transparency. It is vital for governments to enhance accountability, so citizens must be made aware of the PPPs' performance, since they aim to maximize social value. As mentioned above, NPM has been the main public management initiative in recent decades and it is illustrative of the economic rationalism which was developed to ensure a more efficient public sector. However, such private sector concepts were not entirely applicable and could not be fully implemented in the public sector. In the public sector, values such as transparency, protection of rights, fairness, and equity must be dominant, instead of profit or return on investment (Bao *et al.*, 2012). Therefore, there was a need for more contemporary initiatives which take these other factors into consideration. In other words, there was need for good governance.

Governance is a wider concept than management. According to Colley *et al.*, (2005), corporate governance is a concept of structures, rules, procedures and mechanisms for the proper steering and controlling of corporations. Public sector governance includes mechanisms, tools, approaches and structures which define the responsibilities of stakeholders in relation to the organisation, and systems for internal control and external accountability. The difference between private and public governance derives from the social nature of the public sector and from the different interests that the various stakeholders have. Mechanisms and tools are included in both forms of governance, but public governance includes the impact of policies on society. For example, the governors of a public organisation often face greater challenges because they have the responsibility to demonstrate to the public that the organisation performs well, in terms of both economic and social performance. At the same time, they must be accountable to the government, but are also subject to pressure from the political aims of the government.

Some of the critics of NPM have argued that it underestimates the political and social processes which shape the public sector. New Public Governance (NPG) was a value-centred initiative which was developed as a continuation of NPM, but it did not have the same focus on private sector mechanisms. NPG attempted to combine the notions of efficiency and effectiveness with the promotion of the larger common good. The aim of NPG was to coordinate all the stakeholders of the public sector by using institutional arrangements to improve policy-making (Almquist *et al.*, 2013). This is a challenging task because stakeholders have different interests and different perceptions of how best to create public value. Therefore, NPG enables governments to create processes which could facilitate the generation of realistic agreements. NPG also has a crucial role in PPPs as it encourages co-operations between the private and public sectors and focuses on enhancing the ability of governments to develop simple or complex programs for the creation of public goods (Bao *et al.*, 2012). According to Klijn (2012), the main difference between NPM and NPG is that NPM is more hierarchical and it is based on contractual relationships, while NPG recognises the significance of interdependent horizontal relationships and emphasises the synergies that can be created among the stakeholders. Another difference of these initiatives is related to the accounting aims. NPM aims to minimize the cost by managing the outputs, while NPG aims to provide a more complete and consolidated accounting framework. NPG introduces the concept of Whole of Government Accounting (WGA) which is a part of accrual accounting and has had wide international adoption. It places emphasis on decentralization and for this reason, it is a multi-organisational framework of accounting (Almquist *et al.*, 2013).

One of the main concepts of public management is accountability. In NPM, accountability is essential as it ensures the quality of financial information and the quality of management processes in the public sector in the pursuit of efficiency (Wiesel and Modell, 2014). Governance needs a broader definition of accountability which could also examine the provision of services and the impact of policies on society. Additionally, governance takes more stakeholders into consideration, therefore these stakeholders must be accountable for their actions. Accountability represents how governance flows through the hierarchy of public sector and informs citizens regarding the maximization or not of social value. Hodges (2012) identified two forms of accountability: vertical and horizontal.

- Vertical accountability is related to the legal structures of public sector (how accountability flows from institutions to citizens).

- Horizontal accountability refers to the moral and social obligations that the organisations have towards the stakeholders (how different organizations perceive accountability).

However, it is not that straightforward as most developing countries' citizens have low levels of confidence in horizontal mechanisms alongside dissatisfaction with the efficiency of vertical forms of accountability, because of the individual citizen's implementation of electoral choice and the collective effort of pressure by civil society organisations (Goetz and Jenkins, 2004).

Efforts have been made to rectify problems of horizontal and vertical accountability, but since accountability is related to the demand for good performance, to answerability and transparency, there can be various forms of accountability mechanisms such as disclosure statements, annual reports, the requirement for internal or external audit, and the right of the public to information (Bandy, 2011). Thus, the objectives of accountability are very complex in the public sector. In healthcare for example, good performance includes the need for a financially sustainable hospital, but the ultimate target is the ability to provide high quality services. So, hospitals are first of all, accountable for the services that they provide and then for their economic results. However, this is extremely challenging since the health sector is operating with human lives and there is not a perfect equilibrium for the use of economic resources. In this context, the health organisations should demonstrate to the public that the resources are used efficiently, but also that the organisation is fulfilling its social role.

Typically, accountability flows towards the higher echelons of hierarchy and is concerned with the delegation of power from principals to agents and with the ways in which the relationship between them will be defined. Within the public sector, it is not clear who is the principal and who is the agent, because of the existence of citizens, politicians, and managers. Mulgan (2000) defines two relationships of accountability. One is between the citizens as principals and the politicians as agents. In the second, the politicians are the principals and the managers of public organisations are the agents. Consequently, public accountability is more complex than accountability in private sector companies, and additionally there are various heterogeneous interests and stakeholders which can influence public accountability. For this reason, very often we have the distinction between political and managerial accountability. Political accountability includes the ways in which politicians make themselves accountable to the citizens, in order for the citizens to see whether they have fulfilled their promises. Managerial accountability is related to the ways in which managers are accountable to the politicians. This complexity in public accountability illustrates a potential conflict between these two types of accountability as politicians might try to manipulate managers in a way that could help them exploit a situation for political purposes (Chang, 2015). For instance, in the case of public education or health institutions, governments (in a neo-liberal society) implement austerity measures that (in most cases) are against the interests and the will of both the managers and the general public. So, there might be a principal-agent problem as politicians want to pursue agendas which conflict with those of the managers of public sector organisations.

In accounting, financial reporting is the most widespread means of accountability, and this is the same for managerial accountability within public sector. Political accountability can be identified in any form of political discourses (newspapers, interviews, parliamentary debates etc.). In private sector, investors are the main users of financial information. In public sector the users of financial information can be a huge group of heterogeneous stakeholders such as investors, shareholders, lenders, creditors, employees, consumers of services, interest groups, auditors, government, the media and voters (Bandy, 2011). It is evident that each group has different interests and will focus on different elements of accountability and, thus, the conduct of public accountability is a very complex challenge. The objective of public sector financial reporting, apart from providing information to the users, is also to enable the better allocation of resources, and to contribute to political and social decision-making. Regarding specific financial statements, the statement of financial position is different from the typical assets minus liabilities statement of the private sector. In the public sector, ownership interest can be considered as the value of the organisation to the public. The income statement is referred to as income and expenditure statement and it reflects the extent to which, an organisation will need extra funding from taxes, or whether it has a surplus for the year. In other words, it can show the creation of deficits in public sector organisations. Organisations in the public sector operate as subsidiaries of a group. For this reason, the financial reports of each organisation are consolidated to the whole government accounts. Finally, the establishment of a full framework of public sector accounting standards is essential for reliability and comparability to be ensured.

The social role of public governance highlights its crucial position in the contemporary, increasingly complex, public sector. It can increase transparency and accountability, and improve democratic legitimacy and performance simultaneously. It can be considered as an all-around initiative compared to NPM and it can include perspectives which will not only make the public sector more efficient but also can be used for the enhancement of the welfare state. Additionally, governance must ensure that all citizens will have the same rights over the use of resources and contribute to the enhancement of social equality. On the other hand, regardless of the framework of governance, those who govern must be accountable for their actions and accountability is a core value for democratic governance. Accounting mechanisms should be very comprehensive and include information which would be useful for politicians, service users and other stakeholders. This information should not only be related to outputs and services but, it should also focus on the impacts that organisational processes might create (Guthrie *et al.*, 1999). Haque (2006) also argued that, for accountability to be enhanced, financial information must be understandable, comparable, timely, reliable, complete, and accessible to citizens. Thus, it can constitute a tool in the hands of the citizens when examining whether political promises have been fulfilled, and if taxpayers' money has been used in the best possible way.

The role of local governments

The modern public sector is a very complex entity and is very important for the economy, and for this reason, citizens demand greater accountability and efficiency from their governments. Because of the complexity of their public sectors, governments have directed increasing attention to accounting systems as they can provide reliable information for more efficient management of public sector organisations. Decentralization and the enhancement of local government accounting has been the answer to these expectations. The importance of local governments has been highlighted, as central governments undertake big projects, but local governments are responsible for the implementation of policies that can have significant impact on the daily life of citizens. In other words, local governments can create fertile ground for the use of accounting within a micro-management context, which can improve the performance of public sector in a long run (Gomes and Sargiacomo, 2013). However, sometimes there can be a decoupling between local and central governments. Both might have differing interests and might want to achieve different goals. This can cause problems for the management and performance of organisations. In these circumstance, the role of accounting is to provide reliable tools and information which will ensure transparency, accountability, efficiency and effectiveness.

Summary

This chapter has analysed the development of public sector accounting which has happened in line with the growth of the public sector and the influence of the wider environment in which it has operated. Initially, the public sector was the instrument for the development of the welfare state and the main aim was to provide services to citizens. Therefore, the public sector could not have exactly the same managerial tools as the private sector. Economic uncertainty and the complexity of the growing global environment has contributed to the public debate of the need for public sector restructuring. The result of this debate was the emergence of New Public Management during the 1980s, which aimed to improve efficiency and implementation of private sector accounting and managerial tools. This was the main initiative that shaped public policy but not the only one. Initiatives such as Citizen's Charters and New Public Governance attempted to provide a more balanced approach compared to the right-wing oriented NPM.

The turning point for many public sectors across Europe was the economic crisis of 2008 which led to huge pressure for privatisation of some public services and public sector shrinking. This period also led to public expenses being decreased in favour of bank recapitalisation. In this context, the role of accounting has been even more important as it can provide information which will ensure the democratic use of funds and create a context of governance and accountability, which will not only improve efficiency, but also transparency and democratic participation. Regarding democratic participation, the role of citizens has been highlighted, as in democracies they are the only ones who can bring change.

Accounting must be in a comprehensive and understandable language to provide a useful tool to citizens seeking accountability and equity. It is evident that the technical aspects of accounting must be examined at the general social level. The public sector is a constantly changing environment which encompasses many stakeholders with different interests. Thus, any change in accounting practice is influenced by perspectives which do not emerge from economic rationalistic aims.

8

Discussion questions

1   Do you think the public sector faces more scrutiny for being accountable to their citizens as compared to the private sector? For instance, the ownership interest of the public sector is considered a value of the organisation to the public. How does this impact on the social role of public governance?

2   Besides the accountability mechanisms highlighted in the chapter, what additional measures could be used to improve the accountability and governance of the public sector?

3 In your opinion, how successful has New Public Management been in shaping public policies?

4 In your opinion, what has contributed towards the declining public sector in most parts of the world? Is it the growing neoliberal politics? Or is it the austerity measures taken by the governments to manage their budget deficit? Or is it the capitalist framework itself?

References and further reading

ACCA (2016), 50 drivers of change in the public sector, http://www.accaglobal.com/content/dam/ACCA_Global/Technical/Future/drivers-of-change-in-the-public-sector.pdf, accessed 30 May 2017.

Almquist, R., Grossi, G., van Helden, J. and Reichard, C. (2013) Public sector governance and accountability, *Critical Perspectives on Accounting*, **24**(7-8), 479-487.

Bandy, G. (2011) *Financial Management and Accounting in the Public Sector*. Oxford: Routledge.

Bao, G., Wang, X., Larsen, G. and Morgan, D. (2012) Beyond New Public Governance: a value-based global framework for performance management, governance and leadership, *Administration and Society*, **45**(4), 443-467.

Bovens, M. (2005). Public accountability, in: Ferlie, E., Lynn, L.E. and Pollitt, C. (eds.) *The Oxford Handbook of Public Management*. Oxford: Oxford University Press, 182–208.

Bryan, L. and Farrell, D. (1996) *Market Unbound: Unleashing global capitalism*. John Wiley and Sons.

Chang, L. (2015) Accountability, rhetoric, and political interests: twists and turns of NHS performance measurements, *Financial Accountability and Management*, **31**(1), 41-68.

Colley, J.L., Doyle, J.L., Logan, G.W. and Stettinius, W. (2004) *What is Corporate Governance?* New York: McGraw-Hill.

Chomsky, N. (1999) *Profit over People: Neoliberalism and global order*. Seven Stories Press.

Drewry, G. (2005) Citizen's Charters. Service quality chameleons, *Public Management Review*, **7**(3), 321-340.

Edwards, C. (2010) Public-sector unions. *Benefits*, **17**(10.47), 1-68.

Escobar, A. (2011) *Encountering Development: The making and unmaking of the Third World*. Princeton University Press.

Harvey, D. (2007) *A Brief History of Neoliberalism*. Oxford University Press, USA.

Glassner, V. (2010) The public sector in the crisis, ETUI Working Paper No 2010.07, Brussels: ETUI.

Glennerster, H. (1983) *The Future of the Welfare State: Remaking social policy*. London: Heinemann.

Goetz, A.M. and Jenkins, R. (2004). *Reinventing Accountability: Making Democracy Work for Human Development*. Basingstoke, UK: Palgrave.

Gomes, D. and Sargiacomo, M. (2013) Accounting and accountability in local government: An introduction, *Accounting History*, **18**(4), 439-446.

Graham, D., and Woods, N. (2006) Making corporate self-regulation effective in developing countries, *World Development*, **34**(5), 868-883.

Guthrie, J., Olson, O. and Humphrey, C. (1999) Debating developments in new public financial management: the limits of global theorising and some new ways forward, *Financial Accountability and Management*, **15**(3/4): 209–228.

Haque, M. S. (2006) Modernising government: The way forward—An analysis, *International Review of Administrative Sciences*, **72**, 319-325.

Harvey, D. (2007) *A Brief History of Neoliberalism*. Oxford University Press, USA

Hermann, C. (2014) The role of public sector in combating inequality, *International Journal of Labour Research*, **6**(1), 113-158.

Hermann, C. (2015) Crisis and social policy in Europe, *Global Social Policy*, **15**(1), 82-85.

Hodges, R. (2012) Joined-up government and the challenge to accounting and accountability researchers, *Financial Accountability and Management*, **28**(1), 26-51.

Hodges, R. and Lapsley, I. (2016) A private sector failure, a public sector crisis – reflections on the great recession, *Financial Accountability and Management*, **32**(3), 265-280.

Hood, C. (1991) A public management for all seasons?, *Public Administration*, 69, 3-19.

Hood, C. (1995) The New Public Management in the 1980s: Variation on a theme, *Accounting, Organizations and Society*, **20**, 93-109.

Hopwood, A. and Tompkins, C. (1984) *Issues in Public Sector Accounting*. Oxford: Philip Allan Publishers Limited.

Jamali, D. (2004) Success and failure mechanisms of public private partnerships (PPPs) in developing countries: Insights from the Lebanese context, *International Journal of Public Sector Management*, **17**(5), 414-430.

Jenkins, R. and Goetz, A.M. (1999). Accounts and accountability: theoretical implications of the right-to-information movement in India. *Third World Quarterly*, **20**(3), 603-622.

Jessop, B. (2002) Liberalism, neoliberalism, and urban governance: A state–theoretical perspective, *Antipode*, **34**(3), 452-472.

Jones, R. and Pendlebury, M. (2010) *Public Sector Accounting*. Harlow: Pearson Education Limited.

Kamla, R., Gallhofer, S., and Haslam, J. (2012) Understanding Syrian accountants' perceptions of, and attitudes towards, social accounting, *Accounting, Auditing and Accountability Journal*, **25**(7), 1170-1205.

Klijn, E.H. (2012) New public management and governance: a comparison, In: Levi-Faur D, (ed.), *Oxford Handbook of Governance*. Oxford: Oxford University Press.

Malmmose, M. (2015) Management accounting versus medical profession discourse: Hegemony in a public health care debate – A case from Denmark, *Critical Perspectives on Accounting*, **27**, 144-159.

8

McDonald, L. and P. Robinson (2009) *A Colossal Failure of Common Sense: The Incredible Inside Story of the Collapse of Lehman Brothers*. London: Ebury Publishing.

Mitchell-Weaver, C., and Manning, B. (1991) Public-private partnerships in third world development: A conceptual overview. *Studies in Comparative International Development*, **26**(4), 45-67.

Morris, S. (2017) Police cuts: force says it would struggle to respond to terror attack, *The Guardian*, Sept 19, https://www.theguardian.com/uk-news/2017/sep/19/police-cuts-avon-somerset-force-struggle-respond-terror-attack

Mulgan, R. (2003) *Holding Power to Account. Accountability in modern democracies*. New York: Palgrave Macmillan.

Office of National Statistics (2017) Public Sector Finances, report of 2017, available at: https://www.ons.gov.uk/economy/governmentpublicsectorandtaxes/publicsectorfinance/bulletins/publicsectorfinances/september2017.

Oxfam (2015) An Economy for the 99%: It's time to build a human economy that benefits everyone, not just the privileged few, Available at: http://policy-practice.oxfam.org.uk/publications/an-economy-for-the-99-its-time-to-build-a-human-economy-that-benefits-everyone-620170.

Pallot, J. (1992) Elements of a theoretical framework for public sector accounting, *Accounting, Auditing and Accountability Journal*, **5**(1), 38-59.

Pallot, J. (2001) Transparency in local government: Antipodean initiatives, *The European Accounting Review*, **10**(3), 645-660.

Petras, J. (1999) Globalization: A critical analysis, *Journal of Contemporary Asia*, **29**(1), 3-37.

Pierson, C. (1998) *Beyond the Welfare State? A new political economy of welfare*. Penn State Press.

Reinhart, C. M. and K. S. Rogoff (2010) Growth in a time of debt, *American Economic Review*, **100**(2), 573–578.

Reinhart, C. M. and K. S. Rogoff (2011) A decade of debt, Discussion Paper No. 8310 (Centre for Economic Policy Research).

Rodrik, D. (2000) How far will international economic integration go?, *Journal of Economic Perspectives*, **14**(1), 177-186.

Shaoul, J., Stafford, A. and Stapleton, P. (2012) Accountability and corporate governance of public private partnerships, *Critical Perspectives on Accounting*, **23**, 213-229.

Siltala, J. (2013) New Public Management: The evidence-based worst practice?, *Administration and Society*, **45** (4), 468-493.

Steiner, G., Risopoulos, F. and Mulej, M. (2015) Social responsibility and citizen-driven innovation in sustainably mastering global socio-economic crises, *Systems Research and Behavioral Science*, **32**, 160-167.

Wiesel, F. and Modell, S. (2014) From New Public Management to New Public Governance? Hybridization and implications for public sector consumerism, *Financial Accountability and Management*, **30**(2), 175-205.

9 Social Accounting and Third Sector Organisations

Stelios Kotsias, Mercy Denedo, Anees Farrukh, and Vasileios Milios

Introduction

In recent years, much attention has been paid to the roles and the responsibilities of not-for-profit or charitable organisations. These mission-based entities seek social impact rather than profitability for shareholders and comprise what is known as the third sector (TS) of economic activity (Lindsay *et al.*, 2014). Even though the origins of third sector organisations (TSOs) are associated with the birth of the big cities and the industrial revolution in the UK (Emmanuel, 2014), focus on these socially-driven entities and their performance has increased over recent years, primarily due to the alleged failure of not-for-profit organisations to efficiently deploy financially sustainable services and achieve associated programmatic goals.

Like public sector entities, TSOs are under pressure to be accountable for delivering value added services to their constituents. However, the way TSOs are held accountable is different; they are expected to manage a 'double bottom line,' in that they must deliver a measurable and meaningful social impact for their beneficiaries, while also responsibly and transparently accounting for the financial resources entrusted to them by their donors (The Scottish Government, 2011). The TS accounts for a substantial part of many countries' economies. In England and Wales, for example, the TS annual income is estimated at £75 billion, which renders it vulnerable to fraudulent activities and potential misuse of financial resources. Third sector trustees therefore have a duty to manage and protect their organisation's financial resources responsibly; ensure that funds are accurately accounted for and to ensure delivery of their mission as providers of social care and welfare to those in need.

This, however, is not always enacted and has attracted considerable media attention and negative perceptions of TS service social accountability. Indeed, following some recent TS scandals, (such as the Kids Company[1] which collapsed in 2015 triggering a financial and child abuse investigation, Rotherham Children's Services who were accused of a lack of social care and child abuse, and the Cup Trust tax avoidance[2] scandal), the Charities Commission[3] reported "our trust in the third sector has hit an all-time low". This has led to more robust reporting; governance and accountability structures being demanded within this sector.

After introducing the TS in more detail and discussing its nature and purpose in society, this chapter will define what accountability means in this arena and will investigate TSO accountability through three key lenses: reporting frameworks, the 'not-for-profit starvation cycle' and TSO governance. The reporting framework applied by TSOs focuses on the illustration of a not-for-profit organisation's sources and uses of funds, but it fails to highlight how activities performed by the organisation create measurable and meaningful social impact for program beneficiaries. With regard to the 'not-for-profit starvation cycle', donors expect charities to deliver more with less and tend to penalise those charities with high overhead costs. This often results in the delivery of fewer services and an undermining of the organisation's ability to create meaningful and measurable impact (Bedsworth *et al.*, 2008). The manner in which the organisation is governed has a direct impact on its ability to achieve financial and social objectives. Multiple governance methods exist in this sector, which is plagued by poor management, weak control over decision-making and the need to satisfy the interests and expectations of multiple constituencies (Caers *et al.*, 2006). This culminates in agency problems and accountability failures as well as the loss of organisational legitimacy and the erosion of financial support. (Cordery *et al.*, 2017). Following this the chapter will discuss the three forms of accountability typically found in TSOs: upward, downward and holistic. The chapter ends with important remarks, conclusions and critical takeaways.

The nature and purpose of third sector organisations

Using a broad definition, the United Nations (UN) defines the 'civil society' as the 'third' sector (TS) in terms of economic activity, placing it alongside the first and second sectors, or the public and private sectors respectively. Third Sector Organisations (TSOs) are unique in that they do not aim for profit and profit distribution; rather they are self-governed, driven and measured by their social

---

1 https://www.theguardian.com/uk-news/2015/aug/21/kids-company-faces-investigation-over-financial-collapse

2 http://www.thirdsector.co.uk/commission-easily-detected-cup-trust-scandal/governance/article/1184746

3 http://www.managementtoday.co.uk/why-weve-lost-faith-charities/reputation-matters/article/1369094#vKxPBKb7HgYRsTyL.99

impact, and fuelled primarily through gifts of time, insight and capital (Kelly, 2007; Lindsay, 2013). In fact, unlike first and second sector organisations, many consider TSOs to manage a double bottom line (DBL), in that while the achievement of fiscal goals is, of course, essential to the organisation's viability, advancement in its mission is the primary objective.

For these reasons, such organisations are defined as the 'voluntary', or the 'independent' or the 'not-for-profit' sector. Civil society rests upon the community and civic engagement.

> *Civic engagement means working to make a difference in the civic life of our communities and developing the combination of knowledge, skills, values and motivation to make that difference. It means promoting the quality of life in a community, through both political and non-political processes.*
> (New York Times, 2000).

Third sector organisations, therefore have a strong social orientation. An example of which is that of the Gavi-Vaccine Alliance (GVA). The mission of the GVA is to "sav(e) children's lives and protect people's health by improving the availability of vaccines in lower-income countries". GVA is a charity that was launched in 1999 with the mission of immunizing children in poor countries and is funded both by the public and private sources. Civil society organisations play a key role in advancing GVA's vision and mission; and working in partnership with governments in poor countries, they deliver up to 65% of immunization services, helping populations in remote areas and minorities gain access to vaccines.

In general, TSOs aim for sustainable social growth and the advancement of citizens' well-being; and, rather than distributing their profits to shareholders, they reinvest them in pursuit of their mission. This sector consists of community groups, voluntary organisations, charities, social enterprises, co-operatives and individual volunteers, business forums, faith-based associations, labour unions, philanthropic foundations and think tanks. The main sources of funding for TSOs are voluntary donations from gifts-in-kind and financial contributions, grants from government agencies, membership dues, income from fundraising events, sponsorships, donated goods, as well as income from investment activities in the form of dividends, interest and rent (The Charity Commission – GOV.UK; see also Emmanuel, 2014).

The importance of TSOs in the modern economy

The size, composition and scope of TSOs varies across countries and regions. In terms of size, the third sector is largest in Western Europe and in the United States, while it is much smaller in Latin America and in Central and Eastern Europe, with cultural, religious, economic and prevailing political structures driving these differences (Lester *et al.*, 1999). The demand for a social safety net, especially in Northern European countries, has driven civil society organisations to engage mainly with welfare services, while in the US and Japan, the difficulties faced by the middle class in terms of accessing health care and educational services has led not-for-profit organisations to concentrate mainly on health, education and humanitarian services. Income inequalities in Latin American countries drove the activity of not-for-profit organisations toward education and aid support (Lester *et al.*, 1999), while in Central and Eastern European countries, the collapse of the communist regimes and the quest for less state governance and increased self-reliance drove the development of civil associations in cultural, environmental and recreational activities (Bryun, 2000; Lester *et al.*, 1999). The size and scope of the UK's third sector is laid out in Figure 9.1.

Area	Number of organisations	% of total in England		Organisations per 1,000 people
North East	4,492	3.4%		1.7
North West	13,203	9.9%		1.8
Yorkshire and the Humber	10,309	7.7%		1.9
West Midlands	11,525	8.6%		2
East Midlands	10,714	8.0%		2.3
East of England	16,652	12.5%		2.7
London	24,238	18.2%		2.8
South East	24,858	18.6%		2.8
South West	17,389	13.0%		3.2
		% of total		
Scotland	19,215	11.6%		3.6
Northern Ireland	6,126	3.7%		3.3
England	133,380	80.4%		2.4
Wales	7,080	4.3%		2.3
Total in the UK	**165,801**	**100%**		**2.5**

Figure 9.1: Distribution of voluntary organisations by area, 2014/15.

Source: NCVO UK Civil Society Almanac 2017

Over the past 30 years, the importance and influence of civil society in economic and social activity has increased (Costa *et al.*, 2014). In Scotland, for example the third sector accounted for £4.9 billion of the country's income (see Figure 9.2). The main sources of income for this sector include: donations and earned income from the general public; contracts and grants from the public sector; grants from grant-making trusts; and investment income.

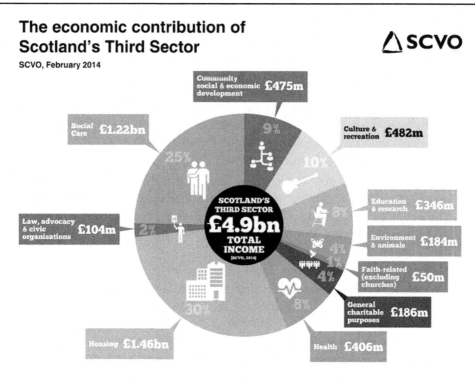

The economic contribution of Scotland's Third Sector

SCVO, February 2014

△SCVO

Community social & economic development £475m

Social Care £1.22bn

Culture & recreation £482m

SCOTLAND'S THIRD SECTOR £4.9bn TOTAL INCOME [SCVO, 2014]

Education & research £346m

Law, advocacy & civic organisations £104m

Environment & animals £184m

Faith-related (excluding churches) £50m

General charitable purposes £186m

Housing £1.46bn

Health £406m

25% 9% 10% 8% 2% 4% 1% 4% 30% 8%

NB: Turnover of Scottish third sector charities based on SCVO classifications and using a sub-set of 2012/2013 charity income data from OSCR.

Figure 9.2: Third sector turnover. *Source*: http://www.scvo.org.uk/

According to the Charity Commission in England and Wales, the number of voluntary organisations in 2017 was 167,027. The total income raised was £74.27bn, with approximately £62bn spent on charitable causes, £3bn generated in voluntary income, £3.5bn used in trading activities and £0.8bn spent to meet governance standards. The sector employed more than 1.5 million paid staff while more than 3.5 million worked as volunteers. In Scotland, there were 23,700 registered charities, meaning that there are 3.4 charities per 1,000 people, the most among UK nations. According to the Scottish Regulator, more than eight out of ten households in Scotland benefited from charitable programs in 2015, while nine out of ten households consistently donated. In Scotland, the sector employs 138,000 paid-staff, while volunteers account for 1,300,000 (Scottish Charity Regulation - OSCR).

Aiming to accomplish the Millennium Development Goals[4], the 2005 UN World Summit Outcome emphasized the importance of democratic governance and efficient public administration in developing countries. Reforming the

4 The Millennium Development Goals aim to eradicate extreme hunger and poverty, achieve universal primary education, promote gender equality and empower women, reduce child mortality, improve maternal health, combat HIV/AIDS, malaria and other diseases, ensure environmental sustainability, develop a global partnership for development. These goals were updated in 2015 but maintain the same social orientation. (See: www.unmillenniumproject.org)

governance systems and redefining the role of the state in economic activity by limiting governmental intervention in selected sectors have been key drivers in the efficient design and implementation of development and financial aid programs. As part of this reformation process, the TSOs have played a substantial role both at local and international levels in promoting democratic governance and the active participation of individuals in developing countries (Cheema, 2010). Indeed, the TS has worked in collaboration with key public sector organisations in the determination and delivery of essential social services, the reason for which is presented next.

Beginning with new public management (NPM) reforms, the welfare social model, as it has predominantly developed in Europe, has been challenged over the public sector's ability to design and efficiently deploy financially sustainable social services, especially under conditions of economic austerity.

> *These are uniquely challenging times with a fragile world economy, (with) sustained pressure on family budgets ... Yet in such times, the power of public services to improve people's quality of life and enhance their opportunities is especially important ... To maintain the quality of public services, we need to do things smarter and better. The financial context and demographic trends are such that incremental improvements in public services are no longer adequate. Fundamental reform is essential ... public services are built around people and communities, public sector organisations work together effectively to achieve outcomes, prioritizing prevention, improved performance and cost reduction, reducing inequalities and promoting equality.* (The Scottish Government, 2011:2-3)

The challenges imposed on the public sector for improved delivery at a lower cost has led successive governments in the developed economies to acknowledge the important role of TSOs in delivering social services (Kelly, 2007). Capacity for innovation and engagement with local communities, as well as the ability to serve citizens facing more complex problems, seem to create the point of differentiation for TSOs in delivering social services in partnership with public sector organisations. In the UK, the relationship between the state and the TS has been redefined with the development of more social services, including welfare benefits, health care, employability and others, being assigned to TSOs (Lindsay *et al.*, 2013:195).

Civil society is "visualized today as a decentralized, voluntary, self-regulating system of civil associations based on a democratic and moral order" (Bryun, 2000:8), having a direct impact not only on the shrinking public sector but also on the private sector and the behaviour and operations of competitive markets. This impact can be realized in several ways, including improving labour skills and the quality of the workforce, creating job opportunities, promoting trust, innovation and entrepreneurship, inducing a new ethos in commercial activities and influencing consumers' preferences (Westall, 2009:18). The fact that the importance and weight of civil society have increased has put charities and TSOs under increasing public scrutiny.

No matter if an organisation is private, public or not-for-profit, it should manage its resources efficiently and transparently. Like public and private sectors, TSOs are under pressure to deliver outcomes effectively and to hold management accountable for serving public purposes and moral objectives. Effective governance codes aim to encourage TSOs to adopt practices that will help them become more efficient in delivering services, creating value for those they serve and being transparent in the sources and the uses of donations utilized to accomplish their objectives (Cabral de Avila and Bertero, 2016). This leads us to consider TS reporting practices and governance challenges.

Reporting practices and governing challenges in third sector organisations

Every charity registered with the Charity Commission for England and Wales or the Scottish Charity Regulator (OSCR), is expected to produce annual reports and accounts that transparently demonstrate the sources and uses of funds. The UK Accounting Standards Board (ASB) regulates financial reporting practices for charities, and it supports the application of reporting standards by issuing Statements of Recommended Practices (SORPs). Financial accounts are prepared on the basis of accrual accounting, which means that charities report income and expenditures when activities take place, rather than when cash is received or spent (see ASB, 2005).

For charities with an annual gross income of £100,000 or more, the statement of accounts incorporates a statement of financial activities, which shows the total incoming resources and spending activities, the balance sheet, the cash flow statement, the notes to the accounts and an annual report. For charities with an annual net income of £500,000 or more or an aggregate value of assets that exceed £2.8 million, the statement of accounts (statements of financial activities, balance sheet, statement of cash flows and notes to the accounts) must be audited. The auditor's statement offers an opinion on whether the statement of accounts complies with the regulations and whether it offers a true and fair view of the financial health of the charity. If no requirement for an audited statement of accounts exists, an independent chartered accountant should examine audited financial accounts. For charities with less than £100,000, the statement of accounts incorporates a receipt and payment account, a statement of balances of accounts, notes to the accounts and the trustees' annual report that compares actual activities against planned activities for the year end (see ASB, 2005, Act 2005).

In the UK, the financial accounts prepared by small charities tend not to meet the minimum reporting standards. Larger charities have financial reports that meet regulatory standards and that are regularly examined or audited by independent bodies. These provide an account of the activities that charities perform for public benefit within the fiscal year. However, despite the reporting practices

9

laid out above, many TS organisations fail to make apparent and disclose evidence on how the activities performed made a difference to their beneficiaries (Charity Commission, 2017). Indeed, a review of many TS organisation annual reports give the impression that charitable organisations comprise a sector characterised by poor management, few efficiency measures and an absence of both professionalism and effective accounting practices that would enhance accountability and transparency (Cabral de Avila and Bertero, 2016). TSOs are mission and value driven organisations; their existence and funding are based on relationships built upon trust and in association with donors who will respond negatively when organisational resources are spent on salaries and administrative expenses. Thus, effective reporting is essential to maintain donor confidence.

The United Way of America, the largest collective recipient of charitable donations, fought a battle to preserve its reputation when it was revealed that donations were distributed to other TSOs without any assessment of the output or contribution offered to their beneficiaries. Its reputation was further damaged when it was also disclosed that its executive management received lucrative salaries and other benefits at the expense of its employees and programs. Donors stopped considering the United Way as trustworthy; and thus, they curbed or reduced their donations. To rebuild trust with donors, the United Way appointed a new CEO and revised its corporate governance procedures, it hired independent companies to review its accounting practices and executive reimbursement policy. As a result, it became more transparent, accountable and reduced its overhead costs, while in 2012, Forbes listed it in its 'Five All Star Charities' (Sontag, 1992; Barret, 2006; see also United Way, 2012).

The non-for-profit starvation cycle

Donors tend to criticize overhead spending and reward charities with minimal overhead costs. The percentage of TSO's overhead expenses that funds administrative costs, including executive director and CEO salaries, training, planning and evaluation investments, as well as support for fundraising activities, has been considered by donors as a key indicator of how effectively a TSO uses the cash raised from donations. Poor accountability and control are attributed to higher overhead costs, as was illustrated in the United Way of America case (Bedsworth *et al.*, 2008).

The validity of using solely financial measurements in evaluating the performance of TSOs in delivering their objectives has been challenged on several fronts. With two open letters sent to donors and to not-for-profit organisations, America's three leading sources of information on TSOs alerted the public that the lack of investment in indirect activities reduces the ability of TSOs to effectively deliver their social objectives (see GuideStar *et al.*, 2013, 2014). GuideStar *et al.*, argue that underinvestment in infrastructure may result in lower operating standards, creating a system that serves fewer beneficiaries by sustaining a smaller network that collects fewer grants because they have not invested in properly supporting or marketing the organisation and its mission. The authors of the letter argue that:

> *in fact, many charities should spend more on overhead. Overhead costs include important investments charities make to improve their work: investments in training, planning, evaluation, and internal systems — as well as their efforts to raise money so they can operate their programs. These expenses allow a charity to sustain itself (the way a family has to pay the electric bill) or to improve itself (the way a family might invest in college tuition).* (GuideStar *et al.*, 2013, 2014)

The not-for-profit starvation cycle is the term used to describe a vicious cycle of persistent underfunding of overhead functions, with the outcome being donors' unrealistic expectations of civil organisations to deliver more with less. This predictable cycle ignores the fact that some overhead expenses (which on average are approximately 10%-15% of total revenues) are necessary and good for the organisation and should, in fact, be seen as an investment in effective program delivery. Many times, allowances are not enough to cover administrative expenses. With an actual overhead spending rate ranging from 17% to 35%, not-for-profit organisations tend to understate indirect expenditures with quite a few charities not reporting fundraising costs, management and general expenses (Goggins *et al.*, 2009).

This is not to say, however, that effective management of overhead has no role in TSO accountability, as the overhead ratio can help identify instances of fraud and mismanagement of funds. In most cases, however, the authors argue, "focusing on overhead without considering other critical dimensions of a charity's financial and organisational performance can do more damage than good" (see GuideStar *et al.*, 2013, 2014).

Governing practices in third sector organisations

9

The pressure exercised by funding institutions, including government agencies, donors and foundations on TSOs to conform to the expectations for lower overhead expenses indicates conflicts of interest between principals and agents. This principal-agent relationship may concern the interaction between trustees and managers or the interaction between donors and trustees. Agents have been assigned the responsibility of managing transparency and the effective management of funds that civil organisations raise. Considered from an agency theory perspective, the prioritization of financial metrics in measuring performance indicates the effort of principals-donors to keep agent-managers/trustees accountable for meeting the mission and scope of the TSO. Financial metrics employed for making the use of donations transparent and enhancing the trust of donors also help TSOs raise and use funds. However, civil society organisations are different from business corporations since they lack the shareholder accountability mechanisms that would hold managers accountable for their actions. Furthermore, TSOs lack profitability objectives, as they do not aim for profit distribution. Their scope and objectives are more complex; they engage with a wider number of stakeholders; and therefore, it is difficult to measure performance output accurately. As a result, in TSOs, agency conflicts may become more acute in relation to profit-seeking entities (Caers *et al.*, 2006). The American Red Cross is an indicative case.

> *The American Red Cross belongs to the American people. The past few weeks have been very challenging for the extraordinarily hardworking and dedicated volunteers, employees and Board members of the American Red Cross. At the end of last year ... a Congressional inquiry regarding several aspects of the governance (was initiated). ... expressing concerns about our Board size, participation and independence, our mission and our organisational culture. What has been difficult for so many of our volunteers who selflessly volunteer their time, energy, money and blood has been the steady stream of very negative media attention about the Red Cross ... something usually reserved for evidence of fraud or criminal malfeasance. This is certainly not the case. We fully support taking any measure that improves how we deliver our vital services and our governance.* (Dan Pallota, 2015)

In profit-seeking entities, corporate governance principles aim to improve relationships and foster fewer conflicts between principal-shareholders and agent-managers. In the private sector, greater need for corporate governance is the result of numerous corporate scandals and the effort to improve transparency and accountability in the management of corporate assets (Cabral de Avila and Bertero, 2016). The TS has not been exempted from fraudulent or unethical behaviour which has fuelled discussion about the governance and accountability of the TS and has led to the development of best practice principles drawn from private sector governance for TSOs. These are principle-based codes aiming to define the role of the board of trustees, or differently, the board of supervisors, which has the legal responsibility for the operations and the conduct of the entities they supervise. Evidence shows that in the not-for-profit sector, the board of trustees tends to exercise weak control over the behaviour of managers. Moreover, they find it difficult to oversee all services provided by the organisation. The activity of the supervisory boards in not-for-profit entities reveals an apparent need for the application of corporate governance structures (Caers *et al.*, 2006).

Third sector organisations are characterised by diversity in scope, goals and operations. Therefore, in the UK different civil organisations such as co-operatives, the National Housing Federation, the Higher Education Funding Council for England and the voluntary and community sector have developed their own codes of best practice. According to the Association of Chief Executives of Voluntary Organisations (2010), the governance code developed for the voluntary and community sector should include the attributes laid out in Box 9.1.

Box 9.1: Voluntary and community sector governance attributes

An effective board will provide good governance and leadership by members:

☐ understanding their role (regarding legal duties, stewardship of assets, safeguarding vision, values and reputation),

☐ ensuring delivery of organisational purpose (by developing and agreeing a long-term strategy evaluating results, assessing outcomes, preparing and reviewing plans and budgets),

☐ working effectively both as individual and a team (among others these will include recruiting new board members with diversified skills providing opportunities for training and development, reviewing performance),

☐ exercising effective control (the board will ensure that the organisation complies with regulatory requirements, have good internal financial and management controls, reviews risks, delegates work effectively),

☐ behaving with integrity and

☐ being open and accountable.

Source: Association of Chief Executives of Voluntary Organisations, 2010

The UK charity Oxfam, provides a good example of this in practice. Oxfam's members of the board of supervisors are responsible for appointing and dismissing the executive director and fixing his or her remuneration, as well as supervising the work of the executive board, approving the annual financial accounts and the code of conduct and approving the strategic plan and mission statement. The executive director, together with the executive board, have the responsibility for managing the organisation's day-to-day activities, coordinating Oxfam and its affiliates, preparing the strategic plan and the annual accountability reports as well as developing the code of conduct and the standard operating rules and procedures. Oxfam signed the first Global Accountability Charter for the TS. The charter sets the values against which it reports its financial, environmental and social report. According to the charter, good governance is founded on a clear mission, organisational structure and decision-making processes. When activities performed are in alignment with the values and processes of the organisation, outcomes are consistent with its mission and reporting complies with the required reporting standards. Oxfam deviates from the principal-agent model, and it recognises accountability rights to a wider number of stakeholders such as people and future generations, the ecosystem, members and supporters, staff and volunteers, partner organisations, regulatory bodies, media and donors (Oxfam International).

9

How these lenses impact accountability in the TS

Defining TS accountability in practice is often difficult due to the diversity and the visibility of the services they deliver (Lehman, 2007; Unerman and O'Dwyer, 2010). Regardless of their form, TSOs have faced increasing scrutiny as to their ability to demonstrate their capacity to effectively manage their double bottom line optimizing the financial resources entrusted to them in pursuit of creating measurable social impact (Cordery *et al.*, 2017; Boomsma and O'Dwyer, 2014).

Experts have argued that it is difficult to monitor or hold the TSOs accountable because they operate in a 'black hole' where their accountability obligations are not distinctly obvious (Yuhas, 2015). TSOs have been accused of wrong-doings ranging from misappropriation of resources to corruption, citing everything from high administrative costs to high executive compensations, wealth accumulation to commercialization and their inability to effectively achieve their mission of raising the social standards in the communities they serve (Ebrahim, 2003a; O'Dwyer and Unerman, 2010). For example, the American Red Cross was accused of mismanagement of funds by diverting its resources for public relations purposes, withholding monies after the 9/11 disaster, delaying the delivery of emergency relief after Hurricane Katrina and providing selective humanitarian aid after Hurricane Sandy in the US (Elliot *et al.*, 2014; Yuhas, 2015).

Despite such criticisms, Lloyds (2005:2) argued that TSOs have strengthened their accountability to increase their legitimacy and overall performance, particularly when they are critical of corporate and government activities. This stems from the fact that their accountability defines their credibility and their independence, particularly when the emphasis is on their funding structure. When TSOs are funded by corporations, their independence and the forms of accounts they provide to their beneficiaries are affected. On the other hand, when they are independently funded by donors and by government agencies, there are regulations that require that accounts be provided to both the donors and the beneficiaries (O'Dwyer and Boomsma, 2015; Agyemang *et al.*, 2009). Regardless of their sources of finance, the absence of accountability undermines their legitimacy and the credibility of their services, the formal accountability they owe their donors and the indirect accountability owed to their beneficiaries (Awio *et al.*, 2011; Gray *et al.*, 2006, 2014).

With regard to accountability, Lloyds (2005) argued that TSOs are investing to improve their accountability and their legitimacy at the international, national and regional levels. TSOs are striving to maintain a balancing act between the accountability that is externally imposed by their regulators, partner TSOs and donors and those that are internally imposed by the TSOs themselves and imposed by their beneficiaries/clients (O'Dwyer and Boomsma, 2015). Accountability in the third sector can be upward, downward and holistic (Unerman and O'Dwyer, 2006; Agyemang *et al.*, 2009; Ebrahim, 2003b), and the shape it takes drives how the TSO is measured in terms of effectiveness, both in terms of financial performance and social impact. Thus, the following section focuses on identifying the forms of accountability in the TS as established in the previous literature and looks specifically at upward, downward and holistic accountability processes.

■ Upward accountability

As discussed so far, TSOs play a significant role in society, providing programs and services that improve the lives of the people in the communities where they operate (O'Dwyer and Unerman, 2007). To provide these services, they are either supported by donors, foundations, partnering TSOs or government agencies that often require them to provide formal accounting of how the resources at their disposal were used and that outline the immediate impact of their services (Agyemang *et al.*, 2009; O'Dwyer and Unerman, 2010). This form of accountability is known as upward, hierarchical or functional accountability (Agyemang *et al.*, 2009; O'Dwyer and Unerman, 2007). Upward accountability enables funders to assert significant financial, governance and/or policy control by demanding accountability for the services provided by the TSOs to assess the efficiency of the funds donated based on pre-determined performance metrics (Agyemang *et al.*, 2017; Gray *et al.*, 2006) in an effort to ensure that the funders understand how their donations were used in pursuit of the TSO's mission. (Ebrahim, 2003b). Additionally, the government often require upward accountability for TSOs seeking tax exemption status. This is done to ensure the organisation provides detailed financial, organisational and programmatic information to illustrate that they are in fact a voluntary organisation and not profit oriented (Ebrahim, 2003b).

Why does it matter?

The requirements for this form of accountability from donors, foundations, and government agencies, particularly for tax purposes and access to governmental and humanitarian aids, often drive this form of accountability over the others (Boomsma and O'Dwyer, 2014). Boomsma and O'Dwyer (2014:161) claim "some organisations have even altered their mission statements to comply with donor desires to maintain funding and thereby secure their survival". The governance requirements for upward accountability enable TSOs to publish their accounts to create a degree of transparency with their donors, clients and government agencies. For instance, in 2005, the American Red Cross was required by the Senate Finance Committee to provide a full accounting on a range of information ranging from its governance to the use of the resources donated for disaster relief after hurricane Katrina (Strom, 2005). Government requirements often compel the TSOs to comply with the regulatory frameworks where they operate and where they are seeking tax exemption status. Failure to disclose such financial information could result in the revocation of their public status and funds (Ebrahim, 2003b; Cordery *et al.*, 2017). This implies that the government can maintain significant surveillance on their activities to prevent fraud and to ensure that they are not profit oriented.

9

What is the impact?

Upward accountability often results in the TSOs emphasizing short-term goals and resource allocation with little to no emphasis on strategic and inclusive engagement that would benefit their clients (see Agyemang *et al.*, 2009). Agyemang *et al.*, (2009), Boomsma and O'Dwyer (2014) and Awio *et al.*, (2011) argued that donors have introduced quantitative mechanisms to ensure mutual accountability and transparency to measure performance and to improve the efficiency of the TSOs' activities. Agyemang *et al.*, (2009) and Ebrahim (2003b) argued that TSOs use annual reports, interim reports (written on a monthly, quarterly or semi-annually basis), performance assessment reports (written during projects) and performance evaluation reports (written at the end of individual projects). They argued that this accountability mechanism has proven counterproductive by damaging the delivery of their services to those they are intended to benefit, and this has compelled scholars to apply a more holistic approach to accountability in the third sector (see O'Dwyer and Unerman, 2008). Ebrahim (2003b:816) claimed "while important, these external approaches have only limited potential for encouraging organisations and individuals to take internal responsibility for shaping their organisational mission, values and performance or for promoting ethical behaviour". However, Agyemang *et al.*, (2009) argued that to ameliorate the ineffectiveness of the upward accountability, TSOs should be downwardly accountable to their beneficiaries/clients.

■ Downward accountability

Downward accountability is used to establish the need for TSOs to share the financial and social impacts of the services they provide to their beneficiaries and the communities they serve (Agyemang *et al.*, 2009; Ebrahim, 2003b). This form of accountability is often used to assess the needs of TSO beneficiaries and to understand whether those needs have been addressed with the services rendered (Boomsma and O'Dwyer, 2014, Agyemang *et al.*, 2009).

Why does it matter?

In the past, downward accountability was often viewed as unnecessary by TSOs because there was no regulatory requirement to share this information with their beneficiary or clients (Ebrahim, 2003b). However, that seems to be changing. For instance, the American Red Cross was accused of misrepresenting its effort to provide humanitarian foreign aid to the survivors of the Haitian earthquake in 2010. Critics argued that the humanitarian aid delivered did not address the needs of the survivors despite a pledge to give 91cents of every dollar raised. This failure is argued to be because the beneficiaries have no feedback/accountability mechanism to access the suitability of the services they received (Yuhas, 2015). Due to criticisms from researchers and policymakers, TSOs are being encouraged to interact and disclose how the resources at their disposal have been disbursed to their beneficiaries beyond their principal-agent relationship with their donors.

What is the impact?

Agyemang *et al.*, (2009) and Ebrahim (2003b) argue that downward accountability should be conducted through participatory dialogues, participatory evaluations and social audits to monitor performance and to establish accounting information systems that would enable the views of their beneficiaries or stakeholders to be considered. Downward accountability enables charities to establish performance indicator metrics to enhance their performance and accountability to stakeholders and to strategically plan future projects tailored to meet the needs of the people they serve. Ebrahim (2003b) goes on to argue that downward accountability measures are more multifaceted and time-bound because they can include participatory rural appraisal visits and participatory learning and action initiatives that could include surveys, public meetings, or a formal dialogue on projects. Nevertheless, Ebrahim (2003b) believes that adopting a consultative approach to downward accountability does not necessarily imply inclusive and effective engagement with beneficiaries, because they have proven to be inadequate in incorporating beneficiaries' needs and views prior to the design and the implementation of their projects. This results in a system that serves to merely validate the views of their funders, rather than reflect the opinions and views of their beneficiaries. However, downward accountability could be enhanced through participatory evaluation, which would enable beneficiaries to assess and hold the TSOs or their donors accountable and therefore increase their leverage or power to seek accountability for the services they are offered (Ebrahim, 2003b). For instance, Lisa Henry, a director of DanChurchAid, a major Danish TSO, argued in 2013 that the only way to prevent corruption and to promote accountability and transparency is to include local communities and local TSOs in the accountability process. This inclusive process enables DanChurchAid to provide services tailored to meet the needs of their beneficiaries and to more effectively promote their mission (Adetunji, 2013).

■ Holistic accountability

Holistic (or social) accountability addresses the accountability relationships of TSOs with their broader stakeholders (Agyemang *et al.*, 2009; O'Dwyer and Unerman, 2007, 2008). It highlights not only the accountability requirements with its funders but also with its beneficiaries, partnering TSOs, communities or regions served, government agencies, staff, members, partnering TSOs and to its mission statement (horizontal accountability). This practice encompasses a broader form of accountability than upward or downward methods. Holistic accountability could include qualitative and quantitative measures of the short and long-term impacts of the TSOs actions to multifaceted stakeholders. O'Dwyer and Unerman (2008:804) argue that "holistic accountability augments the short-term monitoring aspects of accountability focused on isolated campaign achievements/impacts favoured under hierarchical accountability with mechanisms of accountability for the second and third order effects of (TS)O actions".

9

Why does it matter?

Under holistic accountability, individuals with a dominant influence or not over the NGOs are assumed to have the capacity to influence decision making and should be consulted when projects that could directly or indirectly affect their well-being would be implemented (O'Dwyer and Unerman, 2008; Ebrahim, 2003a). Thus, upward and downward accountability could be considered as a subset of holistic accountability (Agyemang *et al.*, 2009). However, O'Dwyer and Unerman (2008) argue that under holistic accountability, the emphasis is often on downward accountability to beneficiaries, despite the multifaceted stakeholders' groups. This implies that emphasis is often on the moral responsiveness of TSOs to the needs of their beneficiaries and also on the moral inclusiveness of their beneficiaries in decision making without discarding the TSOs' responsibilities to its donors and government.

What is the impact?

This form of accountability could include participatory evaluation, stakeholders' forum and surveys, a partnership with beneficiaries to develop and implement their programs and storytelling, which enable beneficiaries to describe their experiences and perceptions of the activities of the organisation. This comprehensive approach enables the TSO to tailor its activities to meet the needs of its beneficiaries, monitor and address their complaints while also striving to address its overall functional accountability to its donors and government (O'Dwyer and Unerman, 2008).

Reflections

Industrialization, urbanization and the subsequent income inequalities set the stage for the development of civil society in the early 19th century. Civil society organisations exist because people are motivated to contribute altruistically with the purpose of improving the lives of others and solving social problems. Civil society exists in the spheres that include humanitarian relief, education and the promotion of democratic reorganisation in countries that are affected by chronic poverty and political crisis. And in addition, not-for-profit organisations strive to provide social services in countries where the public sector is deemed inefficient, its importance in economic activity is in decline, or where the role of the state is only narrowly seen as protecting individual rights and regulating markets.

The importance of TSOs in economic activity has increased, as is evident from the annual turnover of leading charities. Oxfam for example, in 2016, had more than 1 billion Euros in revenue, mainly stemming from fundraising activities and regular giving. At the same time, Oxfam spent 6 million more than its annual revenue in various aid programs, benefiting more than 22 million people in different countries and geographic regions, as well as funding overhead activities, such as administration and fundraising marketing (Oxfam Annual Reports, 2015-2016).

Accountability to financial contributors, volunteers and beneficiaries is high on the agenda both for monitoring the transparent use of the donated financial resources as well as for measuring performance and ensuring a positive contribution to the lives of beneficiaries. Accountability is also important to TSOs for legitimising their activities and for establishing their position in the voluntary sector as entities independent from institutional and private donors as well as for securing a tax exemption status. Like private corporations, governance and financial reporting mechanisms tend to proliferate the rights of those making financial contributions to third sector organisations at the expense of their beneficiaries.

Upward forms of accountability predominantly aim towards providing financial information that enables control and scrutiny on how resources are used (Agyemang *et al.*, 2009). More importantly, they ensure that the scope, mission and activities of civil organisations comply with donors' expectations. These forms of accountability tend to drive managers to focus on short-term objectives, potentially undermining their ability to deliver efficient services to their beneficiaries. This technical form of accountability stands in opposition to more mutual forms of accountability that recognize rights and provide accounts to the communities and groups of people, whose lives the charities aim to improve. The call is for more holistic accountability measurements that will accommodate the needs for information to a wider number of stakeholders and not only the donors and funding government agencies. Such holistic forms of accountability aim to foster a dialogue between not-for-profit organisations, donors, local communities, staff and partners that will cultivate mutual understanding and will enable TSOs to make a true impact in the lives of their beneficiaries (Agyemang *et al.*, 2009; Boomsma and O'Dwyer, 2014).

Summary

This chapter has discussed the scope, composition, size and importance of TSOs in contemporary economies. It gave an overview of the reporting practices and governing codes applied, as well as the accountability implications. As with public sector organisations, TSOs are under pressure to deliver services at low cost. As the cases of United Way of America and the American Red Cross indicate, donors tend to criticise excessive administrative expenses such as spending on salaries, training, and fundraising activities. They also tend to discourage investments in infrastructure that would improve capacity and increase the number of those benefiting from the services TSOs offer. Donors think low overhead costs are a key indicator of how efficiently a TSO uses the amounts donated and they tend to reward charities that report low overhead expenses.

Charities such as Oxfam recognise accountability to a wide number of stakeholders. Accountability in TSOs is predominantly hierarchical, emphasising external control. Reporting is used to evaluate efficiency against predefined targets, with the aim to

9

conform to standards and regulation, with little emphasis on downward accountability and on the impact of their activities on beneficiaries. However, as the chapter argues, the preoccupation with upward accountability could erode value added through their vision and mission statement. This could have a negative impact on the independence and the flexibility of TSOs to meet the needs of their beneficiaries over time. To satisfy their holistic accountability and the dynamic requirements for the services they provide particularly in developing countries, the third sectors need to constantly revisit their mission statements and their role in changing the environment for their beneficiaries through their services.

Discussion questions

1   Define the concept of the 'non-profit starvation cycle'. Discuss why it emerges, and its effect on third sector organisations.

2   Outline and discuss the aims of governance in charities and not-for-profit organisations.

3   Considering the intrinsic developmental roles of BRAC and Grameen Bank and criticisms that they act as parallel states and cannot be challenged because they are accountable to no-one. In your own view, how does the role of NGOs affect the responsibilities of government to provide public goods and to alleviate the poverty of its citizens?

4   Considering the black hole of accountabilities in TSOs, should accountabilities be enforced on TSOs as they are enforced on the private sectors? Should accountabilities to stakeholders be documented or should it be measured based on their impacts on beneficiaries?

References and further reading

Accounting Standards Board (2005). Statement of Recommended Practice, Accounting and Reporting by Charities, Revised, Available at: www.gov.uk/government/uploads/system/uploads/attachment_data/file/354885/sorp05textcolour.pdf [accessed 8 July 2017].

Adetunji, J. (2013). Dealing with corruption in your NGO. *The Guardian* (last updated 28 January at 12.06 GMT). Available at: https://www.theguardian.com/global-development-professionals-network/2013/jan/28/corruption-ngo-development-aid [Accessed 14 September 2017].

Agyemang, G., Awumbila, M., Unerman, J. and O'Dwyer, B. (2009). *NGO Accountability and Aid Delivery*. London: Certified Accountants Educational Trust.

Agyemang, G., O'Dwyer, B., Unerman, J. and Awumbila, M. (2017). Seeking "conversations for accountability" Mediating the impact of non-governmental organisation (NGO) upward accountability processes. *Accounting Auditing Accountability Journal*, **30**(5), 982-1007.

Association of Chief Executives of Voluntary Organisations (2010). Good Governance: A code for the voluntary and community sector, 2nd ed., revised, available: http://greyhoundrescuewales.co.uk/wp-content/uploads/2015/09/Code-of-Governance-Full1-copy-2.pdf [accessed 8 July 2017].

Awio, G. Northcott, D. and Lawrence, S. (2011). Social capital and accountability in grass-roots NGOs: the case of the Uganda community-led HIV/AIDS initiative. *Accounting, Auditing and Accountability Journal*, **24**(1), 63-92.

Barrett, W.P. (2006). United Way's New Way, *Forbes*, January 16. https://www.forbes.com/2006/01/13/united-way-philanthropy-cz_wb_0117unitedway.html [accessed 8 July 2017].

Bedsworth, W. Goggins, A. G. and Howard, D. (2008). Nonprofit overhead costs: breaking the vicious cycle of misleading reporting, unrealistic expectations, and pressure to conform, The Bridgespan Group (April), available: www.bridgespan.org [accessed 8 July 2017].

Bonde, I. and Brandsen, T. (2014). State-Third Sector partnerships. A short overview of key issues in the debate, *Public Management Review*, **16**(8), 1055-1066.

Boomsma, R. and O'Dwyer, B. (2014). The nature of NGO accountability, conceptions, motives, forms and mechanisms. In: J. Bebbington, J. Unerman and B. O'Dwyer, *Sustainability, Accounting and Accountability* (2ed.), pp.157-175. Oxford: Routledge.

Bovaird, T. (2014). Efficiency in third sector partnerships for delivering local government services. The role of economies of scale, scope and learning. *Public Management Review*, **16**(8), 1067-1090.

Bruyn, Severyn Ten Haut. (2000). *Evolving Values for a Capitalist World*, University of Michigan Press.

Burger, R. and Seabe, D. (2014). NGO Accountability in Africa. In: E. Obadare (ed.). *The Handbook of Civil Society in Africa*, pp.77-94, New York: Springer.

Cabral de Avila, L., A. and Bertero, C., O. (2016). Third sector governance: a case study in a university support foundation, *Review of Business Management*, **18**(59), 125-144.

Caers, R., Du Bois, C., Jegers, M., De Gieter, S., Schepers, C. and Pepermans, R. (2006). Principal-agent relationships on the stewardship-agency axis, *Nonprofit Management and Leadership*, 17(1)l.

Charities and Trustee Investment (Scotland) Act 2005, The Charities Accounts (Scotland) Regulations, Scottish Statutory Instruments, No. 218, (May 17, 2006), Available at: www.legislation.gov.uk/ssi/2006/218/pdfs/ssi_20060218_en.pdf [accessed 8 July 2017].

Charity Commission (2017). Charity Commission publishes reviews into the quality of charity annual reports and accounts, Deloitte (24 April), UK accounting plus.

9

Cheema, G.S. (2010). Civil society engagement and democratic governance: An introduction, in Popovski, V. and Cheema, G.S. ed. *Emerging Trends in Democratic Governance*. Tokyo: United Nations University Press.

Cordery, C.J., Sim, D. and van Zijl, T. (2017). Differentiated regulation: the case of charities. *Accounting and Finance*, **57**, 131-164.

Costa, E., Parker, LD. and Andreaus, M. (2014). Accountability and social accounting for social and non-profit organisations. *Advances in Public Interest Accounting*, **17**, 3-21.

Ebrahim, A. (2010). *The Many Faces of Nonprofit Accountability*. Harvard Business School, Working Paper.

Ebrahim, A. (2003a). Making sense of accountability: conceptual perspectives for northern and southern nonprofits. *Nonprofit Management and Leadership*, **14**(2), 191-212.

Ebrahim, A. (2003b). Accountability in practice: mechanisms for NGOs. *World Development*, **31**(5), 813-829.

Elliot, J., Eisinger, J. and Sullivan, L. (2014). The Red Cross' Secret Disaster. ProPublica (last updated 29 October]. Available at: https://www.propublica.org/article/the-red-cross-secret-disaster [Accessed 14 September 2017].

Emmanuel, J. F. (2014). *Financial Sustainability for Nonprofit Organisations*. Springer Publishing Company, New York, e-book ISBN: 978-0-8261-2986-4.

Goggins, A., Howard, G. and Howard, D. (2009). The Nonprofit Starvation Cycle, *Stanford Social Innovation Review*, (Fall), Available at: https://ssir.org/articles/entry/the_nonprofit_starvation_cycle [accessed 8 July 2017].

Gray, R., Bebbington, J. and Collison, D. (2006). NGO, civil society and accountability: making the people accountable to capital. *Accounting Auditing and Accountability Journal*, **19**(3), 319-348.

GuideStar, BBB Wise Giving Alliance, and Charity Navigator (2013). The Overhead Myth, Open letter to the donors of America, Available at: http://overheadmyth.com/ [accessed 8 July 2017].

GuideStar, BBB Wise Giving Alliance, and Charity Navigator (2014). The Overhead Myth. Moving toward and overhead solution, Open letter to nonprofit of America, Available at: http://overheadmyth.com/ [accessed 8 July 2017].

International Non-Governmental Organisations (2005). Accountability Charter (December 20), Available at: www.oxfam.org/sites/www.oxfam.org/files/INGO_accountability_charter_0606_0.pdf [accessed 8 July 2017].

Kelly, J. (2007). Reforming Public Services in the UK: Bringing in the Third Sector, *Public Administration*, **85**(4), 1003-1022.

Lehman, G. (2007). The accountability of NGOs in civil society and its public spheres. *Critical Perspectives on Accounting*, **18**, 645-669.

Lindsay, C., Osborne, S.P, and Bond, S. (2014). New public governance and employability services in an era of crisis: challenges for Third Sector Organizations in Scotland. *Public Administration*, **92**(1), 192-207.

Lloyd, R. (2005). *The Role of NGO Self-Regulation in Increasing Stakeholder Accountability*. London: One World Trust.

New York Times (2000). *Excerpts from Civic Responsibility and Higher Education*, edited by Thomas Ehrlich, Oryx Press, available: http://www.nytimes.com

O'Dwyer, B. (2007). The nature of NGO accountability: motives, mechanisms and practice. In: J. Unerman, J. Bebbington and B. O'Dwyer, *Sustainability Accounting and Accountability* (1ed.), pp.285-306. London: Routledge.

O'Dwyer, B. and Boomsma, R. (2015). The co-construction of NGO accountability: aligning imposed and felt accountability in NGO-funder accountability relationships. *Accounting, Auditing and Accountability Journal*, **28**(1), 36-68.

O'Dwyer, B. and Unerman, J. (2007). From functional to social accountability: transforming the accountability relationship between funders and non-governmental development organisations. *Accounting, Auditing and Accountability Journal*, **20**(3), 446-471.

O'Dwyer, B. and Unerman, J. (2008). The paradox of greater NGO Accountability: a case study of Amnesty Ireland. *Accounting Organisations and Society*, **33**(7-8), 801-824.

O'Dwyer, B. and Unerman, J. (2010). Enhancing the role of accountability in promoting the rights of beneficiaries of development NGOs. *Accounting and Business Research*, **40**(5), 451-471.

Pallota, D. (2015). The way we think about charity is dead wrong, TED talk [March 16], Long Beach California, Available at: https://tedsummaries.com/2015/03/16/ [accessed 8 July 2017].

Quarter, J., Mook, L. and Armstrong, A. (2009). *Understanding the Social Economy: A Canadian Perspective*. University of Toronto Press.

Salamon, L.M., Anheier, H.K., M., List, L., Toepler, S., Sokolowski, S.W and Associates. (1999). Global civil society dimensions of the nonprofit sector, The Johns Hopkins Center for Civil Society Studies, Baltimore, http://ccss.jhu.edu/wp-content/uploads/downloads/2011/08/Global-Civil-Society-I.pdf [accessed 8 July 2017].

Sontag, D. (1992). Affiliates feeling pinch of United Way scandal, *New York Times* (April 22), available at: http://www.nytimes.com/1992/04/22/nyregion/affiliates-feeling-pinch-of-united-way-scandal.html [accessed 8 July 2017].

Strom, S. (2005). Senators Press Red Cross for a Full Accounting. *New York Times* (last updated 30 December). Available at: http://www.nytimes.com/2005/12/30/politics/senators-press-red-cross-for-a-full-accounting.html [Accessed 14 September 2017].

Unerman, J. and O'Dwyer, B. (2010). NGO accountability and sustainability issues in the changing global environment. *Public Management Review*, **12**(4), 475-486.

9

United Way (2012). United Way proud to be Forbes largest U.S. Charity for 2012 and an All-Star Charity. Available at https://uw-mc.org/united-way-proud-to-be-forbes-largest-u-s-charity-for-2012-an-all-star-charity/ [Accessed 3 October 2017].

Westall, A. (2009). Economic analysis and the third sector. Overview of economic analysis in relation to the third sector, Third Sector Research Centre, Working Paper 14.

Yuhas, A. (2015). The Red Cross, Haiti and the 'black hole' of accountability for international aid. *The Guardian* (last updated 5 June). Available at: https://www.theguardian.com/world/2015/jun/05/red-cross-haiti-black-hole-accountability-international-aid [Accessed 14 September 2017].

■   Some useful web links

Charity Commission for England and Wales. https://www.gov.uk/government/organisations/charity-commission

Charity Governance Code. www.charitygovernancecode.org

Gavi, The Vaccine Alliance. http://www.gavi.org

Oxfam International, www.oxfam.org

Scottish Charity Regulator (OSCR). http://www.oscr.org.uk/

The Scottish Government. 2011. Renewing Scotland's Public Services. Priorities for reform in response to the Christie Commission. http://www.gov.scot

The Charity Commission – GOV.UK. www.gov.uk/government/ organisations/ charity-commission.

10 Cooperatives and Family Businesses

Audrey Paterson, Sebastian Paterson,
Eleni Chatzivgeri and Melanie Wilson

Introduction

So far within this book we have considered social accounting within the private, public and third sectors and have explored related concepts and their growing momentum in the drive towards increased organisational and social accountability. In this chapter, we consider two further economic sectors, namely cooperatives and family businesses. Cooperatives and family businesses vary in size and skill and cover a diverse variety of activities ranging from healthcare, social care, and housing to sustainable agricultural and renewable energy sources. Currently in the UK, there are nearly 7,000 independent cooperatives, contributing £36bn to the UK economy. Cooperatives differ from public and private businesses, which exist to produce goods or services in the public interest or to maximise the profits of their owners, respectively. In contrast to public and private companies, the main purpose of a cooperative is the advancement of its members and not the pursuit of public interest or economic gain.

We are, of course, familiar with the profit seeking motives of private business and the social motives of public sector organisations, but cooperatives do not fit well into either of these conceptions due to their hybrid function, which seeks to satisfy both social and economic objectives (Fairbairn 1994).

Governance describes a firm's system of decision-making, direction and control. In the case of cooperatives, effective accountability and governance depends on the pro-active participation of its members. It is recognised that just as traditional businesses, cooperatives should make sure they comply with the accounting as well as the legislative regulations (Jenkins, 2008; Campbell, 2003), and that attention is paid to the level of training of the cooperative board along with their quality (Campbell, 2004) as well as the board's ability to look after the interests of both the cooperatives members and other stakeholders (Cross and Buccola, 2004). Moreover, the board, and the executive team for which it is responsible, directly impact the value proposition that determine members' and other stakeholders' willingness to engage with the cooperative business.

While cooperatives provide a significant contribution to the economy, a large proportion of the UK's economy is also supported by family businesses. Indeed, it is estimated that family businesses account for almost 25% of the UK's gross domestic product (GDP). As such these two areas are of increasing importance when considering the accountability and governance responsibilities of organisations. With new questions arising every day to challenge the contributions that cooperatives and family businesses make to our communities, it is essential that we have the tools to clearly demonstrate their worth. Likewise, given the importance of the role boards play in the success or failure of cooperative organisations and family businesses, and the importance of these organisations in the wider economy, it is prudent to develop some knowledge and understanding of the complexities of the way in which these boards are structured and the role that they play in achieving accountability and governance within their organisation.

In this chapter, we consider the following: who governs; board roles and board relationships with management; board size and director selection processes; the importance of board members' participation; and the input of managers in relation to accountability and governance in these two sectors. The chapter begins with a short overview of the evolution of cooperatives and what constitutes a family business. This is followed by a discussion of the organisational model and governance structures and their effectiveness.

The cooperative movement – evolution and aims

Notwithstanding a recent claim that the origin of the cooperative movement began in 1761 with the creation of the Fenwick Weavers Society in Ayrshire, Scotland and its subsequent formation of a consumer cooperative in 1769 (Carrell, 2007; McFadzean, 2008), the cooperative business model is generally held to have begun amongst grassroot organisations in Western Europe, North America and Japan in the middle of the 18th century. The prototype of the modern cooperative society is commonly considered to be a group of northern English artisans called the Rochdale Pioneers, who opened a store in 1844 (Lambert, 1968). Working in the cotton mills of Rochdale in the 1840s and unable to afford the high prices of food and household goods, they pooled their resources to access basic goods at a lower price. Their enterprise was founded upon the belief that shoppers should be treated with honesty and respect, that they should have a share in the profits and that they should have a democratic right to have a say in the business. Every customer of the shop became a member and thus had a stake in the business.

The International Cooperative Alliance (ICA) recognises that the foundations upon which the Rochdale Pioneers created their business still underpin modern cooperative enterprises today (ICA). The ICA defines a cooperative as "an autonomous association of persons united voluntarily to meet their common economic, social, and cultural needs and aspirations through a jointly-owned and democratically-controlled enterprise" (ICA, 2015). The seven internationally recognised cooperative principles are: voluntary and open membership; democratic member control; member economic participation; autonomy and independence; provision of education; training and information; cooperation among cooperatives, and concern for the community (ICA, 2015). Considering the underpinning principles, cooperative enterprises cannot fit into the current organisational models and are often regarded as unique business models. This is largely because they do not only serve an economic purpose, but a social one as well (Fairbairn, 1994). Correspondingly, the development and implementation of good corporate governance practice for cooperatives is viewed as still being in its early stages (Shaw, 2006).

Cooperatives, like other public and private sector or investor owned firms, have not remained untouched by recent scandals that relate to accountability and corporate governance, nor by the development of codes of good practice. According to Co-operatives UK (2005), the fairly new development of a corporate governance code related to relevant performance measures was encouraged by external governance scandals and acknowledgment that cooperatives had to implement "cutting edge practice in corporate governance" (Co-operatives UK, 2005). The high demand of governance standards as well as increased accountability in different business sectors could not leave the cooperative movement untouched. Yet, the development as well as the implementation of both good accountability and governance practice for cooperatives remains very much in its early stages. The codes adopted by cooperatives so far have been developed based on the codes for companies owned by investors (as explained earlier, these companies serve a different purpose) normally adding in further provisos concerning membership but not substantively reworking them (Shaw, 2006).

A cooperative's main aim is to increase its members' value (professional or household) through the members' use of their facilities, or, in general through their operations, and not to achieve and experience profit. Those who create a cooperative are looking to serve their own needs in terms of goods and services; this means that their main purpose is not to serve people outside the cooperation. However, this is not achievable in practice, and transactions with people outside the cooperation can be justified, because such transactions can help cooperatives to avoid experiencing losses (Kagiamis, 2003).

Having outlined the cooperative movement we now turn our attention to some theoretical perspectives which help to highlight issues cooperatives face in determining governance structures.

10

The cooperative movement – theoretical perspectives

Staatz (1987) identifies areas of conflict and gaps which remain in the theory of agricultural cooperation, notably the disagreement between authors such as Cotterill (1987) and Lopez and Spreen (1985), who view the cooperative as a separate firm maximising a single objective, and other academics, who view cooperatives as organisations of many individuals with each attempting to pursue their own goals (Sexton, 1984; Shaffer, 1987). In terms of gaps, Staatz notes that work needs to be done to incorporate uncertainty into the 'cooperative as a firm' model and 'coalition' models, as well as the more recent 'cooperative as a nexus of contracts' model.

Shaw (2006) provides an excellent and comprehensive overview of corporate governance issues in the cooperative business context. Shaw notes that good governance has been embraced as a vital organ in achieving the United Nations Millennium Development Goals for sustainability and as a precondition of sustainable economic growth. Also, that good governance standards allow better access to external finance, lower cost of capital and lead to better firm performance. And that, although much recognition has been given to the corporate governance agenda, little attention has been given to cooperative sectors and, consequently, the governance challenges of cooperative sectors remain largely unexplored.

Mazzarol *et al.* (2011) developed a conceptual framework that future research could use in the effort to create a business model for cooperatives and their sustainability (Figure 10.1). Cooperative enterprises are often seen as unique business models. Mazzarol examines them from three perspectives; namely, from a member's perspective, as a business entity and at the broader systems level. Mazzerol outlines key units of analysis for every level and takes into consideration three main needs of the cooperative within the model. These needs are:

1   to build identity,

2   to build social capital and

3   to build sustainability.

The application of resilient architecture to facilitate the understanding of the dynamic behaviour of cooperative enterprises over time is also considered (Mazzarol *et al.*, 2011). The work of Mazzarol *et al.* (2011) is definitive as it adds significant knowledge to the understanding of the cooperative enterprise by viewing it as a complex system that must be comprehended on several levels, with economic and social outputs defining its special character, which in turn requires a multi-disciplinary business model research approach.

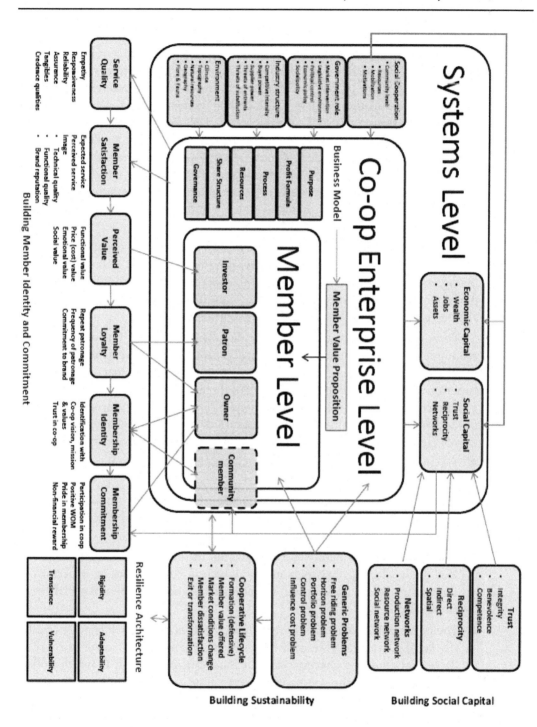

Figure 10.1: Conceptual framework of cooperative enterprise research (Mazzarol *et al.*, 2011:7)

■ Cooperatives, social capital and performance

As already mentioned, cooperatives' main (but not exclusive) aim is to serve its members in terms of their economic needs. However, cooperatives can also serve an educational aim. The importance of education through cooperatives made its appearance during the age of the Rochdale Pioneers; with the memorandum of association stating that 2.5% of the cooperative's surplus should be spent for educational purposes. The leading members had realized that the lack of knowledge would act as an obstacle to the cooperative's growth. The fifth cooperative principle (provision of education, training and information) which, as already mentioned before is internationally recognized and aims to broaden each cooperative's educational impact on its members, can only be successful through the creation of a cooperative ideal and principles.

It should also be noted that their educational aims can target enhancement of their members' educational level on operating related issues or on culture. For this reason, in Germany, even though the cooperatives' principles refer only to the economic benefits, it is clear that they can develop not only educational but also recreation benefits, which add value to the community.

Through cooperatives, and of course though family businesses, small economies have the chance of creating a common enterprise system that will enable them to avoid their exploitation by those corporations that are financially superior. In this way, cooperatives prevent the marginalization of weaker social groups, contribute to the fight against inequality and help in the accomplishment of social equality (Kagiamis, 2003). Cooperatives and family businesses however, do not create only social cohesion but also help in the following ways:

■ The participation and operation of cooperatives and family businesses in the market boosts economic democracy.

■ Such types of organisation increase solidarity (within the economic environment), which in turn contributes to increasing public support in favour of solidarity and mutual aid.

■ Participating in cooperatives helps people to improve their social skills as well as developing their personality, which is very important, especially if we consider that cooperatives' members could come from any social level/ background.

■ The participation of certain types of cooperatives or family businesses in the market, e.g. in agriculture, contributes to the achievement of lower prices than those that could be charged without their participation. It is worth noting that this is due to the cooperatives' operating system (or to the way family businesses operate) and not to the pricing policy itself. In the case of cooperatives, middlemen are not present, which benefits not only the members of the cooperatives, but also society.

One could argue that due to the different structure and nature of cooperatives, it is difficult to measure their social and/or economic impact. However, there have been efforts to capture the impact these types of organisation have. In an effort to identify the impact of Ugandan cooperative societies, Kyazze *et al.* (2017), linked their performance to their corporate governance, by investigating how monitoring rights, ratification of management decisions, innovation and policy compliance affect their social performance. Karthikeyan (2013) tried to measure the social performance of cooperative unions, using as a case study a farmers' cooperative in Ethiopia. By sending out questionnaires to the members of the cooperative, its employees and to the community it was serving, he concluded that the cooperative was a successful case and suggested that it could constitute a paradigm, as other cooperatives could also be successful by offering social benefits. Ruben and Heras (2012) also found a strong correlation between corporate governance policies and the performance of cooperatives in Ethiopia. This implies that if there was a standardization of the evaluation processes of these types of organisation in measuring their social impact, then they could more easily make a business case.

We now turn our attention to family businesses before moving on to consider accountability and governance structures in more detail.

Family businesses

The Institute for Family Business (IFB) estimate that almost 2/3 of UK business is family owned, of which 51% are medium-sized enterprises. These businesses contribute almost 25% of the UK's GDP and provide in the region of 36% of UK employment. As such it is important to understand what constitutes a family business and why it is necessary for them to demonstrate good accountability and governance to stakeholders and society.

The IFB states a firm is considered a family enterprise, if:

1 The majority of votes are owned by the person or persons who established the firm, or those who have acquired the share capital of the firm, or which are in the possession of their spouses, parents, child or child's direct heirs.

2 The majority of votes may be indirect or direct.

3 At least one representative of the family or kin is involved in the management or administration of the firm.

4 Listed companies meet the definition of a family enterprise if the person who established, or acquired, the firm (share capital) or their families or descendants possess 25% of the right to vote as mandated by their share capital.

Examples of companies that fall into the family business category include the Swire group, which was established in 1816 and is still a family concern. Swire's activities span across several areas including the Cathay Pacific airline, marine investments and the property market. One of the UK's largest construction companies, Laine O'Rourke was established in 1967 and remains headed by Ray O'Rourke, the founder of the organisation. Laine O'Rourke has been involved in

10

many large public sector projects including the construction of the facilities for the 2012 Olympic games held in the UK. Associated British Foods, (manufacturer of products such as Kingsmill bread, Patak's, Twining's Tea, etc,) is headed by George Weston, the third Weston CEO since the company was founded in 1935. Established in 1951 as a family business, Stemcor is one of the largest remaining steel manufacturers employing more than 1400 people. The majority of Stemcor's shareholding is still held by family members. Arnold Clark, Europe's largest car dealer, remains in the family of its original founder, Glasgow born Arnold Clark who received a knighthood for his entrepreneurial activity and contributions to society. Other examples include the Bestway cash-and-carry group, which was established in 1956 and the Specialist Computer Holdings (SCH Group) founded in 1975, both of which still hold family members in senior positions.

Family ownership could either be perceived as an opportunity or as a threat. If the controlling family and the company itself can provide reassurance to existent and/or potential investors, the fact that a high percentage of the shares are owned by a family can add value. There is a high probability that investors (creditors and shareholders) will examine in detail such companies before investing in them, due to the high risk of exploitation of other shareholders' rights by the controlling family. La Porta *et al.* (2000) have argued that there have been many cases in which family businesses are characterized by poor transparency and absence of fairness principles and accountability, which has resulted in the abuse of minority controlling shareholders. The key thing that investors are looking for, is reassurance that their interests will be addressed among the family ownership through an appropriate corporate governance strategy.

■   **Family business and social capital**

It is believed that family business can form an appropriate environment for the development of social capital (Coleman, 1988). According to Bubolz (2001:130) "the family is a source, builder and user of social capital". Family members learn how to trust other people (relatives) at a very young age. Family establishes moral behaviour and teaches its members coordination and cooperation, as well as being able to share (Bubolz, 2001). "Increased reciprocity and exchange reinforce the creation and use of social capital that stems from the dynamic factors of stability, interdependence, interactions, and closure common in families" (Arregle *et al.*, 2007:76).

One of the family's characteristics is the provision of stability to children (in terms of the period/time of influence it has upon its younger members), thus creating their very first grounds for socialization (Berger and Luckman, 1967), which enables family members to understand and enhance values that exist within a family. According to Bourdieu (1994:139, cited in Arregle *et al.*, 2007) "this understanding facilitates integration, cohesion and survival of the family unit". As already mentioned above, the interaction between family members throughout their lives, increases the level of trust and sharing values. This means that within the family environment, its members interact with one another; ideas such as solidarity and influence are clearly present. Therefore, unless certain exemptions (such as problems in the family environment), family members can learn how to operate as part of a team through devotion and generosity (Bourdieu, 1994, cited in Arregle *et al.*, 2007).

It would not be realistic to say that there are no economic motives within the family and thus within the family business; family "has a patrimony that unifies family members while it simultaneously instils a competitive spirit among members" (Arregle *et al.*, 2007:77). This means that the probability of a family business' survival is increased through the enhancement of its social capital, which clearly shows how family business can create a powerful form of social capital.

Organisational model and governance structures

Having considered the uniqueness of cooperatives and family businesses we now turn our attention to organisational models and governance structures within these entities. We begin by acknowledging that these organisations face the same accountability and governance problems and issues that appear in the other sectors covered earlier in this book. However, the governance structures in cooperatives have to facilitate the unique interaction that occurs between the membership and the management. Consider a simplified version of the model of cooperative governance, which is reproduced below.

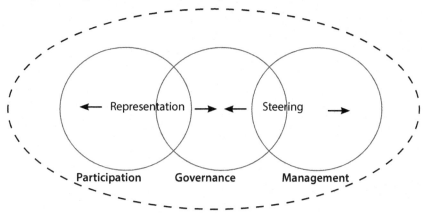

Figure 10.2: Overlaps between participation, governance and executive management. Adapted from the version in Mazzarol et al. (2011:16)

The model shows the interaction between members and management through the governance structures. In the participation sphere the members actively engage with their elected representatives to communicate what they need from the organisation. The members' representatives are then able to, through the committees that subsist within the governance sphere, bring these views to the attention of the organisation's management. Taking account of this representation, managers are then, within their own sphere of influence, able to steer the organisation according to the needs of its members. When seen like this, it becomes clear that the governance structures in cooperatives provide both a mechanism of accountability as well as a mechanism through which direction can be given to management. This added complexity makes it even more challenging to effectively theorise the cooperative model of organisation.

Cornforth (2004) has additionally identified the development of different models of accountability and governance, based on the level of ownership rights and their exercise by members, defined as (i) the compliance, (ii) partnership, (iii) democratic, (iv) stakeholder, (v) co-optation and (vi) 'rubber stamp' models which to varying degrees are relevant to both cooperatives and family businesses.

Specific to the sectors under investigation in this chapter, the organisational model should preferably be one in which a dedicated and enlightened membership votes for a board which will have responsibility for corporate governance and the associated formulation of strategy, policy and procedure, the direction of the business and the supervision of the executive management in the best interests of the membership. The executive management, in turn, carries out the decisions of the board capably but without usurping directorial power and without intruding into its policy-making privileges. However, some complications may arise with this model. LeVay (1983) notes that membership cannot be assumed to be homogeneous; on the contrary it may be heterogeneous, involving many individuals or groups with conflicting ideas and interests, making its purpose difficult to discern and deliver. The membership may be active or passive so that involvement in the affairs of the society may be weak or strong. If it is weak, the board may relax its vigilance, fail to monitor the needs of the members and allow the executive management to dominate, possibly to the extent of permitting it to pursue ends of its own rather than servicing the needs of the membership (LeVay, 1983). On the other hand, if it is strong, it may interfere too much with the executive management and inhibit or prevent the efficient running of the business (Helmberger and Hoos, 1962).

Who governs, board roles and relationships

Having considered organisational and governance structures we now turn our attention to 'who governs' and how the aforementioned theories can drive different board roles. Looking first at who governs and the tensions between representative and expert boards, it can be seen that boards have a difficult balancing act to perform. Taking into consideration the democratic perspective, and to some extent the stakeholder theory view, board members should be selected primarily for their desire to serve the membership, whereas from a stewardship theory view, board members should be selected for their expertise, experience and ability to add value to the enterprise. When examining 'who governs', board size, diversity and director selection processes, terms of engagement and performance evaluation are also important factors to consider. As an example, there is a need to balance directorial experience and organisational memory against recruiting new member talent that may have the ability to see the enterprise from a different perspective and present ideas that are novel, innovative and performance enhancing. In terms of board roles, it is important that board members participate actively and adopt a debating style that is transparent, enquiring and critical. With regard to board relationships with management, boards can benefit from the input of their managers by drawing on their professional experience, business acumen and associations to augment, inform and, in some cases, test the organisational strategy and direction.

Moving on to board roles and their particular emphasis, this is argued by Cornforth (2004) to be most evident in the opposition between agency and stewardship theories or, as Garrat (1996) has described it, the 'conformance' versus 'performance' role of boards. Again, it can be seen that boards have a difficult balancing act to perform. Boards must act in 'conformance' to the interest of owners/members while simultaneously working to add strategic decision-making 'performance' value. Boards therefore must determine how much time to allocate to each of these potentially conflicting roles, often with emphasis on one at the expense of the other.

From a closer examination of Cornforth's (2004) work, it is clear that boards face various important paradoxes in their accountability and governance roles (Cornforth, 2001, 2002, 2003). He notes that the different theories discussed before, when taken individually, are "rather one dimensional, only illuminating a particular aspect of the board's role2, leading to a demand for integration of the insights of these different theories in an effort to develop a new framework (either theoretical or conceptual) (Hung, 1998; Tricker, 2000). Cornforth (2004) claims that if someone takes into consideration all the different perspectives of the theories developed earlier, a new conceptual framework could potentially be developed which could enable boards to deal with the complexities/paradoxes mentioned earlier on. The framework developed by Cornforth for the contrast as well as the comparison of the different theories is provided in Table 10.1. The framework enables a comparison of the different theories in terms of whose interests they serve, who the board members should be, as well as what the role of the board is in each case.

Lastly, looking at board relationships with management, this, according to Cornforth (2004), is viewed quite differently between contrasting theoretical perspectives. Agency, democratic and stakeholder perspectives stress boards' need to control and monitor executive management, whereas stewardship theory emphasises the role of the board as a partner that collaborates with management to improve decision-making. Studies by Sundaramurthy and Lewis (2003)

10

suggest that, when either control or collaboration is overly stressed, there is a risk of a separation of responsibilities or 'groupthink', respectively. Additionally, Kramer (1985) suggests that the relationship between a board and its executive management constantly shifts between consensus, difference and disagreement, depending on prevailing situations and circumstances. Further, as Mole (2003) has pointed out, tension and conflict seem most likely to occur when boards and senior managers have different expectations of their respective roles. To counter this, both board and executive management each need to know who should be doing what and why – essential to this is good bilateral communication.

Table 10.1: A comparison of theoretical perspectives on organisational governance

Theory	Interests	Board members	Board role
Agency theory	Owners/members and managers have different interests	Owners'/members' representatives	Conformance: safeguard owners' interests - oversee management - check compliance
Stewardship theory	Owners/members and managers share interests	Experts	Improve performance: add value to top decisions/strategy - partner/support management
Resource dependency theory	Stakeholders and organisation have different interests	Chosen for influence with key stakeholders	Boundary spanning: secure resources - stakeholder relations - external perspective
Stakeholder theory	Stakeholders have different interests	Stakeholder representatives	Political: balance stakeholder needs - make policy - control management
Managerial hegemony theory	Owners/members' and managers have different interests	Owners/members' representatives	Symbolic: ratify decisions - give legitimacy (managers have real power)
Democratic perspective	Members/the public have different interests	Lay/member representatives	Political: represent member interests - make policy - control executive

Having considered various organizational and governance structures and the who governs, role of the board and relationships we now turn our attention to examples that demonstrate the consequences of poor governance and accountability structures and the importance of the public's trust.

Scandals and public's trust

As mentioned earlier in the chapter, cooperatives and family businesses have not managed to remain immune from scandals over the years. Scandals within family businesses include the Gucci[1] case, where family disputes concerning murder, madness, glamour and greed were all over the news, as well as the case

---

1 http://abcnews.go.com/Entertainment/story?id=115639

of Dassler Brothers[2], who back in 1924 created a shoe company but later, due to tension between the brothers, two different brands were created (Adidas and Puma). Among the scandals that have led to public's mistrust of cooperatives are: the case of Umbrella Co-op in Angkasa, where there were allegations about misuse of funds, the 24 Deposit-Taking Co-ops Scandal, where directors were accused of using the cooperative's funds for their own benefits (to buy land), the Malay Officers Cooperative Credit and Investment Society, where the cooperative was unable to pay salaries and refund its members. So, can these organisations justify the public's trust in them? The answer is yes. Initiatives can be taken to promote the work of these sectors. The impact they have on society and communities could be highlighted to increase public's trust.

One example is the European Confederation of Cooperatives[3] (CECOP-CICOPA), an association founded in 1979, which highlights the importance of industrial and service cooperatives. In one of their recent case studies, they indicated what impact the creation of a farming cooperative had in Italy. The impact study was not based on numbers and figures; rather the cooperative was created with a view to "introduce modern farming methods and new productive activities to restore dignity and value to people through the creation of a social economy, to promote respect for the environment and to develop people's awareness and consumption of local products" (CECOP, 2017). In a world where people have started questioning things requiring transparency and increased accountability, the way businesses can make their case is through evidence of the impact they have on the society. The Committee for the Promotion and Advancement of Cooperatives (COPAC) highlights the people-focused nature of cooperative enterprises, and emphasises the principles of voluntary and open membership which underlie the cooperative movement. It further emphasises democratic member control and member economic participation as being essential features to ensure trust and transparency. These agencies promote and support cooperatives as they provide a valuable space where all people, regardless of race, gender, culture, social background or economic circumstance, can meet their needs and build better communities (CECOP, 2017).

With respect to family businesses the owners have an emotional stake as well as a financial one invested in the business. The implication of this is that there will usually be a preparedness to work through hard times, a desire to make the business work and an innovative and entrepreneurial spirit to ensure the growth of the business with a view to handing it over to the next generation of the family. An example of a successful family owned business that achieved remarkable

10

---

2 http://www.punditarena.com/other-sports/lcairns/dassler-brothers-german-giants-sporting-equipment/

3 It affiliates 26 members in 15 European countries including organizations promoting cooperatives and national confederations or federations of cooperatives representing 50,000 enterprises employing 1.3 million workers. CECOP it is a sectoral member of Cooperatives Europe, the regional organisation of the International Cooperative Alliance (ICA).

growth and success is the Korean consumer electronics giant Samsung which was founded in 1938 by Lee Byung-chul and has grown from its humble beginnings to one of the world's largest electronics providers. Maintaining trust within family business requires determination and positive action. The members must agree on the business strategies and goals, establish and maintain policies and rules regarding working arrangements and compensation plans and act to sustain and build social relations through family retreats or engagement in service projects. To aid them in this endeavour they can recruit external support such as facilitators or councillors to help manage sensitive aspects of the business. Likewise, they can establish a board of directors included in which external expert advisors.

Summary

This chapter has considered two economic sectors, cooperatives and family businesses, and has outlined how they differ from public and private businesses, which exist to produce goods or services in the public interest or to maximise the profits of their owners, respectively. In contrast to public and private companies, the main purpose of a cooperative is the advancement of its members and not the pursuit of public interest or economic gain. Both cooperatives and family businesses face similar governance and social accountability problems to other sectors of the economy. Theoretical perspectives, social capital and performance, organizational and governance structures emphasise the complexity of establishing good governance and social accountability policy and procedures. An analysis and discussion of the perspective of 'who governs'; board roles and board relationships with management; board size and director selection processes; the importance of board members' participation and the input of managers have also been examined. There is no one size fits all approach to ensuring good governance and social accountability. However, initiatives could be taken to promote the work of these sectors. The impact they have on society and communities could be highlighted to increase public's trust.

Discussion questions

1 How do cooperatives and family businesses add value to communities?

2 How can they create social capital out of the money invested in them?

3 Can cooperatives and family businesses measure their social performance and make their business case?

4 How can cooperatives and family businesses justify the public's trust in them?

References and further reading

Arregle, J., Hitt, M.A., Sirmon, D.G., and Very, P. (2007). The development of organizational social capital: attributes of family firms. *Journal of Management Studies*, **44**(1), 73-95.

Berger, P. and Luckman, T. (1967). *The Social Construction of Reality: A Treatise in the Sociology of Knowledge*. London: Penguin.

Berle, A.A. and Means, G.C. (1932). *The Modern Corporation and Private Property*, New York: MacMillan.

Bubolz, M. (2001). Family as source, user, and builder of social capital. *Journal of Socio-Economics*, **30**, 129–131.

Campbell, D. (2003). Congressional hearing focuses on possible need for more flexible co-op business model. *Rural Cooperatives*, **70** (9).

Campbell, D. (2004). Innovative practices focus of Missouri co-op conference. *Rural Cooperatives*, **71**(4), 44-45.

Carrell, S. (2007). History: Strike Rochdale from the record books. The Co-op began in Scotland. *The Guardian* London, England. Available at: http://www.theguardian.com/business/2007/aug/07/retail.uknews.

CECOP (2017). Social farming in Italy: Hoe the social cooperative, Un fiore per la vita, is showing the way forward, available at: http://www.cecop.coop/Social-farming-in-Italy-how-the-social-cooperative-Un-fiore-per-la-vita-is

Co-operatives UK (2005). *Report of the Corporate Governance Review Group*.

Coleman, J. S. (1988). Social capital in the creation of human capital. *American Journal of Sociology*, **93**, 291–321.

Cornforth, C. (2001). *Understanding the governance of non-profit organizations: multiple perspectives and paradoxes*, a paper to be presented to the 30th Annual ARNOVA Conference, November 29 – December 1st, 2001, Miami, USA.

Cornforth, C. (2002). *The Governance of Public and Non-profit Organisations: a paradox perspective*, a paper for the Sixth International Research Symposium on Public Management, 8-10 April, 2002, University of Edinburgh, UK.

Cornforth, C. (2003). Introduction: The changing context of governance – emerging issues and paradoxes, In Cornforth, C. (ed), *The Governance of Public and Non-profit Organizations: What Do Boards Do?*, London: Routledge.

Cornforth, C. (2004). The governance of cooperatives and mutual associations: a paradox perspective. *Annals of Public and Cooperative Economics*, **75**(1), 11-32.

Cotterill, R.W. (1987). Agricultural cooperatives: a unified theory of pricing, finance, and investment. In Royer, J.S. (ed.) *Cooperative Theory: New Approaches*, USDA, Agricultural Cooperative Service Report No. 18, pp. 171-195

Cross, R. and Buccola, S. (2004). Adapting cooperative structure to the new global environment. *American Journal of Agricultural Economics*, **86**(5), 1254-1261.

10

Fairbairn, B. (1994). *The Meaning of Rochdale: The Rochdale Pioneers and the Co-operative Principles*. University of Saskatchewan, Centre for the Study of Co-operatives.

Freeman, E.R. (1986). *Strategic Management: A Stakeholder Approach*, Boston, Pitman.

Garratt, B. (1996). *The Fish Rots from the Head – the Crisis in our Boardrooms: Developing the Crucial Skills of the Competent Director*, London: Harper Collins Pubs.

Helmberger, P.G. and Hoos, S. (1962). Cooperative enterprise and organization theory. *Journal of Farm Economics*, **44**, 275-90.

Helmberger, P.G. (1964). Cooperative enterprise as a structural dimension of farm markets. *Journal of Farm Economics*, **46**, 603-17.

Hung, H. (1998). A typology or theories of the roles of governing boards, *Corporate Governance*, **6**(2), 101-111.

ICA (2015). Cooperative definition. Available at: http://ica.coop/en/whats-co-op/co- operative-identity-values-principles.

Itkonen, R. (1996). My views on cooperative corporate governance. *Review of International Co-operation*, **89**(4), 20-24.

Jenkins, J. (2008). NCBA's Annual Conference to Focus on Cooperatives as the Better Business Model During Cooperative Week. Washington D.C., US Federal News Service.

Jensen, M.C. and Meckling, W.H. (1976). The theory of the firm: managerial behavior, agency costs and ownership structure. *Journal of Financial Economics*, **3**, 305-360.

Kagiamis, G. (2003). *Organisation, Structure and Operation of Cooperations: Super and mini market in Heraclion*, T.E.I. Epirus, School of Accounting, Greece (in Greek).

Karthikeyan, M. (2013). *Social Statement Approach to Cooperative Social Performance Assessment: A Case of Lume Adama Farmer's Cooperative Union in Ethiopia*. 4th EMES International Research Conference on Social Enterprise – Liege.

Kramer, R.M. (1985). Toward a contingency model of board-executive relations. *Administration in Social Work*, **9**(3), 15-33.

Kyazze, L.M., Nkote, I.N. and Wakaisuka-Isingoma, L. (2017). Cooperative governance and social performance of cooperative societies. *Cogent Business Management*, **4**, 1-14.

La Porta, R., Lopez-De-Silanes, F., Shleifer, A. and Vishny, R. (2000). Investor protection and corporate governance. *Journal of Financial Economics*, **58**, 3-27.

Lambert, P. (1968). The Rochdale Pioneers as originators, *Annals of Public and Co-operative Economy*, **39**(4), 559-561.

LeVay, C. (1983). Agricultural cooperative theory: A review, *Journal of Agricultural Economics*, **34**(1), 1-44.

Lopez, R.A. and Spreen, T.H. (1985). Co-ordination strategies and non-members' trade in processing co-operatives. *Journal of Agricultural Economics*, **36**, 385-96.

Mazzarol, T., Simmons, R. and Limnios, M. (2011). *A Conceptual Framework for Research into Co-operative Enterprise*. CEMI Discussion Paper Series, DP 1102, Centre for Entrepreneurial Management and Innovation, www.cemi.com.au

McFadzean, J. (2008). *The Co-operators - A History of the Fenwick Weavers*. East Ayrshire North Communities Federation Ltd

Mole, V. (2003). What are chief executives' expectations and experiences of their board? In C. Cornforth (Ed.). *The Governance of Public and Non-Profit Organizations: What Do Boards Do?* Oxford, UK: Routledge, Taylor and Francis Group.

Pfeffer, J. and Salancik, G.R. (1978). *The External Control of Organizations: A Resource Dependence Perspective*. New York, Harper and Row.

Prakash, D. (2003). *The Principles of Cooperation: A Look at the IGA Cooperative Identity Statement*. New Delhi, Pamda-Network International.

Ruben, R. and Heras, J. (2012). Social capital, governance and performance of Ethiopian coffee cooperatives. *Annals of Public and Corporate Economics*, **83**(4), 463-484.

Sexton, R. J. (1984). *The Formation of Cooperatives: An Analysis of Entry Incentives, Entry Deterrence, Optimal Financing Arrangements, and Stability Requirements*. Ph.D. dissertation, University of Minnesota.

Shaffer, J. D. (1987). Thinking About farmers' cooperatives, contracts, and economic coordination. In Royer, J.S. (ed.) *Cooperative Theory: New Approaches*, USDA, Agricultural Cooperative Service Report No. 18, pp. 61-86.

Shaw, L. (2006). *Overview of Corporate Governance Issues for Co-operatives*. Manchester, UK. The Co-operative College.

Silversten, S. (1996). Governance issues seen from a management perspective. *Review of International Cooperation*, **89**(4), 34-36.

Staatz, J. M. (1987). Recent developments in the theory of agricultural cooperation. *Journal of Agricultural Cooperation*, **2**, 148-155.

Sundaramurthy, C. and Lewis, M. (2003). Control and collaboration: paradoxes of governance, *Academy of Management Review*, **28**(3), 397-415.

Tricker, B. (2000). Editorial: Corporate governance - the subject whose time has come, *Corporate Governance*, **8**(4), 289-296.

10

11 Taxation and Social Accounting

Melanie Wilson, Kate Clements, Darren Jubb and Amber Jackson

Introduction

Taxation is a central component in the operation of modern states and an important societal issue. The payment of taxes is a fundamental concern for individuals, organisations and governments, however, the relationship between taxation and society is complex. For some, taxation is "an essential element in the social contract between government and citizens" (Boden *et al.*, 2010:541). For others, taxation is regarded as an unpleasant governmental intervention that should be minimised (Murphy, 2016). Whichever perspective is adopted, taxation involves transactions between taxpayers and the state and is interwoven into the very fabric of modern society. The centrality of taxation to the operation of modern societies has recently resulted in concern with accountability and transparency, with taxation becoming a high-profile issue for the general public in relation to the activities of several organisations and individuals. For example, as the result of campaigning by several charities and Civil Society Organisations (CSOs), the attention of the public has been drawn to an apparent lack of correlation between the economic success of private sector organisations and the amount of taxation that these organisations have paid (Murphy, 2016). The impact of these campaigns within the private sector has seen organisations and individuals voluntarily paying more taxation but, despite this, there remain several areas of concern regarding the fair payment of taxation and the role of organisations and governments in this regard. With this in mind, the aim of this chapter is to highlight social and ethical issues related to taxation and the responses to such issues. The chapter considers the responses to these issues from the perspective of private, public and third sector organisations to set tax within the context of social accounting and discuss the wider societal impact of taxation, with specific consideration of the social contract between individuals and the state.

To achieve this, the chapter begins by presenting a broad overview of the constituent elements of systems of taxation. It does this by first considering the objectives and scope of taxation before discussing both how taxation is computed and the common issues that arise because of this. Following this, the chapter discusses taxation within the context of social responsibility. It advances the notion of taxation and social responsibility, with a specific emphasis on entities other than private organisations, including NGOs, cooperatives and family businesses. The nature and extent of the activities of these organisations are presented to highlight the numerous initiatives that are in place to address inequality in the payment of taxation. Beyond this, the chapter presents a discussion of the future direction of taxation within the context of social responsibility.

Taxation and tax systems

Before discussing the societal impact of taxation in greater detail, it is important to first understand what taxation is and to consider the key features of the taxation systems that operate within most modern societies. Doing so allows us to consider the wider role of taxation within society. Broadly speaking, taxes can be conceptualised as "a compulsory levy, imposed by the government or other tax raising body, on income, expenditure, wealth or people, for which the taxpayer receives nothing specific in return" (Lymer and Oats, 2015:3). This perspective suggests that taxation is an unavoidable consequence. However, others, such as Murphy (2016), adopt an alternative perspective which suggests that the emphasis on the compulsory nature of taxation is a false perspective as most taxation is paid voluntarily by individuals and organisations. This differentiation is important because the way individuals, organisations and governments view taxation will impact on their commitment to accountability, transparency and fair payment, areas which are covered in more detail later in this chapter.

To fully understand the role of taxation within society, it is important to consider what the overriding objectives of these taxes are. Taxation is often considered to be solely a means of raising revenue for the government. While this is true to a certain extent, there are other objectives that can benefit a wider range of stakeholders. Murphy (2016:77) identifies 'Six Rs' of taxation, which offer a wider view of the role of taxation within society:

- Reclaiming money, the government has spent into the economy for re-use;
- Ratifying the value of money;
- Reorganising the economy;
- Redistributing income and wealth;
- Repricing goods and services considered to be incorrectly priced by the market such as tobacco, alcohol, carbon emissions, etc.; and
- Raising representation.

11

Taxation therefore plays a much wider role within the operation of society. Taxes are set by governments through legislation and policy. Governments decide who and what to tax, the rate of taxation that is applicable, how this taxation will be collected and how compliance with taxation requirements can be enforced. Taxpayers include all types of entities: individuals, corporations, charities, cooperatives and public sector organisations. In the UK, the legal form determines to some extent which taxes are payable. For example, charities are not charged corporation tax on their profits whilst non-corporate entities may pay income tax on their profits, but not corporation tax.

Governments have many, often conflicting, interests to balance when setting tax policies, resulting in increasingly complex taxation systems. Indeed, the development of taxes within taxation systems is often a combination of budgetary requirements to encourage development and avoid austerity, plus anti-avoidance measures to encourage greater compliance or remove unfair advantages to a small section of taxpayers. Over many years, this may result in a system which has lost the underpinning conceptual framework or consistent overall strategy. Thus, the complexity of taxation systems increases the need for accountability and transparency in relation to amount of taxation that is paid and collected.

Taking the objectives together as a whole, the outcome is the creation and operation of a system of taxation. There are several theories concerning what constitutes an appropriate tax system. Famously, Adam Smith outlined four 'canons' of taxation in the *Wealth of Nations* (Mirrlees, 2011: 22). These are: proportional, certain – not arbitrary, convenient and efficient.

While these are widely accepted as good general principles, they do not help decide which objectives of taxation are most important, nor how much tax should be collected. More recently, the ICAEW have argued that taxes need to be properly targeted, regularly reviewed and competitive (ICAEW, n.d.: 4). They highlight the need to improve taxation systems by providing a system which is: statutory; certain; simple; easy to collect and calculate; properly targeted; constant; subject to proper consultation; regularly reviewed; fair and reasonable; and competitive. How systems of taxations are designed and what the purpose of taxation is, are therefore important issues in relation to the overall functioning of taxation within modern societies. This is something that is constantly changing and being updated as societies and governments strive to introduce systems that best reflect their aims and objectives. The aims and objectives of the government responsible for creation and amendment of systems of taxation will impact upon the behaviour of individuals and organisations operating within that system, this will be discussed in detail later in this chapter.

■   Taxation bases and taxation categories

Understanding how taxation is calculated allows us to consider the impact that taxation has on a wide range of stakeholders within society. Central to the understanding of the calculation of taxation is the notion of taxation bases. Taxes are generally levied on four main taxation bases; income, expenditure, wealth and people. An ideal taxation base is one which is clear and distinct, measurable and unavoidable. However, in some instances bases are difficult to measure directly and so proxies are used instead. For example, wealth can be difficult to define and measure, which means that factors which indicate wealth are taxed instead. In relation to this, the Organisation for Economic Co-operation and Development (OECD) identifies six key sources of taxation (Murphy, 2016):

- Income and profits
- Compulsory social security contributions paid to general government
- Payroll and workforce
- Property
- Goods and Services
- Other

Despite a diverse range of areas that are subject to taxation, discussions about taxation and social accountability are often narrowly focused on taxation that is associated with profits. This may be because these taxes are more 'visible' to stakeholders and the wider public as organisations are required to disclose them separately in their financial statements. However, these taxes form only part of government revenues. As an example of this, in the case of OECD countries during the year 2014, taxes on business profits made up on average only 9% of total government tax revenues, while taxes on goods and services were 31% (Murphy, 2016). There are therefore a range of different taxation bases and taxation categories, and we will consider some of the most common of these in the following sections.

Turning attention first to the profits that are generated by businesses, these are, in most instances, subject to taxation. Broadly speaking, if the business is unincorporated (i.e. they are a sole trader or a partnership in the UK), the profits of that business form part of the taxable income of the business owner. In contrast to unincorporated businesses, a limited company is a separate legal entity from its owners and as such is assessed for tax on its profits separately from the individuals who own the company. In addition to these formats, there are other increasingly popular organisational forms such as limited liability partnerships (LLPs), cooperatives, charitable organisations, and social enterprises. These structures may follow the same tax rules as incorporated or unincorporated organisations, or they may be treated as a hybrid combination, allowing them to benefit from tax incentives and savings. What these variety of forms highlight is that within the modern global society, international business is no longer confined to large

11

organisations. In the interests of wider society, it is important to ensure any such tax breaks are awarded only to genuine philanthropically oriented or third sector organisations to ensure fairness and prevent austerity from inappropriate taxation.

In addition to the generation of business profits, there are many other activities that organisations undertake which may also be subject to taxation. These taxes are generally subject to less public scrutiny, but they form a very significant proportion of the total revenues generated from taxation by governments. According to PricewaterhouseCoopers (PWC), for every £1 of tax borne on profits by UK 100 Group Companies, there was another £4 borne in other business taxes (PwC[1]). Indeed, Vodafone state in their 2016 annual report on tax transparency that corporation tax was only one of almost seventy different corporate taxes paid by their operating groups each year (Vodafone, 2016). The range of other taxes paid by organisations will vary to some extent depending on the nature and activities of the business being taxed. Payroll taxes and social security (National Insurance) payments are usually based on employee numbers, or on payroll costs, thereby normally reflecting the number and skills of the workforce. In the UK, the main property-based taxes are Land and Buildings Transaction Tax (LBTT) or Stamp Duty Land Tax (SDLT) on the disposal of land and buildings. Another key property cost for profit making organisations are the non-domestic rate charges paid to the local government (or council). Smaller businesses and third sector organisations may receive a partial concession on this charge. Individuals, businesses and third sector organisations will pay many general taxes and duties such as fuel duties, import/export duties, insurance premium tax, and tax on services and goods (Value Added Tax (VAT) in the UK), to name but a few. It should be noted the public sector is not fully exempt from paying tax. For example, payroll taxes and VAT are due at the same rates by public sector organisations as highly profitable large corporations.

■ Tax borne and collected

In addition to the above, organisations also often act as tax collectors for the tax authorities. They collect taxes such as VAT by charging customers the tax inclusive price and then remitting that tax to the relevant tax agency. Similarly, employer organisations generally deduct income tax from employees' wages at source and remit it directly to tax agencies. This leads to more efficient tax collection, but it can also lead to a lack of awareness of the taxation that has been paid. For example, consumers are often unaware of how much of the price they pay goes to the government through taxes such as VAT, and how much goes directly to the seller. Business entities sometimes exploit this confusion by reporting the tax they have collect and paid to the government, rather than the tax they have directly borne. This applies to all organisations whether they are corporates, charities, or third sector.

---

1 https://www.pwc.co.uk/services/tax/total-tax-contribution-100-group.html

■ Tax expenditures and incentives

Decisions about what to tax and what not to tax are made by governments. There are numerous ways that this can be achieved. One commonly applied method is by setting a zero or reduced rate of tax ('structural incentives') or through ad-hoc incentives (for example, waivers of tax on certain types of income). These incentives are often designed to encourage certain behaviours, such as investment in specific industries or activities. There is a cost to the government of such incentives in terms of tax revenues foregone (sometimes referred to as 'tax expenditures') which is deemed to be offset by the benefits achieved by the policy. However, it is very difficult to measure the costs or benefits directly, leading to a lack of accountability for such incentives. The UK government publishes estimates of the costs of these tax 'expenditures' (also known as reliefs), but acknowledges that the quantification process is difficult and does not consider any behavioural changes brought about by the reliefs.

■ Tax planning, avoidance and evasion

Tax avoidance and evasion are widely used terms whose definitions to some extent depend on the knowledge and perspective of the author. It's useful to think of a spectrum of tax behaviours ranging from legitimate tax planning, through tax avoidance to tax evasion. Where you draw the boundary between the different behaviours depends on your knowledge and perspective, and possibly your definition of tax. Tax planning includes the use of tax reliefs which the law specifically permits. Tax evasion, in contrast, is normally seen as involving illegal deliberate non-compliance with tax laws to decrease a tax liability. Hasseldine and Morris (2013:5) outline two necessary conditions for tax evasion: "a failure to satisfy a tax liability that has crystallised, and an intention, based on an event that has occurred, to be deceitful, fraudulent and/or corrupt with respect to that event". Tax avoidance covers the grey area in between. Tax avoidance is a label that can be used by different interested parties to denote diverse types of behaviour, observing that the same phrase is used in different ways by UK tax authorities, tax advisors and interested NGOs (Hasseldine and Morris, 2013). Attitudes to tax avoidance are shaped by our definition of tax, as "when tax is defined as something we owe by compulsion to a government that is alien to us, out of property all of which is rightfully our own, then we can claim that tax avoidance and evasion are actions to prevent our property being taken from us under duress" (Murphy, 2016:49).

11

These are areas where there has been much public debate that will, no doubt, continue for the foreseeable future. It may be argued that any public sector or third sector organisation has less motive and opportunity than the private sector to participate in tax planning. One of the few routes open to the public and third sector is to minimise social security (national insurance) contributions by hiring contractors instead of employing staff (Sikka, 2013). Issues related to tax avoidance and evasion are significant social concerns within modern societies and these issues have attracted the attention of many organisations, which is discussed in more detail later in the chapter.

■   National tax differences

Tax systems are created by governments regarding their current policy pledges and objectives whilst also incorporating micro and global economic forecasts. This often results in an amalgamation of similarities and differences occurring across different taxation systems. Countries with similar diversity within their economic activity may collect tax revenues in a comparable proportion to GDP. There can, however, be significant variations between high-income and low-income countries. For example, for Organisation for Economic Co-operation and Development (OECD) member states, tax revenues in 2011 were 34% of GDP and have been broadly similar for at least 5 years (OECD, 2017). For low-income countries, tax revenues for the period 2000–2009 were as low as 13.7% of GDP (McNabb and LeMay-Boucher, 2014). There are also differences in the contribution made by different taxes. Low-income countries have traditionally relied more heavily on international trade taxes such as import tariffs which are potentially cheaper and easier to collect than income or consumption taxes. Cobham and Klees, (2016:4) note that "tax revenues in most lower-income countries have not seen any great convergence towards OECD country averages". They identify two main reasons for this international pattern: advice from international organisations (such as the World Bank) that has focused on taxes on sale of goods and services, at the expense of direct taxes on income and profits; and tax havens, which will be discussed shortly.

■   Taxation in the global digital economy

Traditionally, the taxation of business profits depended on the geographical source of these profits and on the residence status of the business entity being taxed (i.e. which country it was directed from). The 'source' country would normally have taxing rights over the profits generated in its location. The country of residence might, however, assert a right to tax all profits, wherever they arose. In such cases, there was usually some form of agreement between countries stating the tax each country is entitled to collect, and to place a limit on the amount of tax payable by the organisation.

With companies now able to trade across the world, often with no physical presence in many countries, it is increasingly difficult to define where activities or bases should be taxed. This gives companies many opportunities for creative structuring of transactions and organisations to minimise tax liabilities. The impact to government forecasting is significant. Private sector organisations are legally entitled to choose their taxation base and taxation structure, and the most appealing option may result in significantly reduced taxes paid in one, or more, locations. Whilst this may benefit the organisations, the impact is a significant loss to the public purse. The public sector requires an amount of income from taxes to fund vital public services and risks prolonged periods of austerity without adequate funds. Countries with a very appealing tax system may attract significant investment and as a result raise increased public funds resulting in a better quality of life for residents.

From the above, we can see that the influence of taxation extends beyond the profits that are generated by individuals and organisations. The societal implications of taxation thus extend throughout modern societies, having a significant impact on the lives of a diverse range of stakeholders. The nature of taxation systems that have been described above highlight the importance of having a fair and just taxation system that treats stakeholders within society in an equal and fair manner. Whether this happens in practice is the focus of the remaining sections of this chapter.

Taxation and social responsibility

As previously stated, the payment of taxes is part of the social contract between individuals, organisations and the state. This is the case not just within one country, but increasingly this occurs across multiple national boundaries as result of increased globalisation. What that share of taxation is, by whom it should be paid and where it should be paid, is part of a wider debate. The lack of transparency surrounding such issues has gathered a significant amount of public attention, resulting in calls for an increase in 'tax justice', which refers to the need for all to pay their 'fair share' of taxation. Attempts to increase tax justice have resulted in the creation of the Tax Justice Network (TJN), which was formed in 2003 in attempt to help redress tax anomalies across the globe.

Whilst the idea of taxation as a central aspect of the social contract between individuals, organisations and the state has been discussed, it is worth considering how this compares with other social responsibility issues. Taxation operates within a legal framework but, as we have seen, there is much scope within this framework for minimising the amount of taxation that is paid. Thus, taxation has similar characteristics to decisions made about other social responsibility issues, particularly if we recognise the 'voluntary' nature of certain elements of tax planning. However, taxation differs from other social responsibility areas in an important respect: for most social responsibility activities, the organisation decides what 'social goods' it is going to 'invest' in – be it reducing the emissions from one of its factories, providing schooling for employee children in a country in which it operates, or offering employees healthcare facilities. Taxation is different – when an organisation pays tax, it hands over resources to a governmental body and the entity has no control over how those resources are spent. The decision-making process may therefore be influenced by the level of trust in the government to use those resources 'wisely' and by political views as to how

11

important the role of government in society is. Alternatively, taxation decisions may be based on a purely financial basis, to satisfy the desires or objectives of one or more stakeholders in the organisation.

Beyond issues of social responsibility, taxation is a key element in sustainability. The United Nation's Sustainable Development Goals (SDGs) require significant public financing which realistically can only come from taxation. Some have estimated that the additional public financing required to achieve these goals is around 27% of GDP in low income countries (Tax Justice Network, 2016). In addition to sustainability, taxation is also an important consideration with respect to the exploitation of finite resources. Taxation revenues are one way of 'replacing' the resources extracted, so that the country maintains the same level of 'wealth'. It is difficult, however, to set an appropriate price on such activities, to take account of the loss of the resources and any other environmental costs, but also any additional benefits received such as employment and investment in infrastructure. Although tax revenues are essential for investment to increase the well-being of societies, there is no guarantee that such funds will be spent on public goods; in corrupt or unstable regimes, the tax may not benefit the poor in society but may be used to fund lavish lifestyles or weapons. There must, therefore be accountability not just by tax payers and but also by governments as to how they spend the taxes they collect.

■ Tax and corporate responsibility: the private sector

Corporate social responsibility (CSR) in relation to taxation has received little attention within academic literature (Sikka, 2010; Dowling, 2014). One of the reasons for this is because of the narrow range of stakeholders – employees, customers and investors – who benefit from tax avoidance (Dowling, 2014). That being said, if the public and the State are also seen as key stakeholders, then tax avoidance will attract more widespread scrutiny (Sikka, 2010). This perspective is one which has been taken by CSOs and, increasingly, by international organisations such as the International Monetary Fund (IMF), the OECD and the World Bank. These organisations have produced many reports in the last twenty years on corporate tax avoidance and its impact on low income countries.

Despite recognition of these issues, more work is required to develop a coherent theoretical framework for the discussion of tax within the context of corporate social responsibility. It is an emotive subject, with impassioned claims made by the CSOs and increasingly rigorous defences of their positions by private sector organisations. The reports by the CSOs contain much economic analysis, but little disclosure of qualitative tax matters, such as tax policy. This has become more common within the past ten years and there are increasing opportunities to evaluate the attitudes of organisations in the private sector, particularly large organisations, to tax and actual practices.

There are different lenses through which the issues surrounding accountability and corporate taxes can be viewed. From a stakeholder perspective, if stakeholders were to be defined narrowly as shareholders, one might believe that an organisation had a duty to minimise its tax liabilities as far as legally possible. However, if one broadens the idea of stakeholders to include wider society, then transparency, fairness and sustainability become key issues. The media attention on tax avoidance and evasion within the private sector has often been predicated on notions of 'fairness' and disregarded the genuine legality of the tactics being used. Many would adopt the viewpoint that it is 'unfair' that these entities, because of their size and international operations, can exploit tax differentials and incentives in a way which is not available to smaller entities. The concern here is with the principle of equity, and whether the tax burden is shared on an equitable basis or is falling increasingly on smaller entities as the larger ones are not paying their 'fair share'. The media, public sector organisations, CSOs and other international bodies all share concerns about lack of transparency on tax matters by private sector organisations and the impact this has on the public purse and local communities.

Beyond this, organisations within the accounting and consultancy sector have also been found to be complicit in this regard. Indeed, several of the large global accountancy and consultancy firms have faced significant fines for promoting aggressive tax avoidance schemes. Following this, they have since sought to re-establish their credibility and that of their clients by producing reports highlighting the wide range of taxes paid by the private sector and the contributions they make to society.

The public sector

As discussed above, national governments are responsible for creating taxation law and for putting in place the infrastructure to collect taxes and encourage compliance. The tax environment and systems they create help to influence 'tax morale', which is defined as the attitude of a taxpayer towards the taxation system and the likelihood they will comply with the regulations and pay the required amount of taxation. The system will be shaped by political considerations, such as how far tax systems should have a redistributive goal, but should also ensure that revenues are maximised as far as possible and all taxpayers are treated equally (ICAEW, n.d).

Governments also wish to create a thriving economy and encourage investment. The tax system is one way of doing this as it can be used to achieve policy objectives through incentives, system requirements, charges or tax rates to encourage certain behaviours and investments. Taxation is also a means of 'charging' for public resources, or 'externalities', such as pollution, to ensure that the organisation pays for its impact as far as possible. It is, however, extremely difficult to measure the cost of tax incentives and to balance those against the benefits (such as employment, or infrastructure) brought by an organisations' investments and activities.

11

The governments of low-income countries face many challenges when negotiating with large globally mobile private sector organisations – the latter may have vast experience and resources in such negotiations. Establishing a robust, skilled and resourced revenue service and infrastructure may not initially appear to be a key priority for low-income countries, but without such a system, the country will not be able to obtain the revenues essential for its growth and development. Equally, developed countries must maintain a robust system to maintain economic stability and 'deal-making' with large private sector organisations is not restricted to low-income countries. In the UK, for example, tax officials are empowered to strike deals with multinational entities when discussing complex tax arrangements. Indeed, relatively recently Vodafone reached an agreement with HMRC regarding the amount of taxation that was due, but this agreement was then reviewed by the Public Accounts Committee. Transparency and accountability are thus key to ensuring that there is trust in tax systems.

Beyond the private and public sector

Issues surrounding taxation and social responsibility extend beyond the private and public sectors. If governments have a 'right' to a share of profits generated by an organisation, which is captured through taxation, we can consider whether this share is different for organisations who primarily operate with social aims and objectives. For example, if these organisations employ staff, should they have to pay the same employment and social security taxes as profit generating organisations? These types of issue primarily relate to the structural reliefs that the government designs within a system and the consequential impact on the public purse. Tax systems are intrinsically linked to government accountability. We can also consider if these organisations view tax as part of their social contract and to what extent. These issues are discussed in the following sections in relation to cooperatives, the third sector and NGOs.

■ Cooperatives and family businesses

From a taxation point of view, one of the key differences between cooperatives and family businesses and more typical private sector organisations is that they are smaller in size and have much simpler organisational structures. Smaller businesses are less likely to have the potential for tax savings significant enough to warrant the setting up of complex structures, or have the necessary funds to be able to afford the fees of tax consultancy firms for advice on advanced tax planning. A family-controlled business, however, can, in some instances, have opportunities for 'tax planning' decisions, such as how to extract funds from a company in a tax-efficient manner. Indeed, a study conducted by Chen et al., (2010) on the tax aggressiveness of US listed firms, comparing family and non-family firms between 1996 and 2000. Their work suggested that family firms were less tax aggressive than non-family firms. However, they attribute this not to any difference in attitude to tax, but to family owners' concerns that these practices might indicate rent extraction (non-value maximising activities decision-makers pursue at the expense of shareholders), which would deter minority investors and so increase the cost of capital.

In addition to family businesses, cooperatives represent another possible business structure. Cooperatives are organisations that are owned by their members, who each have a share in the business. They may therefore have a very wide membership base in contrast to concentrated traditional shareholdings in some limited companies. Currently in the UK, there are nearly 7,000 independent cooperatives, contributing £36 billion to the British economy (Co-operatives UK, 2015). Cooperatives often operate through the structure of limited liability companies and therefore pay taxes on their profits; the profits being calculated before any distributions to members. However, cooperatives have traditionally emphasised sustainability and community responsibility. Indeed, one of their core principles is "giving people more control over the things that matter to them – their work, homes and local area" (Co-operatives UK, 2017[2]). Further, Cooperatives have led the way in fair taxation with the Midcounties Cooperative being a pioneer of the Fair Tax Mark. Further to this, Cooperatives UK state their position regarding fair and transparent taxes and their expectations of their cooperative members clearly with regards to the Fair Tax Mark. They state it is:

> Already adopted by pioneering cooperatives including Midcounties and the Phone Co-op, Cooperatives UK – following a mandate from the cooperative sector at its annual conference in 2014 – has agreed a partnership with the Fair Tax Mark to make it simpler for cooperatives to become accredited, including a 20% discount for Cooperatives UK members. (Co-operatives UK, 2015[3])

This would imply a very clear attitude towards fair taxation within their organisations. The Fair Tax Mark is an effective way for cooperatives to demonstrate that they are fair and ethical businesses, and distinguish themselves from competitors (Co-operatives UK, 2015). Third party organisations are not specifically required to report on their tax policies and it remains a discretionary report for any organisation.

■ The third sector

Third sector organisations can take a variety of legal forms which will determine the tax rules that they are subject to, including any incentives and concessions which may apply. For example, taxation may be due on any surplus income or profits generated, depending on the nature, purpose and structure of the organisation. Whether third sector organisations view paying tax as an appropriate sharing of profits with the government, or whether they view taxes as a loss of funds which would otherwise have been used for the core social purpose is an area which could usefully be explored.

2 See: https://www.uk.coop/promoting-co-ops/fair-tax-mark

3 See: https://ldn.coop/worker-co-ops/reimagine-economy-uk-cooperative-economy-2017/

In the case of charities, they are generally exempt from corporation tax on any surpluses (profits) they make but, like all employers, have to pay social security contributions for employees and often suffer irrecoverable VAT. Thus, charities are not exempt from needing to ensure that they comply with tax regulations. In addition to this, there are also generous tax incentives on donations, benefiting both the charity and (higher rate tax) donors. Further structural reliefs encourage individuals to leave charitable bequests in their wills. Charities are also eligible for relief on non-domestic rates on any properties they occupy. Third sector organisations thus have a slightly different tax contract with society. They benefit from tax exemptions and reliefs so need to be accountable for these tax expenditures as well as any tax they have actually incurred. Thus, from a social accounting point of view, tax disclosures can be as significant for charities as for any other organisations.

■ Civil society organisations and taxation

Over the past twenty-five years, there has been increasing media and CSO attention on issues of tax avoidance by large organisations within the private sector, highlighting the exploitation of loopholes and opportunities presented by globalisation and the growth of intangibles (Murphy, 2016). In 2000, Oxfam published a report *Tax Havens: Releasing the Hidden Billions for Poverty Eradication* linking the issues of tax avoidance by large organisations with welfare and social issues in low and middle-income countries (Oxfam, 2000). Tax havens are jurisdictions which have very low levels of tax and often high levels of secrecy, not exchanging information with other tax jurisdictions. It is argued that corporations artificially shift profits to such locations to avoid tax in other countries.

There has also been increased attention on the agreements between large organisations in the extractive industries and host country governments. In 2002, the CSO 'Publish What You Pay' (PWYP) was formed with the objective of ensuring that extractive industry companies disclosed more information about the payments they make to the governments of the countries in which they operate, so that those governments could be held to account by their citizens for how those funds are used. Other campaigning charities also produced tax-related reports over the next few years. Tax avoidance and tax justice were being clearly positioned on the world political and economic agenda.

Summary and future directions

This chapter has presented taxation in terms of a social contract between governments, organisations and individuals within modern societies. It began by outlining how taxation operates by discussing taxation systems, bases and the various taxes that government seek to collect. Further to this, the chapter highlighted the different reactions to taxation that are witnessed in the private and public sectors. Moving beyond this, it covered the relationship between taxation and organisations existing outside of these sectors, with emphasis placed on cooperatives and family businesses, the public sector and the third sector. Specifically, it highlighted the role of organisations and initiatives designed to challenge the status quo and to campaign for fairer systems of taxations.

Taxes have therefore been presented as more than a means of raising public funds. If we believe fair taxes are essential to the operation of modern societies, we must also assume ethical behaviour in the form of integrity and compliance. The implications of raising or reducing taxes, or creating incentives, may benefit one sector of society whilst disadvantaging another. This is increasingly challenging in a digitally mobile economy, where private sector organisations can effectively choose their tax location to their best advantage. The goal should be a transparent taxation system in which everyone pays their fair share, where adequate funds are raised to avoid austerity, and where a competitive sustainable economic activity, growth and development are encouraged. This would result in a fairly funded and taxed society in which organisations and individuals are all accountable. Incentives and initiatives may be designed within a system to encourage compliance and payment of taxes within the true country of source, and discourage participation in tax avoidance schemes or location in a tax haven. It has been estimated that, in the last five years, over £12 billion has been lost via tax avoidance schemes in the UK alone. Cooperative associations, on the other hand, are demonstrably present in the Fair Tax debate, in addition to showing strong ethical principles. This may be a model some large private sector organisations could learn from.

Taxation is an essential element in the sustainability, development and maintenance of a stable economy and a fundamental aspect of the social contract between taxpayers, government and wider society. Moving forward, we should encourage greater consultation and debate around the issues of taxation and wider participation in these issues beyond specialist expertise. This would allow us to more fully understand the diversity of society and differing perspectives that exist in relation to taxation. Such debate would also be a mechanism to improve communications and transparency and raise awareness of the intrinsic link between taxes paid, public sector funds and the impact on society. Greater engagement with local communities could extend to greater transparency and information sharing with tax havens to effectively remove the tax benefit of utilising tax saving schemes.

11

In relation to transparency, making reporting of the taxation paid by organisations within the private, public and third sector a statutory requirement would engender greater trust and increase understanding of the link between taxation and society. In relation to this, the issues highlighted in the current chapter, including initiatives such as the Fair Tax Mark and the Tax Justice Network have highlighted the demand within society for engagement with issues relating to accountability and social responsibility concerning taxation. In this regard, the role of organisations within the accountancy and consultancy sectors should also be questioned. Indeed, several of the large global accountancy and consultancy firms have faced significant fines for 'promoting' aggressive tax avoidance schemes. Despite attempts to re-establish their credibility and that of their clients their role in lawful and unlawful tax avoidance continues to be an issue within the industry and the practices of such organisations should be placed under greater scrutiny.

Discussion questions

1   Compare taxation with other social accounting issues.

2   Discuss whether the Fair Tax Mark is an appropriate way to encourage better reporting of tax issues.

3   Identify a multinational company which operates across the world. Review the tax disclosures in their financial statements and assess the usefulness of the information for evaluating their attitudes to tax as corporate social responsibility issue.

4   In the global, digital economy what criteria should be used to assess where and how much tax global corporations should pay?

References and further reading

Boden, R., Killian, S., Mulligan, E. and Oats, L. (2010) Critical perspectives on taxation, *Critical Perspectives on Accounting*, **21**(7), 541-544.

Chen, S., Chen, X., Cheng, Q. and Shevlin, T. (2010) Are family firms more tax aggressive than non-family firms?, *Journal of Financial Economics*, **95**(1), 41-61.

Cobham, A. and Klees, S. J. (2016) *Global Taxation: Financing Education and Other Sustainable Development Goals*. Background Paper prepared for the International Commission on Financing Global Education Opportunity, Published by ActionAid International, Oxfam International, and Tax Justice Network. Available at: http://lib.guides.umd.edu/social_justice/economic_development

Co-operatives UK (2017) An incredible 13.6 million people own the UK's cooperatives. https://www.uk.coop/about/what-cooperative. Accessed 21 September 2017.

Co-operatives UK (2015). Fair Tax Mark. https://www.uk.coop/promoting-co-ops/fair-tax-mark. Accessed 21 September 2017.

Dowling, G.R. (2014) The curious case of corporate tax avoidance: Is it socially responsible, *Journal of Business Ethics*, **124**(1), 173-184

Hasseldine, J. and Morris, G. (2013) Corporate social responsibility and tax avoidance: A comment and reflection, *Accounting Forum*, **37**(1), 1-14.

ICAEW (n.d). *Towards a Better Tax System*. London: ICAEW.

Lymer, A. and Oats, L. (2015) *Taxation: Policy and Practice*, 22nd ed., Birmingham: Fiscal Publications.

McNabb, K. and LeMay-Boucher, P. (2014) Tax Structures, Economic Growth and Development, Available at: http://www.ictd.ac/images/ICTD_WP22_2.pdf

Mirrlees, J., and Institute of Fiscal Studies (2011). *Tax by Design: The Mirrlees Review*. Oxford: Oxford University Press.

Murphy, R., (2016). *The Joy of Tax*. London: Transworld Publishers.

OECD (2016) *Revenue Statistics 2016*, Paris: OECD.

OECD (2017). Tax, About the Inclusive Framework on BEPS, available at: http://www.oecd.org/tax/beps-about.htm. Accessed 21 September 2017

Oxfam, (2000). *Tax Havens: Releasing the Hidden Billions for Poverty Eradication*. Oxfam International

Sikka, P. (2010) Smoke and mirrors: Corporate social responsibility and tax avoidance, *Accounting Forum*, **34**(3/4), 153-168.

Sikka, P. (2013) Smoke and mirrors: Corporate social responsibility and tax avoidance—A reply to Hasseldine and Morris, *Accounting Forum*, **37**(1), 15-28.

Tax Justice Network. (2016) Report launch: Global taxation - Financing the Sustainable Development Goals, 2016.

■ Some useful web links

CSO Publish What you Pay - http://www.publishwhatyoupay.org/about/history/

OSCR (Office of the Scottish Charity Regulator) Scotland - https://www.oscr.org.uk/

PWC– https://www.pwc.co.uk/services/tax/total-tax-contribution-100-group.html

Vodafone (2016), Annual Report, Available at: http://www.vodafone.com/content/annualreport/annual_report16/index.html

11

12 Tomorrow's Accounting and Society's Future

Audrey Paterson, Eleni Chatzivgeri, Yasser Eliwa, and William Jackson

Introduction

This book began by introducing you to the notion of accounting for society, the historical development of corporate social responsibility, accountability and ethics and its importance to everyday life. Unlike other mainstream textbooks which predominantly focus on large private sector organisations, we have explored the concept of social accounting, the role of business and accountability from the public sector, third sector, cooperatives and family business perspectives. By doing so, we demonstrate that social accounting and accountability equally applies to these sectors and that its application is just as complex and controversial as it is in the business world. Indeed, examples that demonstrate questionable ethical and moral behaviour within these areas and professional practice are threaded throughout the book. We have also noted that careful reflection and consideration are essential ingredients of a social accounting system when determining socially responsible investments, the role of tax in a fair society and global economy and ensuring professional integrity.

We have shown that accounting is an essential pillar of society, providing the foundations on which organisations and governments base their economic and financial decisions. It provides a mechanism whereby information relevant to stakeholders, managers, investors, etc. can be used to evaluate performance, regardless of the sector in which the organisation is situated. These foundations have come under critical scrutiny in recent years, particularly following the recent spate of global financial crises. Indeed, the reliance, accuracy and compliance of accounting information and the profession were heavily criticised alongside organisations who had also not foreseen or reacted to the global financial crisis adequately. Consequently, the profession has turned its attention to how it can provide solutions that facilitate greater transparency, accountability, reporting, and fair value measurements. Greater attention has also been drawn to corporate accountability over the last couple of decades with increasing importance also being placed on the social impact of organisations' activities.

Despite the growing trend towards greater corporate accountability and increasing revival of social accounting there remains a significant gap between what organisations do, what they are willing to report, and the rights of society. In this concluding chapter, we consider the realities and myths of social accounting in relation to tomorrow's accounting and society's future. The chapter begins with a discussion of accounting as a social and institutional practice. It then moves on to consider the issues raised throughout the book and reflects on how the public sector, third sector, cooperatives and family businesses need to adapt and respond to demands for increased social responsibility and demonstrate this through a social accounting and accountability system. The chapter concludes with a discussion of the changing nature of accountability and social accounting, future directions and potential developments within the social accounting arena.

Accounting as a social and institutional practice

In the past, accounting has been considered as a simple technique that can be used to provide, process and evaluate information and has been characterised as a 'technical topic'. However, accounting establishes a social dimension, since it is a 'more dynamic and sophisticated' discipline (Rudkin, 2007), and is thus not only an institutional but also a social practice (Potter, 2005). In recent decades we have witnessed an extraordinary transformation in the way organisations account for their activities and impact on society. This can be attributed to several factors. First, from an academic perspective, there has been a growing body of research that investigates the pervasive and enabling characteristics of accounting and its impact on organisational activity and consequently society and the environment. This research has not just been contained to the accounting discipline but has appeared within financial economics, psychology, organizational theory, sociology, political theory, anthropology, history, philosophy, linguistic theory, communication theory, theology, and critical theory, thereby creating an interdisciplinary project which furthers our knowledge and understanding of the far-reaching effects of accounting as a social and institutional practice.

Hopwood and Miller have been particularly influential in this regard. It is through their work that an extensive investigation into the socio-historical impact of accounting originated. From such works accounting is shown to be a calculative practice that infiltrates the contemporary world in a myriad of diverse ways (Hopwood and Miller, 1994). Indeed, it is through their work that we can appreciate the genesis of accounting's modern power, how influential accounting

12

has been in the politics of economic measurement and the changing relationship of the accounting profession and the state in regulatory terms.

Following Hopwood and Miller's pioneering work, several strands of research demonstrate the role of accounting: in management motivations for social reporting/disclosure; as a tool for ensuring securing/maintaining legitimacy and societal expectations; in demonstrating ethical and social accountability to stakeholders and the wider community; and as a social accountability tool. Indeed, such work demonstrates the continuing importance of accounting in so many spheres of social life that an understanding of the conditions and consequences of such a calculative technology is vital in an increasingly globalised and connected world.

Accounting, ethics and the business world

The last two decades have witnessed the burgeoning social responsibility and accountability movement. Even organisations that produce questionable goods such as tobacco, alcohol and gambling have joined the bandwagon. As Chapter 2 demonstrates, this has been driven by the recent financial crisis and spate of business scandals in which accounting has been implicated. This has fuelled the perceived need for organisations across all sectors to demonstrate accountability and ethical behaviour in their business activity. However, the concept of accountability is rather a chameleon as it holds different meanings depending on the context and is not simple to define or identify. The question of ethical business behaviour is a subject that has troubled thinkers and policy makers for many decades. Indeed, the subject of business and accounting ethics has become substantially complicated as organisations conduct business across multiple national boundaries and cultural settings. The activities of organisations have the potential to impact on all aspects of society, which drives the need for organisations to demonstrate proper ethical and moral behaviour and accountability. A robust code of conduct/ethics is generally regarded as the hallmark of a profession. This has been recognised by the accounting profession and their implementation of a code, by adherence to which it is expected that members will behave well. Members are expected to comply not only with the letter of the code but also the spirit. Organisations demonstrate varying degrees of responsibility and compliance towards social accountability and ethical behaviour. Those with robust systems can achieve a reduction of unethical or illegal behaviour and can use this to their strategic advantage.

However, we need to recognise that social accounting and corporate social responsibility (CSR) practices have a long history. CSR practices, as Chapter 3 demonstrates, did not develop in a vacuum. Several factors and social actors influenced its development and shaped what it is today, in developed and developing economies. Yet, CSR practices and their implementation in developed countries and developing economies differ in significant ways. Though the broad aims of CSR in developed and developing economies are the same, the manifestation, progression and conceptualisation of CSR between these two broad economic categories differ. Globally, CSR developed mainly from philanthropic practices and social movements, and recently has progressed to a wider range of issues and practices such as fair trade, environmental protection, corporate governance and SRI. In developing economies, CSR is still at the philanthropic phase, because of poor governance and weak institutional structures. However, it is clear from the analysis in Chapter 3, that the CSR decisions and practices of businesses are no longer only motivated by economic benefits but also in response to wider social issues and the changing needs and opinions of a wider section of society.

Whilst CSR has attracted attention from practitioners and academics from different disciplines over the years, the whole idea is yet to be fully integrated. Concepts of what it is, the rationale behind it, and the strategies for achieving it are yet to be synthesised into a coherent whole. This is further complicated by the increased globalisation of organisational activity and rising political uncertainty. Chapter 4 has attempted to demystify several of the issues surrounding CSR. Here we discussed CSR by exploring five major dimensions (environmental, social, economic, stakeholder and voluntary). Consequently, we identify that CSR activities are carried out by organisations from the most basic level (economic responsibility) to the most developed (philanthropic responsibility). The divergent theoretical arguments regarding the ethics and morality of corporate behaviour are utilised to provide greater insight into the complexity of CSR issues and the changing business landscape. Strategic approaches to CSR implementation, which assumes that organisations should embrace CSR as a key business issue rather than as an ad hoc response to corporate social and economic failures are presented. Stakeholder engagement in embedding a strategic approach to CSR in organisations is shown to be essential in developing effective social accountability and CSR. However, it is clear from the evidence covered and examples raised that the concept of social accountability and CSR are somewhat elusive, and that good practice is dependent on the worldview that society and organisations hold.

Up until this point of the text, we focussed on the concepts of social accountability and CSR, how these have been developed and their impact on organisational activity. From here we moved on to consider how these concepts have helped in the drive towards increased social accountability and CSR and their usefulness in achieving sustainability; socially responsible investments; and how organisations, shareholders and stakeholders can evaluate the social accountability of the organisations in which they have a vested interest.

Sustainability, SRI and social audits

For over four decades, social reporting has been under the scope of accounting study, as well as being a concern for major organisations (Milne and Gray, 2012). We identified that during the 1970s, a few organisations were ahead of their time by disclosing social information in their annual reports and (fewer still) by creating a separate social report (Kolk, 2010). Given the current drive by governments and influential interest groups across the world towards ensuring sustainability, it is prudent to develop an understanding of the underlying principles that have contributed to today's developments. Chapter 6, therefore, provides a chronicle of SER, and CSR and sustainability reporting; separating the two and exploring the current state of practice. It provides the historical background to the concerns from which socially and environmentally friendly business, its first attempts at reporting, and the trends of its development emerged. Within this, the very influential triple bottom line (TBL) has been applied to show how sustainability perceptions have changed, not only in terms of accounting and reporting, but also organisational strategies and thinking.

Initiatives promoting integrated thinking and sustainability strategies, which include both voluntary and mandatory guidelines, were formed in the 1970s and 1980s. Today, these initiatives have a significant role in the markets, affecting mainly large organisations. Despite the power and influence this implies, there are many theoretical gaps in the fundamentals of both the TBL and sustainability reporting, and consequently, to the initiatives as well. It is argued that all organisations are accountable to their stakeholders and under that pressure, feel obliged to act and report; in short, to provide an account as to how their actions contribute to a better future. However, the future of sustainability reporting is likely to be volatile. On the one hand, its increased popularity promotes optimism towards the future, as more economies and markets get involved in sustaining resources and communities for future generations. On the other hand, if the criticisms involved in the practices are to be considered valid, there is doubt as to whether what is being done today will maintain and empower the economy, people, and nature in the future. It will be interesting to see, what further developments the EU Commission and governments mandate for sustainability and organisational responsibility on this matter.

In line with the sustainability drive, there have been calls for more detailed measures and indicators that could be used to assess the social and economic processes and outcomes of organisations' sustainable development strategies and plans. Indeed, the adage 'if you want it to count, count it' has underpinned many of the sustainability and socially responsible investment (SRI) debates. Considering this, we have introduced you to the concept of SRI. We have acknowledged that SRI is not a new concept but has evolved over many centuries and has been influenced by several factors including religion, culture and the preference of regions, with each region focusing on areas most important to them. Indeed today, Scandinavian countries have based their policies strongly around issues of environmental and ecological concern, while countries like the UK put issues of community development at the forefront of SRI policies. Campaigners in favour of SRI posit that screens are more than mere tools allowing moral standards of investors to be aligned with investment choices; they argue that by investing in organisations that demonstrate a high level of social responsibility, SRI lowers the cost of capital of such organisations and thereby encourages the focus on improved SRI performance (Vanwalleghem, 2017). It further demonstrates that the SRI movement is increasing in strength and thus forms an integral part of many governments' political agendas.

Having considered these aspects, we turned our attention to ways in which organisations can demonstrate their social responsibility and accountability in an effective way, given the conflict between societal needs and expectations; and organisations who are resistant to being held to account. Our starting point was an overview of the social audit movement, which was presented in Chapter 7. Social audit has been shown here to be multi-faceted in nature and scope and, as a result, three main types of social audit were considered. By looking at the early developments in social audit, the chapter highlighted the origins of social audit as an external mechanism designed to increase transparency and accountability regarding the impact of organisational activities on an array of stakeholders. As stakeholders began to demand greater levels of accountability, coupled with several corporate scandals, organisations started to take responsibility for assessing and reporting on their social, ethical and environmental impact. Along these lines, two further types of social audit: supply chain audits and self-generated audit were developed. The former concerns organisations, mainly from the corporate sector, adopting codes of conduct and external standards to ensure the safety and fair treatment of workers within supply chains. Once adopted, organisations should ensure, through a process of social audit, that these standards are being adhered to by factories and organisations in their supply chains. Finally, the chapter considered the increased adoption of the holistic process of social audit by organisations designed with social, ethical and environmental goals in mind. The chapter details the development of several initiatives in this area that has resulted in moves towards professionalisation of the social audit movement and considers its relevance to the public and third sector as well as to cooperatives and family businesses. However, the effectiveness of these audits to ensure social accountability and transparency are ultimately dependent on the level of stakeholder engagement, regulation and political power.

Social accounting in the public and third sectors

Having considered the relevance of social accounting, business ethics, CSR, sustainability and SRI we then investigated their importance and application in the public and third sectors. We began our analysis with the development of public sector accounting which has always been in line with the growth of the public sector and influence of the wider environment in which it has operated. Initially, the public sector was the instrument for the development of the welfare state and the main aim was to provide services to the citizens. So, this means that the public sector could not have the same managerial tools as the private sector.

12

Economic uncertainty and the complexity of the growing global environment have contributed to the public debate of the need for public sector restructuring. The result of this debate was the emergence of New Public Management (NPM) during the 1980s, which aimed to improve the efficiency and implementation of private sector accounting techniques and their associated managerial tools in the public sector. This was the primary initiative that shaped public policy but not the only one. Initiatives such as Citizen's Charters and New Public Governance attempted to provide a more balanced approach compared to the right-wing orientation of NPM.

The turning point for many public sectors across Europe was the economic crisis of 2008, which led to huge pressure for the privatisation of some public services and the shrinking of others. This period also led to public expenditure being decreased to allow bank recapitalisation. In this context, the role of accounting has been critically important as it can provide information that will promote the democratic use of funds and support a context of strong governance and accountability; which can not only improve efficiency, but also transparency and democratic participation. The role of citizens in democratic participation has also been highlighted, as they are ultimately the only ones who can bring about change. Accounting must be a comprehensive and understandable language to provide an effective tool for citizens seeking accountability and equity. It is evident that the use of every technical aspect of accounting must be examined at the general social level. The public sector is a constantly changing environment that includes many stakeholders with different interests, therefore, changes in accounting practice are influenced by perspectives, which typically do not emerge from economic rationalistic aims.

Third sector organisations (TSOs) form an essential part of the economy and provide essential and valuable services to vulnerable segments of society. To fully appreciate the importance of the third sector, the scope, composition, and size of TSOs in contemporary economies is discussed in some detail in Chapter 9. As with other organisations, TSOs are under pressure to deliver services at low cost. As the cases of United Way of America and the American Red Cross indicate, donors tend to criticise excessive administrative expenses, on items such as salaries, training, and fundraising activities. Also, they tend to discourage investment in infrastructure that would improve capacity and would increase the number of those benefiting from the services TSOs offer. Donors appear to regard low overhead costs as a key indicator of how efficiently a TSO uses the funds donated and tend to support those charities that report low overhead expenses.

Even though charities recognise their accountability to a wide number of stakeholders, accountability in TSOs is predominantly hierarchical, with an external control emphasis. Reporting is used to evaluate efficiency against predefined targets that aim to create conformity to standards and regulation, with little emphasis placed on downward accountability and on the impact of their activities on beneficiaries. However, as the chapter argues, the preoccupation with upward accountability could erode value added through their vision and mission statement. This could have a negative impact on the independence and the flexibility of TSOs to meet the needs of their beneficiaries over time. To satisfy their holistic accountability and the dynamic requirements for the services they provide, particularly in developing countries, the third sector needs to constantly revisit their mission statements and their role in changing the environment for their beneficiaries through their services.

Cooperatives, family businesses and tax

Two other economic sectors, namely cooperatives and family businesses, are also crucial to national economies. Cooperative organisations exist to produce goods or services in the public interest, and/or to maximise the profits of their owners and thus differ from public and private sector organisations. In contrast to public and private organisations, the primary purpose of a cooperative is the advancement of its members and not the pursuit of public interest or economic gain. Family businesses, on the other hand, are driven by profit maximisation in the same way as large multi-national organisations. The main difference lies in the fact that family businesses are managed and controlled within the family. This does not, however, mean that they are not vulnerable to inappropriate, unethical or fraudulent behaviour. Indeed, both cooperatives and family businesses face similar governance and social accountability problems as the other sectors of the economy. Theoretical perspectives, social capital and performance, organisational and governance structures all emphasise the complexity of establishing good governance, and social accountability policy and procedures are considered in relation to these two segments. The role and compositions of boards are important aspects in establishing appropriate and robust systems of CSR and social accountability. Indeed: who governs; board roles and board relationships with management; board size and director selection processes; the importance of board members participation and the input of managers, respectively, are shown to have a significant impact on the performance and social perceptions of the organisation. Chapter 10 analysed and discussed these issues in some detail and demonstrated that there is no 'one size fits all' approach to ensuring good governance and social accountability. However, it also showed that initiatives could be taken to promote the work of these sectors and that the impact they have on society and communities could be highlighted in an effort to increase public trust.

Tax is a core element of a socially responsible organisation. Taxes are the main way to raise public funds, which in turn enable the provision of public services. Tax needs to be seen as a social good and something that organisations of all types are proud to pay. Society needs to have a more sophisticated debate about the role of tax. Social responsibility must be exercised not just by private

12

sector organisations through complying with tax regulations, etc., but also by organisation across economic sectors and governments, and by creating open, equitable tax systems. If we believe fair taxes are essential in a fair society, we must also assume ethical behaviour in the form of integrity and compliance. The implications of raising or reducing taxes, or creating incentives, may benefit one sector of society whilst disadvantaging another. This is increasingly challenging in a digitally mobile economy, where private sector organisations can effectively choose a tax location to maximise their economic advantage. The ultimate tax goal may be defined as a transparent tax system where: everyone pays their fair share; adequate funds are raised to avoid austerity, while maintaining a competitive global platform and; sustainable economic activity, growth and development are encouraged, resulting in a fairly funded and taxed society in which organisations and individuals are all accountable. Incentives and initiatives may be designed within a system to encourage compliance and payment of taxes within the true country of source, and discourage participation in tax avoidance schemes or location in a tax haven. Currently, it is estimated that around £12 billion is lost via tax avoidance schemes. Co-operative associations may be seen as demonstrably present in the Fair Tax debate, in addition to their strong ethical principles. This may be a model some large private sector organisations could learn from.

Future directions/paradigm change

Despite the growing trend of corporate accountability and the increasing revival of social accounting, there remains a significant gap between what organisations do, what they are willing to report, and the rights of society. The history and the dynamics of CSR practices from a wide social context, demonstrate that social accounting and CSR practices have been shaped through different factors, including globalisation. It has been argued that understanding globalisation is not an easy process due to the many different definitions have been developed throughout the years; perhaps attributable to the diverse range of cultural experiences and interpretations applied to it. According to Al-Rodhan (2006:3), for example, it comprises "economic integration; the transfer of policies across borders; the transmission of knowledge; cultural stability; the reproduction, relations, and discourses of power; it is a global process, a concept, a revolution, and 'an establishment of the global market free from socio-political control'." It is claimed that through globalisation, distances become shorter, and interaction becomes easier. However, this raises significant questions particularly about the responsibility and social accountability of governments, organisations and the role of accounting. For example, does globalisation make things easier or not? Does it enable interaction between participants, or is this just a myth we all want to believe? What are the impact and challenges of globalisation on social and environmental practices and consequently society? Moreover, what role does accounting play in this?

Globalisation has increased international investment and trade, which in turn has increased the need for standardisation of accounting practice and greater social accountability and organisational CSR. It has been argued that the use of a common set of accounting principles and CSR disclosures (International Financial Reporting Standards (IFRS)) reduces the risk of missed investment opportunities (Miles and Nobes, 1998) and enables comparability for investors and stakeholders seeking SRI opportunities, not only among a parent company and its subsidiaries, but also among companies operating in the same industry in different countries (Leuz and Verrecchia, 2000). Indeed, the increased quality of accounting information after IFRS adoption has apparently increased transparency and the ability to attract foreign capital (Covrig *et al.*, 2007). The 2005 mandatory adoption of the IFRS by all European listed companies as well as the voluntary one by many different non-EU countries, shows that in the context of the globalisation, accountants need to adjust to new rules (Wei, 2008).

However, the harmonisation of accounting standards reveals that there are different globalisation approaches, since, despite countries adopting IFRS, they are still trying to retain varying degrees of independence over their regulations (Godfrey and Chalmers, 2007). The differences between countries in relation to their economic, legal, political and cultural characteristics also affects globalisation, which in turn, affects the different agendas followed by national standard setters. Thus, globalisation affects accounting and CSR practices and vice-versa. This will, therefore, require continuous investigation, to understand the impact and challenges of globalisation in the wider context and to further evaluate its societal impact, so that the accounting profession can develop appropriate responses to these situational changes.

It is also important to recognise that globalisation has different dimensions: political decisions (such as the General Agreement on Tariffs and Trade back in 1947), technological achievements (such as decreased communication and transportation costs), and economic developments (Scherer and Palazzo, 2008), and also entails risks. For example, globalisation comprises the transfer of policies across different countries, but given the existence of different cultural and legal environments, there is considerable discretion of managers in determining the social and ethical standards of their organisation. This is evident in the numerous social and environmental scandals that frequently appear in the social media and those that were highlighted throughout this book. Therefore, future efforts in standardising social and environmental policies in a globalising world, where multinational companies (MNCs) thrive, should also take into consideration how such discretion can be handled.

Additionally, organisations operating across national borders also face challenges due to different legal practices followed in the different countries in which they operate. It has been argued that MNCs are expected to fill in the gaps of non-existing CSR regulations in developing countries and are seen as the key answer to the need for global regulation (Matten and Crane, 2005). However, the

12

adoption of CSR practices remains largely voluntary and results in differences in MNCs' contributions to international development goals. Even though prior research has found that MNCs "can help their foreign suppliers from developing countries become more socially responsible" (Marano and Kostova, 2016:29) this has not always been translated into action. Rather there are examples of organisations continually sourcing low-cost products from suppliers that have questionable practices, such as child labour, to secure greater profit maximisation, in full knowledge that their use in developed countries is deemed unethical and socially irresponsible. This therefore raises more questions. Is the existing level of regulation sufficient? Can accounting practice help to alleviate these cultural and political differences and facilitate greater social accountability? The solution to the regulation gap might be self-regulation or the development of selected initiatives of third sector globally, which will benefit society in developing countries.

As Cooper and Sherer (1984:208) stated, "any accounting contains a representation of a specific social and political context. Not only is accounting policy essentially political in that it derives from the political struggle in a society as a whole but also the outcomes of accounting policy are essentially political in that they operate for the benefit of some groups in society and to the detriment of others." This implies that any changes in the political scene will influence the discipline and practices of accounting and their outcomes.

The global political landscape also changed significantly during 2016 with the election of Donald Trump in the USA and the vote of UK citizens to leave the European Union (Brexit). In 2015, after many years of negotiation, 195 countries (including the US) signed the Paris Accord, which contained far reaching environmental commitments alongside calls for greater transparency. On the assumption of his Presidency, Donald Trump quickly announced that the US would withdraw from the accord, claiming that going ahead would cost millions of American jobs (Shear, 2017). Apart from the Paris Accord's attempt to account for each country's (and in turn each organisation's) environmental responsibility (and consequently social impact), recent initiatives have also included efforts towards increased transparency of extractive industries and their contribution to the societies/countries in which they operate (accounting for the society). But, given the fact that the UK is now leaving the EU (with the stated view of some members of the Government to reduce the legislative burden from organisations such as the European Court of Justice) and given that Donald Trump campaigned on a platform of reduced regulation to stimulate business (including the repeal of social and environmental initiatives), we have to recognise that the movement towards greater international cooperation in this area may have hit more than just a bump in the road. We also must recognise that the US and UK are important role models in this regard and it may take little more than the perception that they are gaining competitive advantage, by opting out, for others to do the same. In accounting, uniformity and transparency are important bedfellows and stepping away from international agreements is likely to harm both, and unlikely to have positive outcomes for the environment and for many of the least powerful in society. As accountants we must be ready to meet these challenges with forms of accounting that alleviate the potential implications of such issues and we must continue to emphasise and advance the importance of the social accounting and CSR movement.

Summary

We have demonstrated throughout this book that accounting is not a neutral, benign technology reporting the facts of organisational life. Rather accounting practice takes account of the importance of local, time-specific factors, aims at understanding the diverse and complex processes of organisational activity and its relationship with the external world, and is concerned with the calculating what once was thought to be incalculable. In an increasing globalised and unsettled political environment with pressures on governments and organisations across all segments of the economy to ensure sustainability and social accountability, new modes of governance and financial information are needed. As we move forward, to ensure good CSR, social equity, accountability and sustainability for future generations, greater emphasis on the terms on which business behaviour is based is needed. Attention should also be given to the creation of more inclusive and equitable markets.

Organisations across all segments of the economy need to pay more attention to managing their governance and partnership relations, including greater stakeholder participation in a bottom up accountability/audit process. There is also a need to extended work on corporate reporting/disclosure to embrace partnerships and emerging standards for reporting. Likewise, with increasing globalisation, consideration needs to be given to the development of new modes of governance such as co-production, co-operation and the building in of common codes and shared values into the social accounting and CSR system.

As the chapters in this book demonstrate, accounting plays a wide-ranging and complex role within organisations. It is more than just a set of calculative technologies and practices, but rather is central to the social accountability and governance of organisations regardless of which sector these organisations are placed in. Understood in these terms, the scope for extending and developing the possibilities of accounting in a social world remain open for further exploration. As accounting continues to gain in importance in so many spheres of social life, an understanding of the conditions and consequences of calculative technologies is vital.

12

Discussion questions

1 What are the impact and challenges of globalisation on social and environmental practices and consequently society?

2 Can accounting practice help to alleviate cultural and political differences and facilitate greater social accountability? If so, in what ways?

3 How appropriate is social accounting in a globalised world?

4 How can transparency be achieved if not all countries are subject to the same regulations?

References and further reading

Al-Rodhan, N.R.F. (2001) Definitions of Globalisation: A comprehensive overview and a proposed definition, Program on the geopolitical implications of globalisation and transnational security, Geneva Centre for Security Policy, Available at: http://www.css.ethz.ch/en/services/digital-library/publications/publication.html/19462

Cooper, D. J., and Sherer, M. J. (1984) The value of corporate accounting reports: Arguments for a political economy of accounting, *Accounting, Organizations and Society*, **9**(3/4), 207–232.

Covrig, V.M., Defond, M.L., and Hung, M. (2007) Home bias, foreign mutual fund holdings, and the voluntary adoption of international accounting standards, *Journal of Accounting Research*, **45**(1), 41-70.

Godfrey, J.M. and Chalmers, K. (2007) *Globalisation of Accounting Standards*, Edward Elgar Publishing Limited

Hopwood, A. G. and Miller, P., editors, (1994), *Accounting as Social and Institutional Practice*, CUP, Cambridge.

Kolk, A. (2010). Trajectories of sustainability reporting by MNCs. *Journal of World Business*, **45**(4), 367-374.

Leuz, C. and Verrecchia, R.E. (2000) The economic consequences of increased disclosure, *Journal of Accounting Research*, **38**(Supplement), 91-124.

Marano, V. and Kostova, T. (2016) Unpacking the institutional complexity in adoption of CSR practices in multinational enterprises, *Journal of Management Studies*, **53**(1), 28-54.

Matten, D. and Crane, A. (2005) Corporate citizenship: toward an extended theoretical conceptualisation, *Academy of Management Review*, 30(1), 166–179.

Miles, S. and Nobes, C. (1998) The use of foreign accounting data in UK financial institutions, *Journal of Business Finance and Accounting*, **25**(3/4), 309-328.

Milne, M. and Gray, R. (2012). W(h)ither ecology? The triple bottom line, the global reporting initiative, and corporate sustainability reporting. *Journal of Business Ethics*, **118**(1), 13-29.

Potter, B. N. (2005) Accounting as a social and institutional practice: Perspectives to enrich our understanding of accounting change, *ABACUS*, **41**(3), pp. 265–289.

Rudkin, K. (2007) Accounting as myth maker, *The Australasian Accounting, Business and Finance Journal*, **1**(2), 13-24.

Scherer, A.G. and Palazzo, G., (2008). Globalization and corporate social responsibility, In: A. Crane, A. McWilliams, D. Matten, J. Moon and D. Siegel, (eds.), *The Oxford Handbook of Corporate Social Responsibility*, pp. 413-431, Oxford University Press.

Shear, M. (2017) Trump will withdraw U.S. from Paris Climate Agreement, *The New York Times*, 1st June, Available at: https://www.nytimes.com/2017/06/01/climate/trump-paris-climate-agreement.html

Vanwalleghem, D. (2017). The real effects of sustainable and responsible investing? *Economics Letters*, **156**, 10-14.

Wei, H.C. (2008) Globalisation and its effect on accountants, *Journal of Accounting Perspectives*, **1**, 81-84.

Case Studies

Education for a sustainable future: The case of Pakistan

Anees Farrukh

Introduction

The United Nations' Millennium Development Goals (MDGs) were developed in 2000, when 147 countries committed to addressing the issue of extreme poverty throughout the world. This was partly to be achieved by promoting universal access to primary education and reducing gender disparity to support environmental sustainability throughout the globe. These countries set a target to achieve their quantitative targets by the year 2015, however many of the Southern states are yet to achieve the goals discussed in the year 2000.

One of the countries that failed to achieve the Millennium Development Goal relating to universal access to education is Pakistan. The current situation within the education sector in Pakistan is, like many other developing countries, falling short of the targets set by United Nations. Indeed, according to UNESCO, the South Asian region is the second highest in terms of the number of out-of-school children not getting an education, after Sub-Saharan Africa. Despite some serious efforts toward improving the situation, the number of drop out children in Pakistan is close to 25 million. To put this into perspective, the population of Australia is around 25 million. There is therefore much scope for improving education within Pakistan.

The role of education as an influential instrument in eliminating poverty and inequality from society has been extensively recognised. Despite the government's commitments for universal primary education, Pakistan still has one of the highest rates of illiteracy in the world along with major gender disparity in education. Educational reforms in the educational systems of Pakistan are often focused on increased provision of resources and not on improving student-learning outcomes. This raises questions regarding the validity of those reforms which do not lead to sustainable interventions and emphasises the need to make the educational system accountable for learning to the learner, to achieve the MDGs. To highlight these issues, this case study discusses educational reform within the context of Pakistan, specifically focusing on the measures adopted to measure improvement within the education system.

Globalisation, imperialism and education

Implementing the United Nation's MDGs would improve the lives of millions of children. The contempt by the state departments of Pakistan regarding the indigenous needs of the population is one of the numerous reasons why the MDGs have not been met. Additionally, the state has also failed in achieving another commitment: The Education for All (EFA) initiative, which placed major emphasis on the quality of education at the primary level. The review report of the implementation of EFA, published in October 2014, outlines that, despite frequent policy commitments, the primary target of universal primary education in Pakistan would not be achieved.

It is important to note that in addition to the public sector, private institutions and the NGO sector has been actively working to address this crisis of education. However, low-income countries are often caught in the contradiction whereby the education that is promoted by educational institutes is closely aligned to the overall objective of development – namely economic growth and poverty reduction. Most educational institutes, therefore, promote skill development within low-income countries to provide the necessary human capital and industrial processes that would support the neo-liberal politics of institutions such as the IMF and the World Bank. These institutions promote policies in the Southern hemisphere through their Structural Adjustment Programs (SAPs) on the macro level and have found a new role for education, which serves to reinforce imperialism through further limiting the capacity of low-income countries to determine their own educational agendas.

Education, throughout history, has been subjected to a continuous assault from the neo-liberal institutions of the capitalist power bloc, with the intention of building an oppressive system that reinforces capitalism as the only acceptable mode of production (Thomson and Bebbington, 2004). Further, Tikly (2001), notes that much of the literature on education and globalisation focuses on the western industrialised countries and their 'significant other', i.e. the newly industrialised countries of the Pacific Rim. In a similar vein, Goldsmith and King (2013), argue that the product of education in traditional societies, like Pakistan, is qualitatively different from the product of the whole educational process of developed countries, not in terms of individual intellectual achievement and assessment, but in terms of the role of education in relation to their economies. Education plays a direct and active part in the processes of production, skill development and producing such labour force that is needed by capitalist power bloc.

CS

This raises questions about the role and relevance of such reforms in the context of globalisation and its implications on education policy, their resources as well as the process and educational outcomes in countries on the periphery of the global economy and politics. The spread of neo-liberal politics under the guise of globalisation and 'development' becomes contradictory to the key concepts that mark out education's role in relation to the repertoire, namely the development of human and social capital (Tikly, 2001).

The education system of Pakistan is facing tremendous challenges – lack of financial resources, increased drop outs, poor policy implementation, outdated curriculum and an unproductive examination system, that are linked to the role that education plays in a society. As the individual and collective values in the societies are shaped by the system of education, the ability to control educational outcomes becomes significant as it determines the role education plays within society (Thomson and Bebbington, 2004). Subsequently, individuals' understandings of the world are constructed through education and thus powerful actors seek to harness the education system to their own ends. This limits the potential of education to play a transformative role in a society. In this light, a certain role of education within a society is attained under which education is used to maintain the status quo. Therefore, there is a need to broaden our understanding of the implications of globalisation on education.

The measure of success for education?

In one attempt to end this educational crisis, the state of Pakistan committed itself to Vision-2025, which is a long-term plan to revamp the social protection system in the country. To aid public schools in improving their standards, the government has established an alliance through Public Private Partnerships (PPPs) with local successful NGOs, who recognise the needs of the indigenous communities to improve schooling in Pakistan. Although it is a significant issue for the country, there are only a few NGOs who have partnered with the public schools as most NGOs are reluctant to affiliate themselves with state institutions due to the bureaucratic distortion in both government departments and public schools. This has resulted in a trust deficit between government and NGOs. This cycle of inefficiency which affects all other institutions has led to this concern: how to promote education for the sustainable future?

The failure to address the educational crisis has resulted in calls to build an effective and accountable education system that meets the United Nation's MDGs and promotes sustainable education across generations simultaneously. It is vital to develop and adopt an appropriate measure of educational success that promotes learning based outcomes. To address obstacles to achieve such an education system several tools and measures have been adopted by national, international and development agencies but these organisations have failed to promote such educational outcomes that encourages learning. For instance, the Annual Status of Education Report (ASER, 2015), which is the only publicly available dataset relating to this area of education, has only provided a large sample glimpse of the basic status of learning among children in Pakistan. This dataset highlights the inequalities in the education systems of Pakistan (along with a series of other issues that are related to the educational resources that are discussed above), which creates social hierarchies and eventually increases the imbalances in the society. The ASER findings, however, do not address questions about the efficacy of education and how to develop an accountable educational system. Moreover, the tools used by ASER only assess a narrow set of mechanical functions in its computation and lack the ability to recognise characters and to read a sentence or paragraph when assessing reading competencies. ASER adopted easy to use tools to measure children's learning levels based on internationally recognised principles whereby after two years of schooling, children are considered to have developed sufficient reading fluency and acquired basic numeracy skills, but such overreliance on best assessments that are popular or even the assumption that 'what worked there will necessarily work here' raise questions on the validity of such measures.

The problem with the output measures discussed above is the disconnection of social and non-social factors along with the governance mechanisms of the school system. Such indicators might be useful information within the developed world where accountability systems are developed according to their needs, alongside a series of other governance mechanisms, but in the context of developing countries who lack a formal educational infrastructure, such reports do not provide adequate information for interpretation in educationally productive ways. A comparison among schools (systems) is inherently unfair because it is not possible to separate school effects from effects resulting from non-school factors (for instance, overall, 52% of PPP students and 66% of private school students take private tuition compared to only 11% of government school students. Those who undertake private supplementary tuition are on average 86% more likely to succeed on the academic tasks than those not undertaking it (Amjad and MacLeod, 2014). Therefore, more multifaceted interventions are needed that address the faults in the educational process than using statistical tools that only examine the educational resources and their outcomes.

The measure of education for a sustainable future

For an education system to work effectively it is imperative that relevant structures are developed to address the measurement of educational accountability. According to Freire (1996), education often acts as an essence of oppression, controlled by political powers as a tool to extend their oppression of the population. In this context, it is significant to recognise the conception of bureaucratic accountability that has influenced Pakistan's education system. Federal and provisional officers promulgate educational policies with varied rules and regulations as ministers are the legislators and the voice of teachers (professional accountability), while parents and students (market accountability) have little

CS

influence. As noted by Darling-Hammond (2004:1050), "Bureaucratic account-ability does not guarantee results, it concerns itself with procedures; it is effective only when procedures are known to produce the desired outcomes, and when compliance is easily measured and secured", therefore, such mechanisms of accountability are counterproductive and do not result in any institutional or social change.

While it is true that both students and their parents are directly influenced by the measure of accountability for attending school and struggle to meet expecta-tions, it is important to assess their role in the formation of accountability policies (Darling-Hammond, 2004). The issue of teaching, financial aid, curriculum, learn-ing, professional development, and school administration cannot be separated from the issue of accountability. Of all the research on educational outcomes, the study carried out by Westhorp *et al.* (2014), is the most extensive. This study notes that although there are problems with existing power relationships in relation to multiple stakeholders in developing countries, the community-accountability and empowerment interventions can improve education outcomes. An increase in accountability may improve education outcomes by improving:

■ The infrastructure of schools through the availability and allocation of funds where they are most needed, thereby ensuring appropriate school facilities to reduce the gender disparity.

■ The quality of curriculum by making it more relevant to the local needs.

■ the processes for school assessments that can evaluate students' opportunities to learn.

■ The student-teacher relationship by building professional capacity that ensures that teachers have the knowledge and skills they need to teach. The improvement in pedagogy will pay off in improved student outcomes.

■ The student's experience of schooling and building reciprocity between com-munities and education authorities.

■ The relationship between communities and education authorities through establishing a sense of shared vision by promoting the participation of mar-ginalised groups in the decision-making processes. This would also promote their rights and entitlements.

Summary

To achieve universal access to primary education, it is imperative that relevant structures are developed to address the measurement of the educational system. As educational outcomes are highly influenced by the accountability of their resources which determines the role education plays in the society, it becomes significant how to achieve universal access to primary education. As the desire to achieve MDGs is needed, it also influences the educational outcomes. If universal access to primary education is achieved solely based on how many schools are built, how many children are enrolled in the schooling system, or how many pupils passed the standardised tests, then the educational process becomes a route to developing a regimented skill set to preserve the status quo. However, if the desire is to promote critical thinking and empower students that respond to such social conformity, then it is vital to develop such mechanisms that puts learning at the core of the educational process. Only then we can achieve the MDGs and education will be able play its transformative role.

Discussion questions

1 Reflect on your own notion of education. What is the purpose of education and how can education make the future more sustainable? Do you agree (or disagree) that educational accountability is vital in making education sustainable for the future?

2 If you were asked to form an educational policy for Pakistan, which measures would you adopt that would help Pakistan achieve the MDGs?

References

Amjad, R. and MacLeod, G. (2014). Academic effectiveness of private, public and private–public partnership schools in Pakistan. *International Journal of Educational Development*, **37**, 22-31.

ASER Pakistan (2015). *Annual Status of Education Report*, Pakistan.

Darling-Hammond, L. (2004). Standards, accountability, and school reform. *Teachers College Record*, **106**(6), 1047-1085.

Freire, P. (1996). *Pedagogy of the Oppressed*. London: Pelican.

Goldsmith, M. and King, A. (1979). Issues of development: towards a new role for science and technology; proceedings of an International Symposium on Science and Technology for Development, Singapore, January 1979.

Thomson, I. and Bebbington, J. (2004). It doesn't matter what you teach? *Critical Perspectives on Accounting*, **15**(4), 609-628.

Tikly, L. (2001). Globalisation and education in the postcolonial world: Towards a conceptual framework. *Comparative Education*, **37**(2), 151-171.

Westhorp, G., Walker, B., Rogers, P., Overbeeke, N., Ball, D. and Brice, G. (2014). *Enhancing community accountability, empowerment and education outcomes in low and middle-income countries: A realist review*. University of London, Institute of Education, EPPI-Centre, London.

CS

Nigerian Oil Spill Monitor: Accountability hybridisation for sustainable development

Mercy Denedo

Introduction

This case study presents an account of the Oil Spill Monitor (OSM) accountability-sustainability platform which emerged from the external social audit and advocacy work of NGOs in collaboration with public service organisations in the Niger Delta region of Nigeria. Together these organisations built and legitimised the National Oil Spill Detection and Response Agency's (NOSDRA) response to sustainable development and accountability for oil spills in the region. Accounting-sustainability hybridity technologies are used to drive accounting(ability) for sustainable services in organisations whose responsibility is to offer public goods or services equitably to all members of society and all generations (Ball *et al.*, 2012; Grubnic *et al.*, 2015). Thomson *et al.*, (2014) state that accounting-sustainability hybrids are practices that seek to make visible, to govern and to help mediate between accounting and sustainability initiatives in organisational processes. They identify examples of accounting-sustainability hybridisation as including biodiversity audit, carbon accounting, corporate social reporting, energy costing, external social audits, full cost accounting, shadow accounts and sustainable balanced scorecards. The present case study presents a discussion of such mechanisms within the context of oil spills in the Niger Delta region of Nigeria.

Field of study

Nigeria is referred to as the 'Giant of Africa' due to its economy and population, which is estimated at 181.6 million (World FactBook, 2016), but at the same time it is recognised as a mono-product rentier state relying majorly on crude oil production (Abah and Okwori, 2006). Despite the oil and gas industry's contribution to the economy and development of Nigeria, poor practices by the oil producing corporations, third party interference with oil installations, and the ineffectiveness of regulators have resulted in the Niger Delta being ranked as one of the five worst petroleum-damaged ecosystems in the world (Oviasuyi and Uwadiae, 2010; Kafada, 2012).

In Nigeria, the Department of Petroleum Resources (DPR) is the oil industry regulatory agency within the Ministry of Petroleum which is responsible for the maximisation of revenue and the conservation of the environment. On the other hand, NOSDRA is the environmental conservation agency within the Federal Ministry of Environment responsible for the protection of the environment and to respond when there are spills in Nigeria. Generally, NOSDRA is perceived as better positioned to protect the environment because their sole responsibility is environmental management and not the maximisation of oil revenue in Nigeria (SDN, 2015a). NOSDRA was established in 2006 with a mandate under the NOSDRA Act 2006 to conserve and protect the Nigerian environment.

OSM an accounting-sustainability hybridisation technology

Steiner (2010:6) puts forward that "as public and political attention typically focuses more on environmental integrity in developed nations and ignores that in developing ones, company and governmental attention to oil infrastructure integrity and spill risk tends to follow the same pattern". This is especially the case in the Niger Delta region where there has been an extensive oil spill into the environment the indigenous people rely on for their welfare. Oil pollution has affected sustainable development and the ability of the indigenous people to live in a sustainable manner.

Environmental advocacy NGOs and observers have argued that the regulatory mechanism within the oil industry has not been effective. Previous studies have revealed that the regulators lack the funding, equipment and capacity to enforce fines and penalties on those responsible for oil spills, which hinders their effort to effectively solve the problems of environmental pollution (Amnesty International, 2013; SDN, 2016). Consequently, local, regional, national and international NGOs have stated the need for regulatory agencies such as the DPR and NOSDRA to have the power to enforce its environmental standards.

In addition, the lack of adequate funding and conflicts of interest resulting from the joint venture agreement existing between the corporations and the government has had significant implications on the natural environment, social equality and sustainable development for present and future generations' living and depending on the natural resources for their wellbeing (Amnesty International, 2009; Amunwa, 2011). These problems, and their implications, resulted in the launch of the OSM platform in January 2014, via a coalition of advocacy NGOs in partnership with NOSDRA (SDN, 2014).[1] This partnership was to address the problem of missing information on oil spills, the extent of damage, the causes and the volume of spills in the Niger Delta and the remediation strategies adopted.

The OSM monitor is a mediating accounting-sustainability hybridisation technology that monitors and publishes records of oil spills within the Niger Delta region. This can facilitate speedy remediation of impacted sites to protect the stakeholders from the social, economic and environmental cost of such pollution. The OSM platform is maintained and managed by NOSDRA (SDN, 2014). NOSDRA's responsibility is to sustain a zero-tolerance approach to oil spill incidents by monitoring how contingency plans are translated into the sustainable

---

1 See https://oilspillmonitor.ng/

CS

environment of Nigeria. They are also required to address the problems caused by oil spills by embarking on joint investigation visits to polluted sites, to prevent future occurrences and to ensure appropriate remediation are proffered to the polluted sites in Nigeria (Amnesty International, 2013; SDN, 2016).

Before the establishment of this digital accounting-sustainability instrument, Amnesty International (2013) argued that historical data on oil spills by companies were not made publicly available, except for data published by Shell, Nigeria. They concluded that the numbers of onshore and offshore spills and the volume of the spill are under-reported. Due to these problems, environmental NGOs, through their external accounts, highlighted that there is a need for transparency and visibility regarding the extent of environmental damage, the cause and the volume of oil spills in the Delta (see Christian Aid, 2004; Social Action, 2009a, 2009b, 2014). The OSM is an accountability-sustainability mediating technique to deal with the problem of biodiversity, social inequality, economic and environmental degradation that affect health, the standard of living, right to water, and right to earn a living from the natural environment of the Niger Delta across generations. This form of accounting-sustainability hybridisation technologies impact on how NOSDRA engage and account for the oil spill to the stakeholders and the response of the oil corporations and the other stakeholders to the remediation of the polluted sites.

The OSM creates a public transparent platform to account for every oil spill occurring in the Niger Delta region because external accounting evidence revealed that majority of the oil spills are under-reported (Steiner, 2010; Amunwa, 2011). The intricacy and critical evaluation of what is reported or not is beyond the scope of this case study, but the OSM platform was established to address the problems of how oil spills are accounted for or disclosed by the regulatory agencies and the corporations to the other stakeholders.

The OSM was thus established to manage, visualise and map oil spill data in the oil industry of Nigeria to facilitate speedy joint investigation visits as well as to serve as a mediating accounting-sustainability instrument to improve accountability for the oil spill and gas flares. It is a digital mapping technology that gives public access to oil spill data. It serves as a mediating accounting-sustainability instrument due to the non-availability of accountable information on the extent of environmental impact, causes and volume of oil spilled in the Niger Delta (SDN, 2015b). Furthermore, it is aimed at revealing the scale of illegal oil refining and spillage activities by third parties and the environmental impacts this causes in the Delta. Although pioneered by the advocacy NGOs, this technology is managed by NOSDRA to enable government agencies, oil corporations, civil society groups and communities' members to identify and share oil spill information depending on who discovers the spill whenever they occur (SDN, 2014). Oil spill data in this accounting-sustainability platform is updated daily by NOSDRA when oil spills data are sent to the platform and this data are checked and confirmed by NOSDRA in Abuja (headquarters).

Accountability implications of the OSM

The OSM mediates by disclosing oil spills data, which were previously not disclosed or were under-reported, to facilitate a network of accountability and dialogues among the regulators, the oil corporations, civil society, communities and the public on the issue of oil spills in Nigeria. This form of accounting or reporting affects how the local or indigenous people, the corporations and the public perceive, embed and pursue sustainable development to protect and respect the environment and biodiversity for the present and future generations. However, disclosing that there is a spill on the OSM platform does not immediately translate into stopping or containing the spill and remediating the impacted environment for the benefit of the indigenous people who depend on fishing and farming for their welfare.

Furthermore, this does not translate to fines or sanctions being imposed on the corporations or the perpetrators when there is a spill, to ensure preventive measures are installed to avoid further oil spill occurrence. The OSM relies on the voluntary accountability and engagement of the oil corporations to provide data, logistics and estimates of the oil spill, as well as soil or water samples and permission to carry out remediation. Additionally, though the data displayed on the OSM is immensely useful, it does not tell the whole story and challenges in the Niger Delta because it is fraught with insecurity, third party interferences on oil installations and the continuing social, economic and environmental challenges facing indigenous people. Not undermining the harmful impact of third parties' interference on (intra)intergenerational sustainable development in this context but where disclosure is not backed up by remediation action, the accounting-sustainability hybridity impact could be deemed as ineffective.

Despite the accountability and engagement potential of the OSM, (intra)intergenerational equity and sustainable development could be argued to lie outside this safe haven. This is the story external accounting prepared by advocacy NGOs are trying to publicise and to galvanise accountability and dialogic actions towards addressing from the local, regional, national and international audience. This is because managing and accounting for social, economic and environmental sustainability across generations require reactive accounts, ensure effective risk management policies and stakeholders' engagement that could be incorporated into public service (and other) organisational practices to eradicate inequalities and drive sustainable environment across generations.

Summary

The aim of this case study was to explore how the OSM accountability-sustainability platform emerging from the advocacy work of NGOs with the public service organisations has built, guided and legitimised NOSDRA's response to sustainable development and accountability for oil spills in the Niger Delta of Nigeria. Of relevance to sustainability is the noticeable shift in how oil spills

CS

are accounted for by the public service organisation, which is achieved through engagement with the NGOs, corporations, communities and the public. This case study highlighted how public service organisations manage and account for (intra)intergenerational equity for sustainable development and how the OSM serves as a mediating instrument for accountability and sustainability in the public service organisation (Thomson *et al.*, 2014; Grubnic *et al.*, 2015). Despite the significance of the OSM, it is not enough to address the enormous challenges facing the indigenous people, the regulators and the corporations. The OSM makes visible and closes the accountability gaps regarding the extent of environmental damage, the cause and the volume of the spill. Nevertheless, whilst there continues to be no significant corresponding actions to minimise the (intra)intergenerational impacts on biodiversity, pollution of land, water and air, and the operations of the public-sector organisations, it makes this accounting-sustainability technology ineffective in addressing (intra)intergenerational sustainable development.

Discussion questions

1 Discuss the significance of the accounting-sustainability hybridisation platforms in the public sector.

2 In your view, what could have been done to ensure the effectiveness of the OSM to drive sustainable development in this context? What other factors should be considered to drive the effectiveness of the OSM in the future?

References

Abah, O. S. and Okwori, J. Z. (2006). Oil and accountability issues in the Niger Delta. In: P. Newell, and J. Wheeler, (eds.) *Rights, Resources and the Politics of Accountability*. New York: Zed Books Ltd. Chapter 10.

Amnesty International (2009). *Nigeria: Petroleum, Pollution and Poverty in the Niger Delta*. London: Amnesty International Publications.

Amnesty International (2013). *Bad Information: Oil Spill Investigations in the Niger Delta*. London: Amnesty International.

Amunwa, B. (2011). Counting the cost; corporations and human rights abuses in the Niger Delta. *Platform*, October. Available at: http://platformlondon.org/nigeria/Counting_the_Cost.pdf [Accessed 26 February 2014].

Ball, A., Soare, V. and Brewis, J. (2012). Engagement research in public sector accounting. *Financial Accountability and Management*, 28(2), 189-214.

Christian Aid, (2004). *Behind the Mask: The Real Face of Corporate Social Responsibility*. London: Christian-Aid.

Grubnic, S., Thomson, I. and Georgakopoulos, G., (2015). New development: managing and accounting for sustainable development across generations in public services-and call for pap ers. *Public Money and Management*, 35(3), 245-250.

Kadafa, A. A. (2012). Environmental impacts of oil exploration and exploitation in the Niger Delta of Nigeria. *Global Journal of Science Frontier Research,* **12**(3), 18-28.

Oviasuyi, P. O. and Uwadiae, J. (2010). The dilemma of Niger-Delta region as oil-producing states of Nigeria. *Journal of Peace, Conflict and Development,* **16**, 110-126.

SDN, (2014). Dealing with oil spills in the Niger Delta - Towards technology-driven crisis prevention. Stakeholders Democracy Network, http://www.stakeholderdemocracy.org/dealing-with-oil-spills-in-the-niger-delta-towards-technology-driven-crisis-prevention/ [Accessed 9 September 2016].

SDN, (2015a). Improving oil spill response in Nigeria: comparative analysis of the forms, data and related processes of the joint investigation visit (JIV). Stakeholders Democracy Network, http://www.stakeholderdemocracy.org/portfolio/improving-oil-spill-response-in-nigeria/ [Accessed 9 September 2016].

SDN, (2015b). Oil spill monitor takes second place at Innovating Justice Award. Stakeholders Democracy Network, http://www.stakeholderdemocracy.org/oil-spill-monitor-takes-second-place-at-innovating-justice-awards/ [Accessed 9 September 2016].

SDN, (2016). Towards improving the Joint Investigation Visit following oil spills in Nigeria: narrative report and recommendations. Stakeholders Democracy Network, http://www.stakeholderdemocracy.org/wp-content/uploads/2016/06/Towards-Improving-the-JIV.pdf [Accessed 9 September 2016].

Social Action, (2009a). Flames of Hell, gas flaring in the Niger Delta. Port Harcourt: Social Development Integrated Centre (Social Action). http://saction.org/home/ [Accessed 10 March 2015].

Social Action, (2009b). Fuelling discord, oil and conflict in three Niger Delta communities. Port Harcourt: Social Development Integrated Centre (Social Action). http://saction.org/home/ [Accessed 10 March 2015].

Social Action, (2014). Still Polluted: monitoring government and Shell's response to UNEP's environmental assessment of Ogoniland. Port Harcourt: Social Development Integrated Centre (Social Action). http://saction.org/home/ [Accessed 10 March 2015].

Steiner, R., (2010). Double Standard: Shell practices in Nigeria compared with international standards to prevent and control pipeline oil spills and the deepwater horizon oil spill. Friends of the Earth International, http://members.foei.org/en/resources/publications/pdfs/2010/double-standard-shell-practices-in-nigeria-compared-with-international-standards/view [Accessed 12 March 2014].

World FactBook, (2016). Africa: Nigeria. Central Intelligence Agency, (last updated on 7th September). Available at: https://www.cia.gov/library/publications/the-world-factbook/geos/ni.html [Accessed 17 September 2016].

Thomson, I., Grubnic, S. and Georgakopoulos, G., (2014). Exploring accounting-sustainability hybridisation in the UK public sector. *Accounting Organizations and Society,* **39**(6), 453-476.

CS

Hospital reforms in a period of economic and political uncertainty

Vasileios Milios

Introduction

The economic crisis of 2008 revealed structural problems with the hospital sector, which had caused high inefficiency and impaired the services that were being provided to citizens. Reforms were necessary, but the incumbent socialist party did not have the willingness to implement these reforms. In 2012, the recently elected right-wing party decided to implement some reforms to tackle the identified inefficiencies. They suggested new hospital structures along with some measures which could make the hospitals efficient. However, the fear of political costs associated with these policies prevented the right-wing government from insisting on these reforms. This case study[1] examines hospital reforms in a period of fiscal crisis. It aims to show how the changing global environment can affect the performance and objectives of the public sector. In this case study we will discuss how the socialist party, which was in power from 2004 until 2012, tried to exploit the hospital sector for political purposes.

Socialist party period (2004 – 2012)

Socialist parties prefer large public sectors (Borge *et al.*, 2008). During the first four years of the period in question, the government expanded the quality of services in the public sector and placed an increased emphasis on healthcare and the hospital sector. The amount of public money allocated to hospitals was increased and, for this reason, new hospitals were established, existing hospitals were supplied with new equipment and additional personnel were recruited. The citizens were very happy with the healthcare system, which made a significant contribution to the good image of the government. Therefore, the socialist party used healthcare in the political debate to highlight the success of the government. The government argued that the increased spending for healthcare illustrates the philosophy of the government and proves its social awareness. Thus, the socialist party was re-elected in 2008 and the role of healthcare expansion was very decisive in this decision by the citizens. After the elections, the socialist government stated that one of the main priorities was the further improvement of health services. In the following Government Budget, there was a subsequent increase in hospital expenditure.

---

1 This is a fictional case based on a real life and time example.

The fiscal crisis and the necessity of change

The fiscal crisis of 2008 changed the plans of the government. The banking sector needed recapitalization and, similar to other countries, pressure was placed upon public expenditure (Hodges and Lapsley, 2016). The public debate turned towards improving the competitiveness of the private sector and freezing the expansion of public sector. For this reason, the socialist government decided to take some measures for the stabilization of the economy. These measures included full performance evaluation of the public sector and the creation of a task force whose findings highlighted significant problems within the health sector, which had previously been underestimated. There was a significant quantitative expansion of the hospital sector but, the quality of services was not improved at the same time. Further, the hospital sector was creating deficits every year, which, in the period of crisis, influenced the fiscal performance of the state. A very large hospital sector is expected to result inefficiency (Afonso *et al.*, 2003), therefore it was necessary for the hospital sector to zero the deficits and decrease their annual cost. The detailed report from the task force revealed weak hospital management structures, and inadequate audit and control from the central government. Furthermore, it revealed that the doctors had almost absolute freedom within the hospitals regarding the consumption of materials and decision making. Management was not able to restrict the doctors who were invoking their medical knowledge and thus, they were the main drivers of operations. It was clear that the hospitals needed a management reform. The proposed changes included significant cuts in the amounts that were given to hospitals, better recruitment of managerial staff, more comprehensive budgets and annual reports which must be monitored by the Ministry of Health, and better management which could monitor the doctors and implement elements of economic rationalism in the daily management of hospitals. The task force proposed a full framework of co-operation between each hospital and the Ministry, but they also proposed measures which should be implemented in the daily operations of each hospital, underlining in this way the importance of management in hospitals.

Political reaction to change

Almost all members of the socialist party did not agree with these reforms as they believed that they are not in line with their ideological beliefs. So, even though the government decided to implement these reforms, the fear of the political cost influenced the implementation. The reforms were thus incomplete, and they did not have the expected results. The government was creating impediments to the process as well as it did not carry out the monitoring role as it should have whilst also trying to preserve the size of hospital sector. As a result, the hospital sector was continuing to create deficits and there was inability from the government to reduce the cost. This inefficiency problem and the lack of modern management impaired the social role of the hospitals as the quality of services was decreased due of the irrational distribution of resources and the inefficient use of them.

CS

Additionally, the Ministry of Health received pressures from the Ministry of Finance for the proper implementation of the proposed measures. Although the Minister of Finance feared the political cost of such measures, he understood that these measures are necessary for the sustainability of hospital system. He believed that an inefficient hospital sector could infect the remainder of the public sector. For this reason, the Minister of Finance demanded the implementation of the measures and the gathering of more comprehensive information regarding the performance of hospitals. However, the wider political environment rejected the measures and preferred the political survival.

Right-wing party period

In 2012, the right-wing party won the elections and the new Prime Minister promised a radical reform in healthcare, including the proposals of the task force from 2009. The main promise of the PM before the elections was an efficient public sector. Adams *et al.* (2011) argued that countries with right-wing governments are likely to have higher efficiency rates compared to socialist governments. So, the government promised a public sector which could deliver high quality services to the citizens at a much lower cost. For this reason, he believed that the implementation of the reforms would be highly important to show that his government is in line with the promises that it made to the citizens. In his first meeting with the Minister of Health (MoH), the PM argued that: "it is very important for us to succeed in hospital reform. As we have seen, it is a key driver for the success of our government and our re-election. I want you to be in charge of this reform. All hospital managers must be accountable to you and then, I want constant updates regarding the progress of the reform. The most important task is the cost reduction. We have to tackle inefficiency and only then, we will improve the services."

The hospital reforms

The MoH took into consideration the report of the task force from a few years earlier, but he believed that the reform could be more comprehensive. He decided to go back to a basic concept of public sector: New Public Management, which constituted a weapon in the hands of right wing governments in the pursuit of public sector efficiency (Hood, 1991, 1995). For this reason, he established a committee for hospital reform which was constituted by five technocrats with experience in health management (two from the public sector and three from the private sector). The aim of the committee was to create a management framework for hospitals by using private sector tools as well. They set expected results for hospitals which were related to both quality and financial performance. The mechanisms that they set for the hospitals were mainly related to the monitoring of costs and evaluation of services. For the better monitoring of the hospitals, the committee established Hospital Boards to enhance management of each hospital. The chairman of the board (or manager) was the one who had the responsibility to inform the committee about the results of the hospital. Boards had responsibility for individual hospitals, undertaking strategic planning, monitoring performance and the achievement of targets, ensuring quality standards, appointing and appraising senior management, and engaging with local community. The board members were appointed directly from the committee.

To address inefficiencies, they asked hospitals managers to conduct better negotiations with suppliers. Additionally, they asked the managers to reduce hospitalization stays as the ministry pays more for each further day. In monitoring costs, the parliament voted for a new regulation for public sector budgeting. Hospitals should prepare budgets every year in which they have to provide very detailed information regarding the expenses that will be incurred. These budgets should include costs relating to personnel, operations, pharmaceutical and supplies. Every month, the hospitals had to submit interim reports to the committee to show if they are in line with their targets. If there was any differentiation from the initial budget, then the hospital will suffer from reductions in funding.

The reform established a uniform framework of operations for public hospitals. It included an organizational chart which should be implemented by all hospitals and it specified the jurisdictions of each actor. The Hospital Board was the head of the hospital and the manager was in charge. In the lower echelons, the hospital was divided to three main departments: medical, nursing and administrative. The medical department included the different clinical departments in the hospital (ophthalmological, pathological, etc.). The nursing department includes all nursing operations of the hospital and the keeping of simple statistical records regarding the patients. Administrative services include the staff manager who is responsible for the staff, excluding doctors. Additionally, they include the administrative department which is responsible for the daily management of the hospital. The administrative department is working in co-operation with the finance department which is responsible for the economic aspect of each decision. The following diagram illustrates the organisational structure of hospitals:

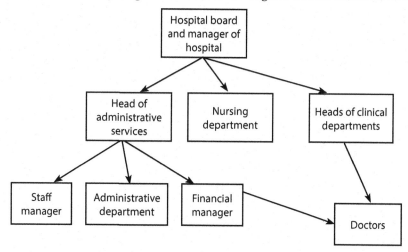

This structure is very similar to the prior structure of hospitals. The problem previously was the lack of a clear organisational chart with specified responsibilities and, moreover, the committee wanted to add one more element to hospital function. Doctors should be accountable not only for their medical practice, but also for the economic implications of their actions. Doctors previously had excessive freedom in their practice without taking into consideration the economic aspects of their decisions. This was leading to waste of resources and it was major factor in the prevailing inefficiencies. For this reason, each doctor now had a personal budget and a personal number of patients to account for each month. Thus, they could not cause artificial demands and due to budget restrictions, they had to buy only the materials which are essential. Furthermore, each month, before the submission of the interim reports, doctors will have meetings with the financial manager to discuss the economic results of their practice.

Issues with the reform

The measures put in place regarding the economic restriction of doctors were not successful. There were cases in which the doctors did not have the necessary materials for surgeries because of economic restrictions, and the process for applying for additional funds was very time consuming. Additionally, due to the restriction on the specific number of patients that each doctor could have, there were a lot of people who could not find doctors and thus they ended up waiting for a long time. There was a fierce frustration in the doctors who believed that the State did not trust them. Additionally, a lot of people were lodging complaints with the local MPs claiming that the new government worsened the condition of public hospitals. However, the main target of the government was to reduce the cost and make the hospital sector efficient. During the first months, the interim reports that hospitals were submitting to the committee were in line with the targets that were set. The cost started to decline but, after some months there was a stagnation of deficits. That means that the cost was decreased but not that much. This happened because of the problems which were mentioned before. The need for extra funds for doctors changed the expected cost that was originally set out within the budget. This reform resulted in the deregulation of the function of hospitals as it represented a failed effort of austerity much as measures of austerity failed in several countries because of their narrow view (Cohen *et al.*, 2013)

The end of the reform

One year after the implementation of the reform, in the first meeting between the MoH and the committee, it was evident that the targets had not been achieved as the hospital sector seemed to have stagnated, deficits had been generated and there had been a gradual decrease in the services provided. However, the committee insisted on the reform counting as they claimed that this was the correct solution and only some amendments were needed for the improvement of the hospital sector. The MoH took this on board but he would reply only after his meeting with the PM. In this meeting, the Minister claimed that the committee might be right, and it could be a chance for the government to demonstrate its faith to liberal politics and to the efforts against inefficiency. PM argued: "I cannot talk to the voters only for efficiency. These are complex issues for them. But, they can definitely understand the fact that they do not have proper treatment in a hospital. Besides there is a narrative that we can use. We can say that we managed to reduce the cost without mentioning specific numbers. Did you see what happened with the socialist party? When they could show good performance of hospital sector, they won the elections. But when they seemed to be unable to protect the health of the citizens, it turned to a disaster. So, we cannot have the same fate. We must abandon the huge part of this reform and we will keep some elements to make sure that the cost will not be increased. Under a stable situation we can start improving the provided services again." Consequently, the Minister of Health terminated the committee and once more the reforms remain unimplemented.

Summary

There was not a strong political will to create the necessary fertile ground for the success of the reform. In both eras, politicians, who are one of the main stakeholders within the public sector, considered their political future as more important than the reform. Regardless of the ideological beliefs of each party, the aims of accounting were influenced by political survival. This notion is in line with Chang (2005) who argued that politicians might attempt to manipulate accounting to achieve political targets.

Discussion questions

1   Identify the chains of accountability and mention the type of accountability (political, managerial, vertical, horizontal). Do you believe that there were any conflicts because of the interests which derive from the types of accountability?

2   The right-wing government attempted to implement some liberal reforms under the prism of New Public Management. Why do you think that these reforms failed?

References

Adam, A., Delis, M.D. and Kammas, P. (2008) Public sector efficiency: levelling the playing field between OECD Countries, *Munich Personal RePEc Archive* (MPRA), **16493**, 1–27.

Afonso, A., Schuknecht, L. and Tanzi, V. (2003) Public sector efficiency: an international comparison, European Central Bank Working Paper Series, 242.

Borge, L.E., Falch, T. and Tovmo, P. (2008) Public sector efficiency: the roles of political and budgetary institutions, fiscal capacity, and democratic participation, *Public Choice*, **136**, 475-495.

CS

Cohen, S., Guillamon, L. D., Lapsley, I. and Robbins, G. (2015) Accounting for austerity: the troika in the Eurozone, *Accounting, Auditing and Accountability Journal,* **28** (6), 966-992.

Chang, L. (2015) Accountability, rhetoric, and political interests: twists and turns of NHS performance measurements, *Financial Accountability and Management,* **31**(1), 41-68.

Hodges, R. and Lapsley, I. (2016) A private sector failure, a public sector crisis – reflections on the great recession, *Financial Accountability and Management,* **32**(3), 265-280.

Hood, C. (1991) A public management for all seasons?, *Public Administration,* **69**, 3-19.

Hood, C. (1995) The New Public Management in the 1980s: Variation on a theme, *Accounting, Organizations and Society,* **20**, 93-109.

Management control in Indonesia's local government

Alexander Anggono

Introduction

Many public sectors across the world have undergone considerable reform over the last few decades. This has been in response to increasing government deficits and criticisms over the use (and misuse) of financial resources and accusations of the mismanagement of public services. The following case study focuses on concern of central government to build systems to enhance transparency and accountability that had been neglected by previous regimes; particularly on financial decentralisation by employing social accounting that consider organisational culture, ethical and moral issues in Indonesia.

Initiation of the government reform

Historically, Indonesian politics has experienced turmoil: specifically, in 1998 the military regime that had been ruling for 32 years was obliged to step down (Lewis, 2005). The financial crisis affected Indonesia severely both economically and politically, all of which served to weaken the central government (Green and Campos, 2001); hence, a separatist sentiment emerged. To cope with this situation, in May 1999 the Indonesian Parliament passed laws concerning regional autonomy and fiscal decentralisation. These reforms were expected to bring improvements and efficiency to government services because the local governments are closer and more accessible to the people they serve (Coaffee and Johnston, 2005; Lewis, 2005; Turner, Imbaruddin, and Sutiyono, 2009; Young and Padovani, 2009). All of those programmes were outlined by many international institutions that came to give assistance to the GOI to accelerate its recovery from the crisis, such as the IMF (the International Monetary Fund) and USAID.

Following the IMF programmes, the Indonesian central government undertook government reform gradually, and determined which institutions need to be reformed. Its first priority was public organisations responsible for state revenues; the second priority was the audit institutions; the third was law enforcement institutions and the judiciary. After that, other ministries or agencies would follow that were regarded as 'less important'. For example, the Ministry of Finance became the priority, followed by the supreme audit board as the second priority. The IMF formally encouraged empowering the supreme audit board (the SAB) to improve the accountability and transparency of the government's financial management by referring to international best practices and reinstate the position of the SAB, which previously was weakened. Then,

CS

on 17th January 2005, the SAB proposed a government accounting standards to the president (Simanjuntak, 2005). The government accounting standard is being implemented gradually, and is aimed at making a transition from cash-based accounting towards the application of a full-accrual method (Harun and Kamase, 2012; Indonesia, 2003). Each local government must provide an income statement, balance sheet, cash flow and notes in its financial statement, which is then the mechanism that central government uses to oversee the financial performance of local government. Consequently, local government need to improve the competency of their officials (Harun and Kamase, 2012).

Another agenda of the IMF was the reform of budgeting processes, because, in the previous era, the Indonesian administration had been running without a budget. The philosophy at that time was, "Give me the money, and we do the job. When we entered, it was important to ask, Why should I give you the money? What job is it?"' (Salim, 2009), and even ministries or government agencies had off-budget accounts to cover any unexpected expenditures (Green and Campos, 2001). The IMF required financial transparency, and hence off-budget accounts were identified, audited, and brought under a consolidated budget. This task was assigned to the State Audit Board (the StAB), which is responsible for internal audits of government institutions. In addition, the IMF suggested establishing the Anti-Corruption Commission, which came into operation in 2004. This new body was named the Commission of Corruption Eradication (the CCE) (Schutte, 2012). The institution has responsibility for preventing, investigating, and prosecuting corruption cases. In order to facilitate the carrying-out of these duties, a special court for dealing with corruption cases was established (Jacobs and Wagner, 2007). The court has maintained a 100% conviction rate of corruption cases particularly for suspects who have been caught red-handed, and the KPK has prosecuted many prominent politicians, ministers, and governors, as well as officials of the Indonesian central bank (Butt, 2011).

The World Bank also played a role in the reformation by working with the Ministry of State Apparatus Empowerment and Bureaucratic Reform along with other ministries to hold a forum for sharing and learning with many experts from various countries to accelerate organisational restructuring to make it more efficient and more effective. To this end, employing technology was a priority at that time in Indonesia's reforms. The first reason was to minimise personal interactions that could possibly create a temptation to behave corruptly. The second reason was the need to build information systems to support human resource administrations, since the current information system was fragmented and negatively affected both the quality and accuracy of data. This meant that the data could not be relied on; for example, there was a lack of data pertinent to the competence and background of staff (Nurbaya, 2010).

In 2000, the Indonesia government held a meeting with the CGI (Consultative Group on Indonesia) that was supported by the World Bank and the CIDA (Canadian International Development Agency) to endorse the implementation of the decentralisation process by determined planning and staging. The meeting decided upon the stages of implementation, breaking them down into initiation, instalment, consolidation, and stabilisation; they also decided on relevant targets. The initiation stage was undertaken in 2000; 2001 and 2002 were designated for the instalment period; 2003 and 2004 were for the consolidation period; and finally, 2007 was expected to be the stabilisation period. However, the implementation plan did not go as well as expected, due to a lack of effective communication between the central government and local governments (Nurbaya, 2010).

Another international institution involved in the reformation was GTZ (German Agency for Technical Cooperation), especially in running 'good governance' programmes. Donor institutions such as GTZ did not impose their programmes, but raised awareness of and gave insight into the reformation of all levels of government. This process also involved bilateral donors such as Australia and New Zealand, which assisted in designing government organisations that would eliminate corruption or financial irregularities practices (Hamilton-Hart, 2001). As a result, the structure of the ministries and agencies in Indonesian public administration has been transformed; it is now more regimented and rigid in order to enhance the performance of the bureaucracy so as to deliver an effective and efficient public service (Datu and Nawawi, 2014).

Decentralisation policy

The main agenda of the IMF was devolution of power from central government to local government. Legislation was arranged carefully to establish a legal basis before proceeding with decentralisation reform and administrative decentralisation, as well as the expenditures and revenues that might be incurred or accrue from the policy respectively. The UNDP (United Nations Development Programme) was also involved in promoting the decentralisation agenda. For the implementation of the programme, the Government of Indonesia provided a budget of about IDR1.02 trillion, equal to around US$1 billion at that time, plus IDR94 billion, which was roughly US$94 million from donor countries, channelled through the UNDP.

These conditions stoked up enthusiasm for the creation of new districts or new provinces, but without any consideration being given to the region's developmental potential. As consequence, new districts or cities increased the number of local governments from 420 in 1998 to a current total of 514. The main idea of creation of new districts of provinces was to get as much money as possible from central government (Devas, 1997). Once obtained, the funds from central government were then used for administrative spending, such as on government officials' salary and government offices, rather than investment or infrastructure to generate new opportunities(Sjahrir, Kis-Katos, and Schulze, 2014).

Since decentralisation is directed at the municipal rather than the provincial level, this raises a problem regarding the extent of central government's reach over the municipalities. Therefore, central government delegates its coordination

CS

function to its representatives at the provincial level. However, there is no formal, subordinate relationship between the municipalities and the provinces; hence, the municipal administration might well ignore the intervention of a governor, who has no legal power over either the districts or cities in their region / province because the municipalities are structurally responsible to central government rather than to provincial governments. Initially, the President considered that if power were devolved only to the provinces, these would then still have the power to demand independence from central government; but if devolution were extended to the lower levels of districts and cities, any intention of separatism could be eliminated, as the municipal regions are too small.

In these decentralisation processes, the Ministry of Home Affairs also dealt with the transfer of assets and government officials from central government to local governments. A new law, marked out clearly which areas were to be managed by central government and which areas would be managed by local government. This law determines six areas controlled by central government: i.e. national monetary and fiscal affairs; foreign affairs; religion; national security; defence; and the judiciary. Referring to this regulation, central government determines the assets, personnel, and administrative tasks to be devolved to local government. This makes decision-making much easier, because of the geographical constraints in Indonesia (Klinken, 2013).

Issues on organisational culture

Many leaders of government institutions lack an understanding of what the reform is because the reform is perceived as offering increasing remuneration and solely focusing on regulations and policies; it is thus regarded as being an inherently incomplete reform. The reformation needs to be started by overhauling business processes for improving public services that are expected to regain the public's trust. For example, reformation of the Ministry of Finance began with reviewing the standard operating procedures and then simplifying the business processes and automating some areas by combining IT with certain procedures. These steps were followed by reviewing job descriptions, analysing jobs and workload, building an assessment centre that would affect any additional bonuses, setting up a human resource information system, and then enhancing the quality of human resources by recruiting new staff from the pool of high-quality new graduates.

The governance reforms at this moment are relatively complex, as they not only focus on hard-control related to procedures, laws and regulations, but also to soft-control emphasising socio-cultural aspects currently encountered in government: for example, ineffective infrastructure development and government spending are induced and facilitated by counter-productive bureaucracies either in central and/or local government. Therefore, to change the cultures of internal organisations, the leaders must have the courage to challenge those officials who hold established positions and who are regarded as ruling little kingdoms in a ministry or department. However, this approach is not supported by existing regulation, and it is not easy to discharge a government official unless he is caught red-handed committing a serious crime, or is in grave violation of civil service regulations. Therefore, open commitment of the leaders to governance reform needs to be initiated by the President and all ministers, parliament members and local government leaders, and all judicial branches. The commitment must be embodied by giving positive examples, such as not practising cronyism, and by respecting laws, bureaucracy and meritocracy, because clear examples can make the concept of reform easier to understand. Moreover, consistency is also needed in structuring, closely monitoring, evaluating and restructuring the governance system, all of which demonstrate the leaders' concern with reform.

In addition, concerning the organisational culture of government organisations, that is still perceived to be high power distance. It is necessary to establish an egalitarianism climate in which an individual can speak up if something wrong occurs, and where any ensuing judgements are not based on ethnic or religious affinities. This bureaucratic mentality is still dominant among government officials, inherited from the previous era where the working environment tended to impede the critical and creative thinking of officials (Harun and Kamase, 2012). Moreover, socio-cultural structures in Indonesian government institutions are very strong, an esprit de corps, meaning that it is considered inappropriate to shame a member of the group, and hence attitudes are very permissive towards underperforming staff or even those violating the rules (Irawanto, Ramsey, and Tweed, 2012). Hence, it is now a preferable option to recruit new personnel, rather than attempt to re-educate the old staff; young, talented workers can be shaped easily, and are perceived to be able to change socio-cultural attitudes and values in public organisations, enabling them to become more open-minded.

Issues on interactions among government institutions

Another issue relating to governance reform is interaction among departments or ministries. There is rivalry between departments. The government officials do not really belong to the government, but belong to a department that demands the officials' loyalty. The whole system of government is very much ego-sectoral (Salim, 2009). Hence, it is not easy to draw personnel from other departments, as the current system encourages departmental loyalty rather than a wider inter-departmental perspective. To deal with this issue, the ministries or agencies are compelled to formulate an integrated system. At the national level, there is the National Reform Team, which make up a coordinating forum to discuss policies and regulations across institutions in a more structured way. This forum can also revisit policies that have been implemented. However, this kind of forum is susceptible to political dynamics, because the current political system encourages domination by national elites (Faguet, 2013). When many political parties are involved and hold power in many departments, then conflicts of interest will be prominent. This condition is due to the composition of ministries in the

CS

Indonesian government, as approximately 61% of ministers are from political parties (Echwan, 2009). The historical roots of each political party affect the behaviour of each political actor differently (Barley and Tolbert, 1997; Blau, 1970; Peters, 1999) because each party has own values that affect the activities and relationships within the organisation (Barley and Tolbert, 1997). When a political actor has a position in a ministry, the values of his/her party affect them significantly. As indicated that parties will tend to fight for their own interests within the existing systems (Eisenstadt, 1964), and use the systems as vehicles for their political benefit (Dix, 1992).

Lack of coordination does not only occur between ministries, but also between ministries and local governments, leading to public funds being spent without considering the benefit for the local government (Mello, 2000). As formal organisations, ministries and local governments must have a system to coordinate and control activities (DiMaggio and Powell, 1983; Meyer and Rowan, 1977). Local government is required to conform to the regulations and policies that have been established by central government (Meulen, 1998). However, in many cases, local governments reluctantly adopt the prescribed systems, which might not fit with their needs because every local government has its own different characteristics. As a result, interrelationships among ministries, local government and local government agencies may seem to be attached, but in some aspects they remain circumscribed, separate and slow to respond (Weick, 1976).

Summary

The Indonesia government has been developing control systems since the government initiated a decentralisation policy. The policy has been dealing with organisational, ethical and cultural issues. As an attempt to bridge those issues with structural control, the central government needs to implement social accounting approach to reduce internal conflicts in government organisation.

Discussion questions

1 Identify the important government institutions in this case. Display this in an organisational chart and discuss how the institutions affect each other in the control of municipalities.

2 Reflecting on the issues, organisational culture and interaction among government institutions outlined in the case, what are your recommendations for the decentralisation policy? Please provide explanation in each of your recommendations.

References

Barley, S. R. and Tolbert, P. S. (1997). *Institutionalization and Structuration: Studying the Link between Action and Institution*. Cornel University.

Blau, P. M. (1970). A formal theory of differentiation in organizations. *American Sociological Review,* **35**(2), 201-218.

Butt, S. (2011). Anti-corruption reform in Indonesia: An obituary. *Bulletin of Indonesian Economic Studies,* **47**(3), 381-394.

Coaffee, J. and Johnston, L. (2005). The management of local government modernisation: area decentralisation and pragmatic localism. *International Journal of Public Sector Management,* **18**(2), 164-177.

Datu, T. T., and Nawawi, H. J. (2014). Implementation of good governance and bureaucratic reform in Indonesia. *International Journal of Academic Research,* **6**(3), 5-9.

Devas, N. (1997). Indonesia: What do we mean by decentralization? *Public Administration and Development,* **17**, 351-367.

DiMaggio, P. J., and Powell, W. W. (1983). The iron cage revisited: institutional isomorphism and collective rationality in organizational field. *American Sociological Review,* **48**(2), 147-160.

Dix, R. H. (1992). Democratization and the institutionalization of Latin American political parties. *Comparative Political Studies,* **24**, 488-511.

Echwan. (2009). Inilah 34 Menteri Kabinet Indonesia Bersatu II dan Catatannya. Nusantaranews, October 21. https://nusantaranews.wordpress.com/2009/10/21/inilah-menteri-kabinet-indonesia-bersatu-ii-catatannya/

Eisenstadt, S. N. (1964). Institutionalization and Change. *American Sociological Review,* **29**(2).

Faguet, J.-P. (2013). Decentralization and governance. *World Development,* **53**, 2-13.

Green, D. J. and Campos, J. E. (2001). Fiscal lessons from the East Asian Financial Crisis. *Journal of Asian Economics,* **12**, 309-329.

Hamilton-Hart, N. (2001). Anti-corruption sStrategies in Indonesia. *Bulletin of Indonesian Economic Studies,* **37**(1), 65-82.

Harun, H. and Kamase, H. P. (2012). Accounting change and institutional capacity: the case of a provincial government in Indonesia. *Australasian Accounting Business and Finance Journal,* **6**(2), 35-49.

Indonesia. (2003). *Law No.17/2003: Keuangan Negara.*

Irawanto, D. W., Ramsey, P. L. and Tweed, D. C. (2012). Exploring paternalistic leadership and its application to the Indonesian public sector. *The International Journal of Leadership in Public Services,* **8**(1), 4-20.

Jacobs, L. G., and Wagner, B. B. (2007). Limits to the independent anti-corruption commission model of corruption reform: lessons from Indonesia. Pacific McGeorge School of Law. Retrieved from http://scholarlycommons.pacific.edu/cgi/viewcontent.cgi?article=1013&context=facultyarticles

CS

Klinken, G. v. (2013). Brokerage and the making of Middle Indonesia. *City and Society,* **25**(1), 135-155.

Lewis, B. D. (2005). Indonesian local government spending, taxing and saving: an explanation of pre and post-decentralization fiscal outcomes. *Asian Economic Journal,* **19**(3), 291-317.

Mello, J. L. R. D. (2000). Fiscal decentralization and intergovernmental fiscal relations: a cross-country analysis. *World Development,* **28**(2), 365-380.

Meulen, B. V. d. (1998). Science policies as principal - agent games : institutionalization and path dependency in the relation between government and science. *Research Policy,* **27**, 397-414.

Meyer, J. W. and Rowan, B. (1977). Institutionalized organizations: formal structure as myth and ceremony. *American Journal of Sociology,* **83**(2), 340-363.

Nurbaya, S. (2010). *Innovation for Successful Societies.* New Jersey: Princeton University.

Peters, B. G. (1999). *Institutional Theory in Political Science: The 'New Institutionalism'.* London: Biddles Ltd.

Salim, E. (2009). Innovations for Successful Societies, Bobst Center for Peace and Justice. *Interviewed by Martin Devlin 6 July.* New Jersey: Princeton University.

Schutte, S. A. (2012). Against the odds: Anti-corruption reform in Indonesia. *Public Administration and Development,* **32**, 38-48.

Simanjuntak, B. H. (2005). Menyongsong Era Baru Akuntansi Pemerintahan di Indonesia. Retrieved from http://www.ksap.org/sap/menyongsong-era-baru -akuntansi-pemerintahan-di-indonesia/

Sjahrir, B. S., Kis-Katos, K. and Schulze, G. G. (2014). Administrative overspending in Indonesian districts: the role of local politics. *World Development,* **59**, 166/183.

Turner, M., Imbaruddin, A. and Sutiyono, W. (2009). Human resource management: the forgoten dimension of decentralization in Indonesia. *Bulletin of Indonesian Economic Studies,* **45**(2), 231-249.

Weick, K. E. (1976). Educational organizations as loosely coupled systems. *Administrative Science Quarterly,* **21**, 1-17.

Young, D. W., and Padovani, E. (2009). Moving toward the New Public Management paradigm. *Social Science Research Network,* 1-23.

Fair tax in a modern society

Melanie Wilson

Introduction

Tax avoidance is the legitimate, legal utilisation of loopholes or effective planning to reduce tax liabilities and increase the wealth of individuals or organisations. In this case study, we shall focus on tax avoidance only. In Blaufus *et al.*, (2016), the difference between tax evasion and tax avoidance is described as the difference in legality whereby tax evasion is an illegal activity, whereas tax avoidance is the legal minimisation of taxation. Further, HM Revenue and Customs (HMRC) define tax avoidance as "bending the rules of the tax system to gain a tax advantage that Parliament never intended. It often involves contrived, artificial transactions that serve little or no purpose other than to produce this advantage. It involves operating within the letter, but not the spirit, of the law. Most tax avoidance schemes simply do not work, and those who engage in them can find they pay more than the tax they attempted to save, once HM Revenue and Customs (HMRC) has successfully challenged them" (HMRC, 2016a). HMRC state tax avoidance is technically legal as it complies with the actual wording of the legislation, yet not the spirit.

How tax avoidance works

Tax avoidance may take many forms including asset planning, deferral of income, planning schemes, transferring prices, or manoeuvring funds to take advantage of different tax systems in multiple countries. These schemes are predominantly popular in industries with extremely high income such as popular music, sports or acting; or by large companies able to take advantage of global mobility.

Large corporations often operate with a global reach and multiple branches across several countries. In such organisations, a pricing method is required to re-charge other branches for services or products. Transfer pricing enables organisations to operate inter-company charges for services and/or products that have been provided to each branch of the organisation. The relationship between transfer pricing and tax minimisation has been has been highlighted in various studies. Transfer pricing policies may enable the artificial shifting of profits into a more tax advantageous regime. Klassen *et al.*, (2017) examine the direct link between transfer pricing policies. Their research determines that:

> some firms set their transfer pricing strategy to minimize tax payments, but more firms focus on tax compliance. We estimate that a firm focusing on minimizing taxes has an effective tax rate that is 6.6 percentage points lower and generates about $43 million more in tax savings, on average, than a firm focusing on tax

CS

compliance. Available data on sample firms confirm our survey-based inferences. We also find that transfer pricing-related tax savings are greater when higher foreign income, tax haven use, and R&D activities are combined with a tax minimization strategy. (Klassen *et al.*, 2017:1)

This review highlights the significant tax losses arising due to transfer pricing policies. In addition to this, Sikka and Willmott (2010) review the relationship between transfer pricing and taxation, concluding that:

> *Transfer pricing practices are responsive to opportunities for determining values in ways that are consequential for enhancing private gains, and thereby contributing to relative social impoverishment, by avoiding the payment of public taxes. Evidence is provided by examining some of the transfer prices practices used by corporations to avoid taxes in developing and developed economies.* (Sikka and Willmott, 2010:1)

Transfer pricing, tax minimisation and Starbucks

The use of transfer pricing and tax minimisation came to the attention of the public in 2012 when coffee giant Starbucks was the focus of media attention and public outcry after it emerged Starbucks had paid just £8.6m in Corporation Tax (tax on company profits) in 14 years and zero for 3 years despite sales of £400m in 2011.[1]

The case surrounding Starbucks UK Ltd. alleged the organisation had artificially reduced the profits taxable in the UK via the utilisation of transfer pricing policies. In Rossing *et al.*, (2016), the relationship between the transfer pricing policies adopted and the resultant allegations of tax avoidance was reviewed. The distinction between legal compliance and moral interpretation was also considered. Rossing *et al.*, (2016) state that:

> *despite Starbucks arguing that its transfer pricing practices were in full compliance with regulatory requirements, public pressure for higher corporate tax payments led Starbucks to increase its UK tax payment on transfer pricing income beyond regulatory requirements. This case study suggests that MNE tax behaviour on international transfer pricing is not strictly a matter of compliance with formal tax regulation. We demonstrate the way an MNE attempts to re-establish its 'corporate social license' with technically legitimate arguments of appropriate transfer pricing and, when such arguments fail to moderate social pressures, an MNE may experiment with voluntary responses.* (Rossing *et al.*, 2016:1)

This shows the allegations and social pressures Starbucks faced despite complete legal compliance. Society did not accept Starbucks' defence that legal compliance was enough.

Starbucks is not the only company participating in optimal transfer pricing policies to utilise beneficial tax loopholes and different global systems. As a result of Starbucks being a widely recognised global brand, the media were able to

---

1   http://www.bbc.co.uk/news/business-20624857

publicise the existence of such tax avoidance and society expressed their opinion with public boycotts and 'shaming'. Starbucks, along with Amazon and Google became a catalyst for 'tax shaming' and morality beyond basic legal compliance in the UK tax system.

Tax minimisation and Amazon

Amazon originally came to the public attention after announcing sales in the UK of £3.35bn in 2011 and a tax expense of £1.8m.[2] Members of society demanded an explanation. In a case similar to that of Starbucks, Amazon transferred, or routed, profits from Amazon UK to its parent company in Luxembourg. This practice had neither started nor ceased in the 2011 accounts year and resulted in significant reductions to the tax liability annually. A compromise was reached resulting in increased tax bills paid in 2015 and 2016. However, Amazon reached the news again in August 2017 when their corporation tax bill decreased by 50% despite continual growth.[3] The decrease in tax was a result of a significant decrease in taxable profits, raising questions why the profits have decreased when turnover has increased. This time, the reason is not related to transferring profits. Amazon have simply changed the way employees are paid, replacing a proportion of salary with Amazon shares. Salary and shares reduce the taxable profit position for Amazon, whilst shares may not carry any immediate tax liability for the employee. A legal and popular employee remuneration system.

Global tax systems and Google

Google is another fast-growing multinational enterprise (MNE) with ongoing tax disputes arising due to differing global tax systems. Google declares sales and pays tax in multiple countries, however, there appears to be confusion between the different reporting systems which led to allegations surrounding the correct value of the sales, profits and taxes due in the UK. After an ongoing period of negotiations between HMRC and Google, in January 2016, Google agreed to pay £130m in tax to cover the liability of £46.2m for the 18 months to June 2015 plus alleged underpayments spanning the previous decade.[4] Google also agreed to pay higher taxes in the future. In a newspaper article in January 2016, Eric Schmidt, the executive chairman of Google's parent company Alphabet stated, "Google was not doing anything wrong because it complied with tax laws around the world" (Rawlinson, 2016).

High-profile individual examples

Tax avoidance receiving media attention is not restricted to MNEs. Several high-profile individuals have also been 'named and shamed' for participation in tax avoidance schemes including musician Gary Barlow and comedian Jimmy

---

2   www.bbc.co.uk/news/magazine-20560359

3   www.bbc.co.uk/news/business-40884753

4   www.theguardian.com/technology/2016/jan/22/google-agrees-to-pay-hmrc-130m-in-back-taxes

CS

Carr. Both Messrs Barlow and Carr voluntarily paid additional taxes to appease society.[56]

Social responsibility and tax schemes

Schemes and plans are legal, in fact many tax authorities' charters, including the UK, state the taxpayer has the right to arrange his or her affairs in any manner he or she chooses to minimise their tax liabilities. Other countries have far more lenient attitudes, almost implying taxpayers may choose the level of tax they may pay. The argument remains whether tax should be based on the strict letter of the law or the spirit of the law.

The counter argument to these legal proposals are these schemes enable wealthy individuals and companies to have more disposable income which may be utilised for job creation, to donate to charitable causes and support community based projects reducing reliance on the public purse for welfare support. The arguments further to say such companies and individuals are attracted to the UK and the competitive environment it creates. This creates significant levels of employment which results in increased payment of payroll based taxes (tax on employees' earnings) and reduced unemployment and the associated dependency on welfare. This becomes an increasing challenge in a mobile, digital global economy where individuals and organisations are easily able to re-locate. Society remains dividend on the acceptability of this current situation.

The impact of tax avoidance on society

The sums involved in tax avoidance are significant. According to HMRC's ongoing work to measure the tax gap in the UK, the 2016 publication estimates the tax loss to the UK exchequer in 2014/15 (6/4/14 – 5/4/15) to be £36 billion, of which 6.5% is theoretical liabilities (HMRC, 2016b). This includes all forms of tax loss including avoidance, evasion, debt, uncollected liabilities and theoretical liabilities. The *tax gap* is the term used to define the measure of the difference between the tax collected and the sum of theoretical tax liabilities. According to HMRC, this figure has decreased annually because of increased targeting. However, according to independent research this figure is challenged as severely under-estimated. In a report conducted by Tax Research UK[7] on behalf of the Public and Commercial Services Union (PCS) the tax gap is estimated at £119.4 billion for the tax year 2013/14 (Murphy, 2014). This includes HMRC reduction in both tax avoidance and debt, but increases the estimated loss due to tax evasion. Whilst HMRC claim tax avoidance is reducing, the public believe it is increasing.

---

5   https://www.thetimes.co.uk/article/jimmy-carr-i-took-tax-flak-because-gary-barlow-is-a-national-treasure-vcqhf5lqk

6   http://www.bbc.co.uk/news/uk-politics-18531008

7   www.taxresearch.org.uk/Documents/PCSTaxGap2014.pdf

Is this fair? Whilst tax avoidance is completely legal, many believe it is neither fair nor ethical. Increasingly society imposes moral pressure on such individuals and organisations to 'pay their fair share' of taxation. In a modern economy of a democratic country, is it reasonable to assume the law achieves fairness, and that if someone is compliant with the law they are paying their fair share? Many members of society feel the current tax system is unjust, inequitable and morally lacking.

Taxes are used to fund many areas within the public sector including healthcare, hospitals, education, social welfare, law and order, transport, culture, sport, environment, and food and rural affairs. Reduced taxes results in a loss to the exchequer, as identified above, which has an impact on the public purse. Significant losses have a potential to cause austerity and divides society between those who have and those who haven't. Some factions of society argue such schemes and opportunities should be made illegal to eradicate such planning and savings, enforcing full compliance and achieving a moral adherent fair system.

The ability to participate in such schemes and tax avoidance is not equally available to all organisations and individuals. Smaller businesses are unlikely to have adequate profits, size or global presence to warrant, or be eligible for, expensive schemes. Third sector organisations such as social enterprises, co-ops, charities and associations share the same problem as smaller businesses plus their missions and ethos would determine such planning repugnant to their stakeholders. The loss to the public sector affects the public, many of whom are unable or unwilling to participate or benefit from, nor prevent, tax avoidance schemes. This lack of equitability may result in small family owned businesses and third sector organisations ceasing to exist as they are unable to compete with larger firms who are able to lower prices due to monies saved from reduced taxes paid.

Community led action

To raise awareness and highlight the different options available to large organisations versus smaller and third sector organisations, projects such as the Fair Tax Mark[8] and the Tax Justice Network[9] commenced. The premise behind the Fair Tax Mark is that companies may apply to the scheme to demonstrate to their customers they are ethical and moral with their tax affairs and pay a full share.

The Fair Tax Mark scheme is available to UK-based businesses trading in the UK and overseas who meet core criteria regarding their corporation tax compliance. Businesses are required to demonstrate transparency in structure and ownership; open communications regarding their accounts; understanding tax obligations and policies reflecting good practice; plus, country-specific reporting for multinationals. Those businesses which meet the criteria may show the Fair

8   https://fairtaxmark.net/

9   www.taxjustice.net/

CS

Tax Mark on their communications to demonstrate to their stakeholders and the community that they are fair and transparent in their tax affairs.

The Tax Justice Network (TJN) launched in 2003 to encourage systemic change to the current international tax basis, with a focus on tax havens and financial globalisation. The TJN describes its role is to:

> conduct high-level research, analysis and advocacy on international tax; on the international aspects of financial regulations; on the role of tax in society; and on the impacts of tax evasion, tax avoidance, tax 'competition' and tax havens.
> (Tax Justice Network, 2003)

The TJN strive to create a politically neutral environment designed to "create understanding and debate, and to promote reform, especially in poorer countries" (Tax Justice Network, 2003). Society welcomes initiatives such as the Fair Tax Mark and the Tax Justice Network and their work to achieve fair tax systems. Tax reform is increasingly complex in a global economy with different tax systems, economies and cultural attitudes towards taxation.

Summary

Tax avoidance is predominantly evident in large multinational companies or extremely wealthy individuals. Whilst the participation in tax schemes is available to few, the implications are wide reaching across all society. Tax avoidance is legal; however, it is not accepted as socially responsible moral behaviour.

Discussion questions

1   Discuss the implications of transparency within tax systems in a global economy and the impact of tax avoidance on public sector funding.

2   Debate the concept of 'fair' taxation and whether tax 'compliance' should be legal or ethical and the effectiveness of the Fair Tax Mark and Tax Justice network in the context of a fair and equitable tax system.

References and further reading

Blaufus, Hundsdoerfer, Jacob, and Sünwoldt. (2016). Does legality matter? The case of tax avoidance and evasion. *Journal of Economic Behavior and Organization*, **127**, 182-206.

HMRC (2016a). Tax Avoidance: an introduction, https://www.gov.uk/guidance/tax-avoidance-an-introduction, HM Revenue and Customs:London.

HMRC(2016b) – Measuring Tax Gaps 2016 edition, https://www.gov.uk/government/uploads/system/uploads/attachment_data/file/561312/HMRC-measuring-tax-gaps-2016.pdf, HM Revenue and Customs: London.

Klassen, K., Lisowsky, P. and Mescall, D. (2017). Transfer pricing: strategies, practices, and tax minimization. *Contemporary Accounting Research*, **34**(1), 455-493.

Murphy, R. (2014), *The Tax Gap: Tax evasion in 2014 – and what can be done about it*, Public and Commercial Services Union: London.

Rawlinson, K. (2016). Google agrees to pay British authorities £130m in back taxes. *The Guardian*, January 23. Retrieved from http://www.theguardian.com/technology/2016/jan/22/google-agrees-to-pay-hmrc-130m-in-back-taxes

Rossing, C.P., Riise Johansen, T. and Pearson, T.C. (2016), Tax anti-avoidance through transfer pricing: the case of Starbucks U.K. in Twenty-Eighth Asian-Pacific Conference on International Accounting Issues: Program and Proceedings. Asian-Pacific Conference, Fresno, pp. 98. *Proceedings of the Asian-Pacific Conference on International Accounting Issues*, vol. 28

Sikka,P. and Willmott, H. (2010). The dark side of transfer pricing: Its role in tax avoidance and wealth retentiveness. *Critical Perspectives on Accounting*, **21**(4), 342-356.

Tax Justice Network (2003). Available at: http://www.taxjustice.net/

CS

Corporate governance and social accountability in cooperatives

Sebastian Paterson and Audrey Paterson

Introduction

Corporate governance and social accountability are firmly recognised as being essential components of organisational structures. Cooperatives differ from public and private businesses, which exist to produce goods or services in the public interest or to maximise the profits of their owners, respectively. In contrast to public and private companies, the main purpose of a cooperative is the advancement of its members and not the pursuit of public interest or economic gain. This mini case study seeks to examine corporate governance and social accountability in the context of the cooperative business model utilising the Conceptual Framework for Research into Cooperative Enterprise developed by Mazzarol, Simmons and Limnios (2011) that was presented in Chapter 10.

Given the importance of the role boards play in the success or failure of cooperative organisations, and the importance of these organisations in the wider economy, this case study examines board behaviour in relation to its governance and social accountability responsibility. Board behaviour has been criticised for over-reliance on one source of data, usually the perceptions of board members gathered through interviews or questionnaires (Peck, 1995). Peck's criticisms are twofold: first, he suggests board members are unlikely to 'reveal their own irrelevance' and so are likely to over-emphasise the relevance of their role, and second, the studies lack any independent confirmation of actors' accounts[1]. Utilising the Mazzarol *et al.* (2011) framework, this case examines the impact of governance and social accountability on three rural agricultural supply cooperatives and raises some questions regarding the effectiveness of cooperatives in achieving good governance and demonstrating social accountability. The case has been anonymised in accordance with agreements laid out by the participating cooperatives.

Case overview

The land mass covered by the northern part of the country, on which this case is based, comprises of 3 million hectares, making up 48% of the country; however, 90% of this land is rough grazing, compared with 67% the country as a whole. Grassland of some kind makes up 79% of the North (64% of the country's total). Within the North there are 23,000 agricultural holdings (45% of the country's

---

1   For fuller details see Peck (1995), p 139-140

total). A sizeable proportion of the holdings are under 50 hectares or, indeed, in most remote cases, under 20 hectares in size. This land area issue is important if one looks at the situation in terms of employment and European Size Units (ESUs). It is calculated that, to provide full-time employment for one farmer, there is a requirement for land, dependent on quality, in the range of 8-40 ESUs. Two thirds of the holdings in the North have less than this critical 8 ESU size and only 10% are over the 40 ESU mark.

Whilst the density of sheep is significantly lower in the North than in the rest of the country, the region is nonetheless heavily reliant on sheep farming, with sheep making up 71% of livestock (60% for the country as a whole). It is estimated that there are some 3 million sheep in the North, making up one third of the country's total sheep. About 1.3 million of these sheep are breeding ewes and, despite a lambing rate below the rest of country, it is calculated that they produce some 1.225 million lambs annually. The only area of the North where cattle dominate is Region 1 (see *Region 1 Farmers* below).

Overall, the North has 380,000 cattle, amounting to 18% of the country's total. The bulk of these beasts are for beef production, with only around 33,000 involved in dairy production. The geography and topography of the North clearly dictates the nature of its agriculture. Apart from Region 1, the whole area is devoid of lush pasture. Quite apart from the many rural areas, the various parts of the North's mainland are severely constrained with regard to the communications infrastructure and, consequently, in terms of connections to major centres across the remainder of the country and other potential markets. In terms of farming output, livestock production dominates, comprising three-quarters of the overall agricultural output for the region. Beef cattle make up virtually half of the total agricultural output, while lambs make up just over one quarter. Traditionally, however, most of these livestock have been sold to more lowland areas of the country and beyond, as store stock. While limited facilities exist within the region, slaughter and any further processing most often take place outside the region, particularly in Eastern parts of the country.

Region 1 Farmers

Region 1 Farmers started in 1958 as a fertiliser-buying group as a Region 1 Bulk Buying Group, with only 12 members. However, due to popular demand, it soon expanded into buying other farm requisites. Additional farmers joined to get the benefit of the better pricing and, in 1968, Region 1 Farmers was born out of the original group. Since that time the company has continued to grow and now has over 750 active members and an annual turnover of £7 million. It is now one of two major agricultural retailers in the North, selling a comprehensive range of farm requisites. It is also open to non-members and is well used by the public. It is still run on cooperative principles, with low margins and profits which are returned to the membership as a dividend on purchases.

CS

Region 2 Farmers

The cooperative was founded in 1964 and has more than 400 members. As the name would suggest, the cooperative has its roots in livestock marketing; while this continues to the present day, it has subsequently expanded into the area of agricultural supplies. The business now services the North with a wide range of agricultural inputs, including feeds, fertiliser, fencing and agricultural accessories. The diversified nature of the business has helped it to continue to function profitably through difficult periods in agriculture.

Region 3 Crofters

Region 3 Crofters cooperative was established in 1958 and was initially set up to supply the crofters in a remote location with animal feed, fertilisers, fencing and drainage materials, as well as other general farm requisites. The company has developed and expanded over the years and now supplies a comprehensive range of farming-associated products. It also has a large retail outlet supplying a diverse range of non-agricultural products for the wider community.

Governance and social accountability

Region 1 Farmers

In Region 1, the management team reported that they were in control of all operational aspects of the business and that in their opinion they were doing an excellent job. The general manager did, however, make it clear that relations with the board were "currently not so good", with the view taken that the board had recently undermined the position and authority of management through their direct involvement in an HR matter and the consequent appointment of an external consultant. Given the general manager's 30-year successful track record of running the business, it was evident that the apparent interference and perceived "lack of trust and support" had resulted in significant discontent.

Given the size of the business (£7m turnover) and substantial number of members, the chairman stated that member participation in the affairs of the cooperative was "poor"; nonetheless, the board was fully staffed with 12 members, "the same old faces", elected to office. The chairman pointed out that, while the board was quite large, it was "seldom the case that all board members could attend meetings". In terms of board representation, qualifications and experience, it was mentioned that "it was difficult to find the right people who were prepared to commit the time"; that said, it was discovered that the board did have an independent accountant in its ranks and farmers running large farms with substantial business acumen. The Chairman had no formal board training.

In response to significant changes in farming brought about by recent Common Agricultural Policy reforms and its effect on Single Farm Payments and other associated grants the Chairman appointed an external consultant to carry out a comprehensive business review. The chairman stated, "the review was deemed necessary to get an independent opinion of whether the business was capable of withstanding and responding to the significant changes in farming brought about by the recent Policy reforms, its effect on Single Farm Payments and other associated grants". The report was not shared with the executive management; however, one of the outcomes of the review was a raise in pay for the general and assistant managers.

Reviewing the organisational structures of Region 1 Farmers revealed an apparent blurring of director versus management roles, poor bilateral communication and a perceived breakdown of trust on the part of the executive management. This was evidenced by the board's decision to directly intervene in management matters (i.e. the HR case and the subsequent or associated decision to instruct an independent business review) without first informing the executive management of its intended purpose or latterly subsequent findings. While there may have been valid reasons for the actions taken or misunderstanding surrounding the motives, the consequences nonetheless appear to have damaged the relationship between the board and management. The recent pay rise awarded to management, for whatever reason, may go some way to repairing the relationship. The relationship between the board and the membership also seemed to be poor, with few members attending meetings and no formal communication strategy in place to keep members informed concerning the affairs of the cooperative. Notwithstanding these criticisms, the business boasts a successful track record and continuing growth. All of the above were deemed to be having a negative impact on stakeholder perceptions of their governance and social accountability.

Region 2 Farmers

From Region 2 managers' perspective, it was clear that they felt that they were in operational control of the business and that, under their management, it was performing and responding effectively to customer needs and market forces. A survey of staff and customers appear to corroborate that view with no distinct dissatisfaction being reported. However, the management team were forthright in stating their reluctance to facilitate board involvement in the day-to-day running of the business "we like to keep them at arm's length"; however there was no impression of antipathy towards or resistance to the board. The view was merely that piecemeal board interference would potentially be detrimental to the enterprise and make their job unduly difficult, given the perception that board members would not have a holistic understanding of the operational side of the business comparable to that which the management team had built up in over 15 years in post.

A review of the board structure indicated that a well-staffed, appropriately trained, qualified, experienced and technically representative board was in place and that board members understood their role and were diligent and skilled in the execution of their specific individual duties. The board also demonstrated understanding of the need to keep members at the forefront of their thinking

CS

while balancing this with the needs of other stakeholders and, importantly, employees, in the latter case ensuring pay and conditions remained competitive with competing owner-investor firms to guarantee recruitment, selection and retention of suitably qualified and motivated personnel. The board left the operational level to the management team, deeming their role to be more concerned with the mission and strategic direction of the organisation. In relation to governance issues, the board had uncovered problems in the past which had led to serious financial difficulties, resulting in the business being "placed under extraordinary measures" by its bank for three years. These were thought to be related to recruitment of staff without the necessary skills.

In terms of the relationship between the board and the executive management, this was assessed overall as excellent, with regular dialogue and the sharing of ideas and opinions evident in an inclusive strategic decision-making process. Likewise. the relationship between the board and the membership also seemed to be good, although this was evidenced paradoxically by the lack of member participation at meetings. As stated by the chairman "if you have a large attendance at an AGM here it's because something has gone wrong". Notwithstanding poor attendance at meetings, regular communication with members concerning the affairs of the cooperative was maintained through the medium of the chairman's quarterly newsletters and annual report.

Region 3 Farmers

The general manager of Region 3 had been in post for 35 years. In terms of day-to-day operational control of the business, this clearly rested with the general manager: "the board don't get involved in the operational side of the business, but they are there for guidance and support as and when needed". When questioned about strategy, the general manager reported that "final decisions rest with the board but they involve input from the accountant as well as me as manager". Regarding strategic direction, the general manager was well informed, having a clear appreciation of the cooperative's mission and vision; that is: "keeping farm input costs fair and working to promote and retain crofting as a viable community occupation for future generations". When questioned on performance measurement and his relationship with the board, the general manager said he was assessed against "year on year turnover and membership trading" and that his relationship with the board was "cordial".

The chairman reported he had only been in post for a year; nonetheless, he was able to demonstrate considerable and impressive knowledge of all matters pertaining to the business and, importantly, the cooperative principles and values that underpin the enterprise. It was also evident that the chairman had a great deal of wider, valuable strategic level knowledge and contacts which could in part be ascribed to his primary employment as an estate factor. The chairman additionally showed a sound general understanding of corporate governance, stating that he and other members of the board had "received cooperative corporate governance training". With respect to board matters, it became clear that the board had extensive and diverse expertise and experience, with members qualified in areas covering law, banking, accounting, engineering, business management and farming. The chairman mentioned that the board followed a "formal democratic process" for seeking and appointing board members and adhered to appointment terms as "detailed in the rules for the cooperative" drawn up initially under the framework of the Industrial and Provident Act 1965. The chairman stated that, while there was "no formal performance appraisal system in place", board members were nevertheless assessed informally against their contribution in relation to annual trading results. Board meetings in Region 3 take place quarterly throughout the year to which the manager is always invited to attend and contribute to meetings.

Summary

All three case studies have some form of governance policy and procedure in place which is applied to varying degrees to direct and control the cooperative enterprises with the interests of all stakeholders, who include management, members and the wider community, taken into consideration and balanced appropriately. Two of the cases reported formal board training, one did not. Each case has encountered problems within their operations.

Discussion questions

1   Reflecting on the cases above evaluate and discuss the usefulness of the framework developed by Mazzarol *et al.* (2011) to cooperative board structures and their effectiveness.

2   To what extent do you believe a corporate governance policy and procedure facilitates cooperative to fulfil and demonstrate their social accountability obligations?

References:

Mazzarol, T., Simmons R. and Limnios, M. (2011). *A Conceptual Framework for Research into Co-operative Enterprise.* CEMI Discussion Paper Series, DP 1102, Centre for Entrepreneurial Management and Innovation, www.cemi.com.au

Peck, E. (1995). The performance of a NHS trust board: actors' accounts, minutes and observation, *British Journal of Management*, **6**, 135-156.

CS

Index

Printed in the United States
By Bookmasters